SARAPIQUI
CHRONICLE

SARAPIQUI
CHRONICLE

A NATURALIST IN COSTA RICA

ALLEN M. YOUNG

SMITHSONIAN INSTITUTION PRESS
Washington and London

Editor: Matthew Abbate
Designer: Janice Wheeler

Library of Congress Cataloging-in-Publication Data

Young, Allen M.
    Sarapiquí chronicle : a naturalist in Costa Rica / by Allen M. Young.
    p.   cm.
    Includes index.
    ISBN 1–56098–014–1 (cloth)   ISBN 1–56098–047–8 (ppb)
    1. Natural history—Costa Rica—Sarapiqui.   2. Butterflies—Costa Rica
—Sarapiqui.   I. Title.
QH108.C6Y68   1991
508.7286'4—dc20   90–39532

British Library Cataloguing-in-Publication Data is available

Manufactured in the United States of America

98   97   96   95   94   93   92   91   5   4   3   2   1

♾ The paper used in this publication meets the minimum requirements
of the American National Standard for Permanence of Paper for Printed
Library Materials Z39.48–1984.

This book is for the people
and other organisms of Sarapiquí
and the rest of the *Vertiente Atlantico*

CONTENTS

ACKNOWLEDGMENTS

A student's long-standing interest in nature usually starts out as a little seed, a kernel of interest, that is nourished and encouraged into being with the help of others. I am very grateful to those individuals who, between 1952 and 1968 especially, believed in my interest and desire to study organismic biology. They include Stanley Starr, Ruth Johns, Arnold Nemerofsky, James Gray, Lynn Throckmorton, Thomas Park, Margaret Young, the late Marion Cormier, Charles Brieant, and George Young. I thank Dan Janzen for providing my first opportunity to study nature in Costa Rica through the Organization for Tropical Studies, Inc. (1968–70). For logistical support and general assistance while I was on the faculty of Lawrence University (1970–75), I am grateful to Drs. J. Robert (Bob) Hunter and Ridgway Satterthwaite, former directors of the Costa Rican Field Studies Program of The Associated Colleges of the Midwest. Since joining the staff of the Milwaukee Public Museum (1975), I have appreciated the hospitality and logistical assistance in Costa Rica of Hans and Yudi Van Der Wielen of the Amstel Hotel (formerly) and Bougain-villea Hotel, and of the people of Sarapiquí, especially those at Cariblanco and Finca La Tirimbina. My research in Costa Rica has been supported by the Organization for Tropical Studies, Inc., Lawrence University, The Associated Colleges of the Midwest, Bache

Fund of The National Academy of Sciences (U.S.), the National Science Foundation, Friends of the Milwaukee Public Museum (including donations from James R. Neidhoefer and Robert Veenendaal to study insects in Sarapiquí), the Milwaukee Public Museum of Milwaukee County, and the American Cocoa Research Institute. I thank Thomas Moore, Thomas Emmel, Paul Opler, Lincoln Brower, Murray Blum, Charles Hogue, Luis Diego Gómez, Gary Hartshorn, Alberto Muyshondt, Keith Brown, Norris Williams, Mark Whitten, Alvaro Wille, Peter Raven, the late Manuel Chavarría, and Rafael Lucas Rodríguez for their interest, encouragement, wisdom, and humanity. For insightful discussions about the uniqueness of Costa Rica and its people, I thank José Giralt, Jorge Coto, Hans Van Der Wielen, and Nancy and Bob Hunter. And my heartfelt thanks to the late Jorge Campabadal, who I wish had lived to read this book, for his friendship over many years. To the members of the Invertebrate Zoology Section at the Milwaukee Public Museum—Susan Borkin, Joan Jass, and Gary Noonan—I am grateful for the unabridged dedication to natural history studies that they have demonstrated over the many years I have been associated with the museum. Special thanks to many others in Costa Rica who have helped me with great patience in many ways, especially Luis Diego Gómez, Dorothy Lankester, Jerry James, Francisco Vásquez, Carlos Valerio, Darién Zuñiga, Maria Schlicker, Charles Hunter, Luis Poveda, Jorge Gómez Laurito, Richard Mullins, Andrés Montalto, Jorge Mejías, Pablo Sánchez, Daniel Hernández, Ramón (Moncho) Morales, Javier Angulo, the Gonzalo González Baquero family, and the late Dagoberto Alfaro.

I could not have written this book without the longstanding friendship and encouragement of Bob and Nancy Hunter, who generously welcomed me to live and study at La Tirimbina over many years, an experience forming the major part of the core substance of this book. Bob also kindly shared with me many of his observations and experiences concerning Sarapiquí.

Christine Coradini provided excellent assistance and professional diligence in typing and editing the book. I thank Drs. Lincoln P.

Brower and Thomas C. Emmel for their review of sample chapters and for their enthusiastic support for this project. For much initial encouragement, I thank Theresa Slowik, former science editor at the Smithsonian Institution Press. I thank the editorial staff of the Press, especially the current natural science editor, Peter Cannell, for his patience, advice, and professionalism in making this book a reality. Matthew Abbate did an outstanding and thorough job of copyediting the entire manuscript, for which I am extremely grateful.

Allen M. Young
Milwaukee, Wisconsin

PROLOGUE

I have spent part of each of the past twenty years in the Sarapiquí Valley of northeastern Costa Rica, studying the abundant insect life of that region's tropical rain forests. In this book I describe discoveries in insect natural history and also personal experiences and impressions of this special place in Central America.

The impetus for the book began with a peculiarly vivid dream. In it, my old friend Jorge Campabadal, a Costa Rican, led me down a familiar garden path toward a quaint blue wooden house with a bright red corrugated metal roof. As we neared the house, "Campa's" eyes gazed upward, locking upon a gnarled citrus tree whose foliage shaded a worn, chicken-scratched patch of hardened earth. He pointed up to an enormous paper comb wasp nest. Crawling over the exposed gray-brown cells of the nest were enormous metallic-green wasps of a kind I had never seen. In fact, until he died at the age of fifty-three in September 1989, Campa lived in San José, Costa Rica's capital. But the house and its setting seemed to belong to another longtime friend, "Challa" González Serrano, who lived in the Sarapiquí Valley, some seventy kilometers from San José.

Dreams tend to jumble diverse bits of memory into a single vivid moment. This particular dream remained in my mind, fusing images of people and natural history that I had experienced for close to two decades in the Sarapiquí Valley. Like my dream, this book is a composite of many elements from my science, my Costa Rican friends, and the Sarapiquí countryside.

The Sarapiquí experience, a chronicle of nature and people in a particular place, became a medium for self-fulfillment and enjoyment for me, although it has not been without its frustrations, disappointments, and mistakes. I consider myself fortunate. I relish the thought of field work in the tropics, in the rain and sunshine, amidst the brambles of dense brush, wandering through primeval forests. Probing into nature has been a big part of living for me since I was eight years old. The inner contentment with my choice of what to do with my life is very similar today to what it was at that age. The happiness of a child exploring the world for the first time, seeking out every insect and new creature that showed itself in the garden or neighborhood marsh or park, became a new dimension to my life as an adult exploring nature in the world's last terrestrial frontier, the tropical rain forest.

Until my special dream occurred, bringing together the elements of a long-standing friendship with the Costa Rican people, the humble beauty of Sarapiquí's countryside, and the alluring beauty of its insects, I had not given any thought to writing a book such as this one. I could only imagine that the other U.S. biologists who have devoted much of their lives to studying tropical nature had similar experiences to mine. Each could give his or her own account of what it is like to do field work in the tropics for many years. At the same time, I believe all of us would agree that our experience could hardly have been called "work." There's an inner drive to study nature, and the feeling overtakes the psyche, especially in the species-saturated tropics of Central America. It is fun and excitement; it is not work.

Looking back, I became aware of just how fortunate I had been to study tropical nature in Sarapiquí for such a long time. But along much of the way, I seldom thought about the whole picture. I had read the many articles and books that describe the complex workings of tropical ecosystems and the tremendous diversity of plants and animals comprising tropical forest communities. All of this was valuable and useful information. But only by spending a lot of time in one place, such as Sarapiquí, and experiencing a whole constellation of nature's cycles, through days, seasons, and years, is it possible to develop an understanding and appreciation of the inherent complexities and marvels of tropical nature. This, too, is what *Sarapiquí Chronicle* is about. In such an account it is not possible to include all of the experiences and incidents of my field work in Sarapiquí. However, I attempt to highlight some of the most interesting and memorable ones.

This book is based upon twenty-one years of field work excursions into northeastern Costa Rica, chiefly into the Sarapiquí Valley. Initially I came to Costa Rica as a postdoctoral research associate with the Organization for Tropical Studies, Inc., spending two years (1968–70) at the Finca La Selva biological station situated on the Río Puerto Viejo. Following this period, I made intermittent trips into the region two or three times every year, staying from two weeks to two months each time. For this reason, my book deals chiefly with my field experiences in Sarapiquí from 1971 through 1989, which occurred mainly at Cariblanco (technically not in Sarapiquí, but close to it) and Finca La Tirimbina near the town of La Virgen de Socorro. The book is a journey into Sarapiquí, a composite of many overland adventures taking place over many years. The first two chapters combine what I recall from my very first foray into Sarapiquí, but interwoven with vignettes of other experiences up to the present.

Finally, and quite unabashedly, my book is about the fusion of natural history and science with the physical beauty of tropical nature. Too often science and scientists are detached from the emotional content of the organisms they study. What I have learned in Sarapiquí is the inherent value in stepping back, away from strict objectivity, and taking time to appreciate the physical beauty of nature. Whether seen through the dazzling iridescence of a *Morpho* butterfly's wings, the drumming call of the cicada, the chemical-mediated elegance of courtship in orchid bees, or the design of a pod of the cacao tree, an appreciation of nature's physical beauty reinforces the need for scientific inquiry into nature's workings, and vice versa. After all, the information obtained through scientific research really represents another form of beauty in our world, what I call "knowledge beauty." So, really, the total human experience is the fusion of physical beauty, in its many, seemingly unlimited varieties, with the knowledge beauty within each creature waiting to be discovered. It is my belief that a cognizance of both kinds of beauty heightens our awareness of the importance of conserving nature, in the tropics and everywhere else.

S^A R^A PIQUI
CHRONICLE

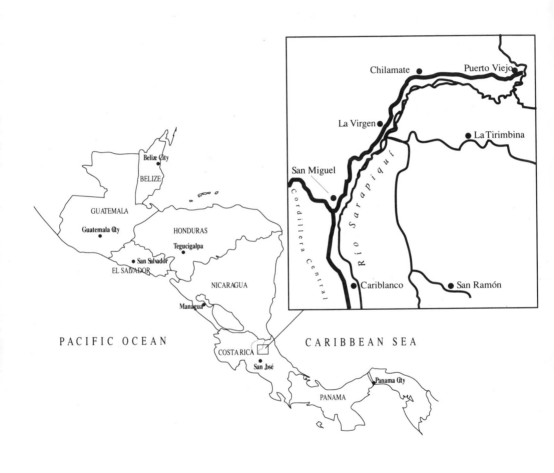

PACIFIC OCEAN

CARIBBEAN SEA

Chilamate
Puerto Viejo
La Virgen
La Tirimbina
San Miguel
Cariblanco
San Ramón

Cordillera Central

Río Sarapiquí

Belize City
BELIZE

GUATEMALA

Guatemala City

HONDURAS

Tegucigalpa

San Salvador
EL SALVADOR

NICARAGUA

Managua

COSTA RICA
San José

PANAMA

Panama City

LEEWARD INTO THE LAND OF CLOUDS

1

There is something special about the journey into Sarapiquí, across the rugged mountains and the massive forest-lined river gorge, with its early morning wisps of white mist slipping away from the dense forest foliage and its incessant evening rains. The scenes are unlike any I had seen before I first came here, whether as a youth in the northern suburbs of New York City, attending college in upstate New York, or spending four years on the south side of Chicago.

Peering down on that steep gorge, formed over millions of years by the raging, powerful waters of the Sarapiquí River cascading down from an ancient volcano, I am transfixed by the mist-studded greenery of the forest. This region must be one of nature's most complex theaters of biological adaptation, where every mode of adaptive ingenuity is reflected in the tremendous diversity of life thriving here. Naturally I had read about the great Amazonian forests and the discoveries of the early naturalists in such places; but over the years I would come to understand that even smaller corners of the American tropics, such as the Sarapiquí Valley with its little-studied forests, can be effective learning theaters for understanding the complexities of tropical nature.

Although the Sarapiquí District of Heredia Province was officially created in November 1970 under the administration of President José Figueres Ferrer, records on the origin of the name Sarapiquí date back at least to the seventeenth century. The precise origin remains sketchy, however, and what little is known about it relates to the river after which the district was named in modern times. The Indians native to the *Vertiente Atlantico* (the Atlantic slope) of Costa Rica originally named a great river that flowed into the Río San Juan the Jori River in their own language, the name also known for the river in 1640 when Spaniards first explored the region. But the Mosquito Indians living in the coastal region at the Río San Juan viewed the Río Jori as a tributary of the mighty San Juan, referring to it as Piquí, roughly translating into Spanish as *rio pequeño* (small river). This river, near its entrance into the San Juan, was also referred to as Serpi Creek, and from this the name Seripiqui and later Sarapiquí was derived. Both the river and the region were largely ignored until 1820, when Joaquín Mora, the brother of Costa Rica's first president, Juan Mora, explored the region, entering it from the Meseta Central. In this book I use Sarapiquí in a broader context than just the administrative district. For the purposes of my discussions, Sarapiquí is much of the *Vertiente Atlantico* region through which the river flows.

Ten million years ago, Central America was a series of unconnected islands that served as stepping stones for plants and animals as they traveled between the continents. Massive volcanism and movement of the Earth's plates eventually established a thin but continuous land mass, modern-day Central America. Chains of mountains, the *cordilleras*, with hundreds of fiery volcanoes formed the backbone of this new land, a formation continuing into North America as the Rockies. The land continued to change as it still does today. As the great fires subsided and the land cooled, water-soaked clouds and warm temperatures, modulated in part by the advance and retreat of glaciers in North America during the Pleistocene, transformed the isthmus into a ribbon of verdancy. Because of the moist trade winds out of the east, the Caribbean side of the mountains became covered with tropical rain forest. Rivers flowing down from the tops of volcanoes carved deep gashes in the terrain, converting rock into soil and carrying it away to the floodplains. In what would become Costa Rica, one such colossal gash on a mountainside, established millions of years ago, became the Sarapiquí Valley. From the cold mountaintops of old volcanoes to the very hot, tropical lowlands fanning out toward the Caribbean Sea and Pacific Ocean, much of Central America became a mosaic testing ground for evolutionary processes shaping the development and expression of species.

When I started traveling to Costa Rica in 1968, I would take the LACSA (the Costa Rican national airline) flight that, in those days, left Miami at about six o'clock in the morning. What incredible sunrises there are over the Caribbean! By the time we were over the Cayman Islands, where in the old days LACSA would refuel, the skies were illuminated, blocked here and there by smudges of smoke-black clouds that appeared and disappeared along the way.

As the jetliner began a slow descent at the Caribbean coast of Central America, my geography lesson really blossomed. As it would on more than six-score future flights to Costa Rica, the coast came up as a thin line of white surf in front of a ribbon of dark beach. For as far as one can see, this double line of frothy water and earth, the boundary between sea and land, curves ever so slightly along what seems to be an even, monotonous coast. It is broken abruptly by the gaping mouth of the muddy San Juan River, a natural boundary between Nicaragua and Costa Rica.

A glitter of mirrorlike sunlight dances off the San Juan and other neighboring rivers as the big plane is jostled by endless updrafts of gusty tropical air. The thin line of beachfront quickly succumbs to a lush mat of greenery that from the air appears as a grayish black succession of low ridges, like the webbing of a duck's foot. These are the tropical rain forests of Costa Rica's Caribbean floodplain, the *tierra caliente*.

Twenty years ago, there were only occasional small clearings for little farms (*fincas*) within this sea of forest. Today, the same flight

The first jetliner, a BAC-111, of Costa Rica's flag carrier airline, LACSA (Líneas Aéreas Costaricensis, Sociedad Anónimo), at the El Coco Airport in 1971. The plane was christened El Tico, after *ticos*, the popular, affectionate name for the Costa Ricans.

path reveals a very different scene. There are many more farms and much deforested land. From the air, the low hills and ridges appear as bald scalps, places where the trunks of once-great forest trees, some more than thirty meters tall and certainly several centuries old, lie on the ground, strewn about like tiny matchsticks neatly splayed in rosette patterns. Here and there are small pockets of forest, ecological minutia of what was once a rich, unbroken story of tropical nature. But as before, the bright red roofs of humble dwellings come into view as we cross over rugged mountains ringed in dense clouds. Sometimes the clouds block out the mountains entirely, but I know that beneath them lies a special place, a "land of clouds," where ancient oak forests once stood and where naturalists over the last two centuries have roamed in search of birds, orchids, and much more.

The mountains loom ahead of the jetliner, appearing as massive bluish black pinnacles with motionless halos of waferlike clouds. More than once, the *simpático* LACSA crew have permitted me to view these mountains from the flight deck. Nestled high in their windward slopes are the birthplaces of Costa Rica's mighty Caribbean-watershed rivers, including the Río Sarapiquí. Before the plane crosses the volcanoes there is a clear view of a huge waterfall, a ribbon of pure white slicing through an incredibly steep, almost vertical wall of rain forest. It is the birthplace, the headwaters, of the Sarapiquí in all its primeval glory, a sentinel to tropical nature's untold story, to this special land's charms. From this view it seems as if the mighty river was born of the dense clouds that bathe the valley in perpetual rain and fog. During the rainy season especially, these persistent clouds nestle at the tops of cragged volcanoes, as they have for eons, fueling the sprawling network of rivers flowing into Sarapiquí and other points east. Here, one can appreciate the role of clouds, rain, and rivers in establishing the conditions necessary, along with consistently warm temperatures near the ground, to promote the evolutionary diversification of life. It is not difficult to appreciate the power of incessant rain to carve the river's gorge from volcanic rock, an event that linked the steamy heights of great volcanoes with the unfolding of nature on the silted floodplains farther east.

With the nose of the aircraft jostling against the wind, we slide through the mist between the towering peaks of the twin volcanoes, Barba and Poás, nature's gateway to the Central Valley and the bustling metropolis of San José. Once we pass through those peaks, we leave behind the world of Sarapiquí, so tiny from up here, and enter into another one, all within this beautiful little country. Coming down through the dense clouds of the rainy season, the broad vistas of the coffee farms finally come into view only moments before the plane touches down at the airport, about eighteen kilometers outside San José. The jetliner provides a perspective unavailable to the ancient peoples of this region, or to the Spanish explorers of the sixteenth century or the great naturalists like Thomas Belt of the nineteenth. As we descend rapidly from sea to land, slicing through thousands of feet of sky in minutes, the broad swath of tropical nature's heterogeneity on the isthmus of southern Central America is forged and replayed over relatively small distances on the geographical landscape of this planet. Many of the species of plants and animals thriving in forests at higher elevations are not the same as thrive at lower elevations.

Finca La Selva in the northeastern corner of Sarapiquí and the Braulio Carillo National Park in the Cordillera Central are the two endpoint ecological reserves for a continuous band of tropical rain forest spanning the entire elevational gradient of the Sarapiquí region. With international support from The Nature Conservancy, World Wildlife Fund, and the MacArthur Foundation, the region between these two localities has been purchased as one huge ecological reserve by the Costa Rican government. It is the last such remnant of forest in all of Central America's Caribbean coastal region. Field research studies by biologists in Costa Rica suggest that many species of mobile animals actually move between higher and lower elevations according to seasonal changes in food supplies and other resources required for survival and breeding. Thus many bird species found at Finca La Selva (La Selva Biological Reserve), at one of the lowest elevations in Sarapiquí, probably migrate to higher points as the seasonally related flowering and fruiting patterns of forest trees alter the availability of their food.

It has taken me years to appreciate the Costa Rican tropics as a total experience, an immersion in the countryside where people, their ways, and the natural history of the country blend together into one unforgettable experience. A special facet of this unique charm of Costa Rica is experienced as the jetliner touches down in the Central Valley. Mirth and friendliness permeate the plane, always completely filled with passengers and incredible assortments of carry-on luggage. Within moments after the rugged Cordillera Central gives way to the bowl configurations of the Central Valley, as the jarring wheels of the jetliner screech to a halt, the passengers break out into loud applause, heard well above the aircraft's engines as it taxis to the gate. LACSA is this way. In the old days, when airport security across the world was less of a problem, throngs of people would crowd on an open balcony of the old airport terminal, waving and clapping as passengers disembarked onto the tarmac. But what is still the same, after all these years, is the special fragrance of the dense tropical air felt immediately on stepping off the plane. It is from the dampened, mold-soaked earth of this fertile valley, a blend of thousands of years of rain and abundance of rotting plants, a natural end product of the luxuriance of vegetation here, and the foodstuff for new life. Nature is felt quickly in Costa Rica.

Early morning takeoffs are equally spectacular. The LACSA plane snakes its way around in an upward spiral, coming up eye-level first with coffee farms, then dairy farms, followed by cloud forest and the tops of volcanoes. Oftentimes, the route is directly over the Poás Volcano. At this point we are perhaps only a few hundred feet above the colorful crater of Poás. Sometimes the pilot deliberately banks the climbing plane over the blue-green crater, with its strands of white steam gusting in the wind. The plane shudders against the strong winds as it climbs higher and meets the clouds. The peaks of other, neighboring mountaintops and ancient craters protrude through the clouds, little patches of bluish black darkness against the dense white clouds and the rich blue hues above. I look down and often think about the many times I have stood at the lip of the Poás crater, with friends or in stark solitude, to peer into the crust over Earth's inner being.

Soon after the plane passes over the volcano, Sarapiquí unfolds below, first the craggy shadows of the land's wrinkled escarpment, then the rolling foothills of San Miguel and La Virgen, and finally the flattened floodplain and Puerto Viejo. During the long rainy season of this region, which generally lasts from April through November or early December each year, the rivers are swollen. From the plane, they now appear as reddish brown flat ribbons, not unlike smooth glass, almost as if frozen. During the brief dry season or *verano,* the rivers are narrower and the water crystal clear. It is during the rainy season that nature shows an exuberance of power and force. Great flows of water crush and grind stone into soil. Over long periods, this pulverized rock becomes the anchorage for life, providing a substrate on which microfloras and forests develop and take hold.

It is surprising what one can learn about the broad sweep of tropical nature from the perspective of a jetliner cabin. From the air, in a few minutes' time, the whole geography of Sarapiquí passes by, from the flat floodplains and ripples of the foothills beyond to the deep swales and ridges of the mountain escarpment. Rivers stand out as silver, shimmering threads against the darkness of the surrounding rain forest. The steep, shaded sides of the Sarapiquí River gorge stand out boldly against everything else in this aerial panorama. Everything suggests a special story to share, from the highly textured landscape and vegetation and the animal life it supports to the people living there. Sarapiquí is a region of change and metamorphosis, one of the last of its kind along the ribbed backbone of Central America, where forest still blends with *fincas*. For in the rest of Central America, rain forest has been almost totally replaced with agriculture and people. But still Sarapiquí ripples in the morning sun or evening rain with bonds to its past, its natural heritage fused with its people.

The winding road of Sarapiquí, as tameless as these ancient mountains, hugs the ridges of the great *cordillera*, making its arduous way from the valley to the steamy lowlands of the *tierra caliente* farther east. From the air, the road seems effortless and easy to travel. The ashen, muddy hues of that road, well known to many of us decades ago, today are supplanted by a smooth, pothole-free ribbon of asphalt along virtually its entire length. What a deprivation now for all of those naturalists and new biologists who come this way, making their way overland from the Central Valley to points east such as Finca La Selva. My bones and muscles will always remember the bouncing of the jeep on the road of yesterday, the scores of roadside repairs to jeeps thrashed about mercilessly by the potholes and gravel.

But nowadays, sleek autos and taxis make their way to Puerto Viejo with little challenge. Has the life of that historic road been extinguished? I do not think so. It still clings to the same hills and valleys, swings through the same hamlets, and still calls out what travel through here must have been like centuries ago. Such things, life's exquisite details, cannot be scoured from the road by layers of fresh asphalt. Yet it is too bad the biologists and natural history lovers of today cannot feel that special taste of this land by being jostled around in an old jeep. As one of my colleagues once remarked years ago about the Sarapiquí road, "It's a terrible, awfully long haul for such a short distance!"

Coming from San José, the region Costa Ricans call Sarapiquí begins immediately northeast of the Cordillera Central, where the village of San Miguel sits along the Sarapiquí road, at the beginning of the foothills into the *tierra caliente*. From the Central Valley up to Vara Blanca at the base of the Poás Volcano, the leeward side of the *cordillera*, the land is bathed in clouds most of the time. From Vara Blanca through Cariblanco and down off the escarpment to San Miguel is the windward side of the *cordillera*, the gateway to Sarapiquí. The road to Sarapiquí follows a mighty ridge that sits on one side of the Río Sarapiquí gorge, most evident at Cuesta Angel or La Cinchona near Cariblanco.

Twenty years ago, a rough gravel road connected the small hamlet of Vara Blanca with the last village at the end of the Sarapiquí road, Puerto Viejo (Old Port). Between these two points, a distance of about sixty kilometers, several small towns exist along the road. What must it have been like when early explorers slowly and arduously made their way through this rugged terrain on foot and horseback? When Columbus set foot on the Caribbean shore, on his fourth voyage to the New World in 1502, most likely there was little else here than a wall of tropical rain forest. Very little is known about the native people of this region of Costa Rica, but it is likely that these early explorers encountered only a sparse population scattered throughout the coastal area and inland foothills. From the coast, the Spanish established a settlement just below the point where the Sarapiquí and Puerto Viejo rivers come together before joining the San Juan. Thus Puerto Viejo became an early overland entry point into Sarapiquí, and in subsequent years a route from the Central Valley was established, where the major settlement of Costa Rica would occur in the seventeenth through nineteenth centuries.

The authentic journey into Sarapiquí still begins after the airport—the overland adventure. Even after twenty years, my first overland trip to Sarapiquí still remains one of my most memorable moments there. What brought me to Costa Rica in 1968 was my appointment to a postdoctoral research associate position with the National Science Foundation–sponsored Comparative Ecosystem Study conducted through the Organization for Tropical Studies, Inc. I was offered this position by Daniel H. Janzen. Finishing doctoral studies in population ecology at the University of Chicago in the summer of 1968, I arrived in San José one sunny morning in September. The Organization for Tropical Studies, Inc., a consortium of U.S. universities engaged in graduate-level teaching and research programs in tropical biology in Costa Rica, would be my host and contact in Costa Rica.

A stocky, round-faced, friendly man, Edgar Murillo, a jeep driver and all-around man Friday for OTS, greeted me warmly at the airport that morning and drove me to the Boston Hotel in San José. On the way to the hotel, Edgar livened up the thirty-minute ride in the jeep with a crash course on the landscape. As it was a clear morning, the view of the ring of mountains surrounding the Central Valley was most impressive. In the east, the Three Marias, a triplet of pointed volcano peaks, was a landmark I would come to know very well over the years. Closer in, low strata of mist were suspended motionless over the rolling hills of coffee and sugar cane. It was the rainy season and there was lushness all around us.

I saw a beautiful sight that I would enjoy many times over the years. In the Central Valley during the morning, billowing white clouds were just starting to ebb across the mountains to the east. Here, clouds take on a special character all their own, so majestic against the striking blue sky. This majesty too was evident in the way these churning clouds hugged the tops of the volcanoes. Driving along, it was easy to feel a sense of urgency, to want to race up the leeward side of these mountains and embrace the magnificence of the clouds! These clouds just were that way, every day here, as they surely have been for millennia. But you must come out here early, because later in the day the clouds show their full hand, often enshrouding the Central Valley with a total veil of whiteness and rain.

Aside from a three-month field course in tropical island biogeography in the Caribbean a year before, this was my first time in the tropics. Everything seemed so strange and exotic. After all, just off the streets of Hyde Park, Chicago's southside university community and the backdrop of the tumultuous Democratic Convention, I was suddenly immersed in a new culture and place. The soft, cooling breezes of the Central Valley, whistling and humming through the cracks of the rattling jeep fervently commanded by Edgar, a man eager to talk about his country, were a pleasant change of pace in spite of the strangeness and my disorientation to this place.

Much of the eighteen-kilometer stretch of highway between the airport (called El Coco in those days) and the city was bordered with coffee *fincas* and thickets of secondary-growth forest. Today, much of this has been replaced with five-star hotels and resort complexes, and with housing developments.

Today occasional parcels of coffee plantations are wedged in between light textile mills closer in to the city, and *Erythrina* trees (*poro*), once used as a shade cover for coffee bushes, still dot much of the landscape, even on the grounds of relatively new country clubs and resorts. During the intense dry season (*verano*) of the Central Valley, the tall, stately *Erythrina* drops much of its leaves and bursts into flower. The bright orange-red inflorescences brighten up the entire sun-parched landscape, especially in February and March. When everything else seems quiescent, baked, and dead, these big leguminous trees with their canopies of red (Costa Ricans call the tree the "Flame in the Forest") signal that the quenching rains of the wet season (*invierno* or tropical winter) are not far off. But for the Costa Rican summer in the Central Valley, the "Flame in the Forest" trees, together with a host of other trees and shrubs in full flower, match the exuberance with which the Costa Ricans reacquaint themselves with the sun following the long rainy season ending in December.

It took me several trips to Costa Rica to appreciate the stark contrasts in the vegetation between the rainy and dry seasons that typify
much of the countryside, and to some extent the hills and plains of
Sarapiquí as well. Vast vistas of a parched landscape, dotted with
vivacious clots of inflorescences that give away, from a distance, the
locations of certain species of forest trees, such as the *Tabebuia* with
its shocking floral canopy of yellow or lavender, easily spotted miles
away, give way in the rainy season to a tapestry of lush greenery largely
devoid of bright reds, yellows, and other floral hues. I had not been
instructed in the ways of tropical seasonality before, and even in 1968
our understanding of this phenomenon was largely rudimentary.

Daniel H. Janzen pointed out in 1967, in a paper published in the
journal *Evolution*, the adaptive significance of the synchronization of
flowering in many tropical tree species with the dry season of Central
America, based largely upon his field studies in Costa Rica. Indeed,
at the very height of the dry season, when everything is brown and
bare, many insects and other animals are active, pollinating the flowers of various tree species in bloom at that time. It seems so sensible
scientifically to consider the timing of insect activity in connection
with the availability of pollen, nectar, and other floral rewards, that
it took even longer to appreciate that many other plant species bloom
in the rainy season. I carefully poke through flowers whenever I have
the chance, coming up amazed at the great variety of bees, flies,
wasps, beetles, and other insects I find there.

I had never seen such biological diversity when I examined flowers
in the weed patches and forest reserves around Chicago and the Indiana sand dunes. Nor did I see things this way as a boy poking around
goldenrods, joe-pye weed, milkweeds, and other field plants near
my home in New York. For me, the Central American tropics became
a highly sensual experience aside from the science and the discoveries
to be made by myself and many other biologists. Edgar Murillo
that sunny morning in 1968, in his delightful *simpático* way, opened
my eyes to the beauty of his country along that highway into town.

Checking into the Boston Hotel I was greeted by Manuel Tobella, a hard-working, industrious Spaniard who, together with his wife, ran the little hotel. The hotel and the kindness of the Tobella family were home for many U.S. biologists in these early years of the Organization for Tropical Studies. The building is wedged tightly between a barber shop and butcher shop on a very busy side street. By no means fancy, its rooms were spotless and the cooking excellent.

The Tobellas quickly adapted themselves and their hotel to the unusual requests and antics of their biologist guests. Their storeroom was filled with all manner of field collecting gear, insect nets, mist nets, jars of pickled amphibians, lots of Schmitt insect boxes, bottles, and duffel bags. In short, this place was a blend of hotel, biology laboratory, classroom, and field station. Jorge Campabadal, who at that time was the local in-country director of OTS, undoubtedly paved the way for the Tobellas to adopt tropical biologists into the familiar atmosphere that permeated their hotel. We were certainly treated as if, indeed, part of their family.

What I remember most about this hotel was the versatility of the members of the Tobella family, especially Don Manuel himself. An hour or so after greeting guests and unloading their luggage, he was behind the bar fetching drinks. After this, he was the waiter serving dinner. At dinner time, Manuel and his family sat at a table near us. He'd look over to check our reactions to the food, which was always great. A large, ornate square can of Spanish olive oil was the centerpiece of his table. He always poured the clear liquid on his salad with the greatest of *gusto,* moving the can around so that the thin stream of oil dabbled all of the greens. It was one of Manuel's links to his native Spain.

All night long, he snoozed on the sofa in the reception area, waiting to unlock the door for the last guest exploring the night life of San José. Coming into town from the field, we would find him hammering and sawing away in the afternoon, doing things like building extra storage space for biologists to store their gear. For the people associated with OTS in the late 1960s, the Boston Hotel was one of those delightful places to return to after a long stint in the bush. The Tobella family made it that way.

Having a home base in San José where people were *muy simpático* and understanding of the often unusual needs of visiting *gringo* biologists has always been an important aspect of tropical field studies. Over the many years beyond my initial association with the Boston Hotel through OTS, I have been very fortunate in this regard. Allow me to explain.

Between 1971 and 1976 I was spending as much as six months each year in Costa Rica, chiefly in Sarapiquí, on field research, usually in two separate trips each year. During this time I obtained a low-rent apartment in the Apartamentos Miami in the San José suburb of Los Yoses, not far from the Costa Rica Field Studies Program office of The Associated Colleges of the Midwest (ACM) in San Pedro. Ofelia Achung, the affable and wise manager of the apartments, allowed me to convert an apartment on each visit into a makeshift laboratory, providing something of very curious interest to the building's other *gringo* residents (in Costa Rica for various reasons, I am sure). It was here that I met Franklin Barnwell, a biologist from the University of Minnesota who was conducting field studies of fiddler crabs. He and his students also used the apartments as a lab between stints in the field. Later, when I reduced the length of my stays in Costa Rica, I switched to the Amstel Hotel in downtown San José for interims between field trips. Yudi and Hans Van Der Wielen, who owned and operated the Amstel until 1984, allowed me to store boxes of field gear in the little *bodega* (storage room) at the hotel when I was in the U.S.

The Van Der Wielens expressed great interest in my studies and became fascinated with the various kinds of live insects I brought to their hotel from Sarapiquí. The housemaids never knew quite what to expect. Nor did some biologists. I recall one instance in which Philip J. DeVries, then a Peace Corps worker studying the distribution of butterfly species in Costa Rica in association with the Museo Nacional, stopped by one evening when I was in town. I had mentioned to him that I was rearing *Morpho granadensis* in my room. Skeptical, he suggested I might be confusing this rare species with a common one, *peleides* (see chapter 3); I raced up to my room and retrieved the female butterfly I was using to obtain eggs. After carefully examining the color patterns on the undersides of its wings, we agreed that the butterfly was indeed *granadensis*.

What was especially handy about staying at the Amstel was its ideal location. From it, I could walk a block to the photo studio of my friend Jorge Coto to have close-up pictures taken of butterfly eggs, using his special equipment to catch their fine details. Next door is the travel agency where Jorge Campabadal worked and took care of my airline reservations and those of many other U.S. biologists. Across the street is the Escorial Restaurant, a meeting place for many *gringos* and local folk, and where I often stop for *café con leche* (coffee with milk) or *té negro con limón* (tea with lemon) with one of the two Jorges, or both! And from these places it is a ten-minute walk to the Museo Nacional where I often go to have plants identified from field work. Carrying plastic bags filled with plant cuttings and caterpillars through the streets of San José, from the Amstel to the museum and vice versa, seldom failed to elicit stares and smiles of curiosity toward this *gringo loco!* If I stopped along the way, opened the bags, and showed interested people what I had, a common remark was *"qué raro este bicho"* (what a strange bug)!

The Van Der Wielens were immensely supportive of my studies, even allowing me to inaugurate the new freezer of their new hotel, the Bougainvillea, with my ice chests filled with specimens and research samples, which I did many times after that, stuffing the shelves of the new hotel's *bodega* with a dozen boxes of research supplies, because they valued the quest for knowledge about the natural history of Costa Rica. In their eyes, as in those of many people, Costa Rica's greatest assets were its kind, gentle people and the natural beauty of its landscapes. Clearly I have been the lucky one to have such cooperation, friendship, and logistical support from special people in Costa Rica over the years.

Monte Lloyd, an ecologist from the University of Chicago, and I left for Finca La Selva in Sarapiquí early one morning a few days after my first arrival in Costa Rica in 1968. La Selva would be my home in Sarapiquí for the next two years. And although most of my work in Sarapiquí over the past two decades has been conducted at Cariblanco and La Tirimbina, my first experience in the region took place at La Selva.

Edgar showed up at six in the morning to pick us up. He drove through a maze of narrow streets. Colorful signs over small shops, an occasional large store, hordes of people walking along, and the noise washed away any remaining sleepiness I had. We edged our way down Central Avenue, through the marketplace. Here, I saw sides of beef covered with flies and huge, gaping fresh fish suspended in the windows of shops. So narrow and congested was the market-place strip that I could easily spot exotic fruits and vegetables being hawked from little wooden carts. Small trucks, brimming over with bananas, plantains, and chickens, challenged Edgar in squeezing through some tight spots. Street vendors sold orchids, parrots, and other wildlife. But the most impressive thing about this place was the press of people everywhere. Not even the streets of Chicago had been this swollen with people.

After Edgar got us through the city, I felt that my first journey to Sarapiquí had really begun. I had no idea what to expect and I only knew a few vague facts about our final destination, La Selva. Within minutes, we were once again out on the open road, with Edgar bearing down hard on the gas pedal, pushing it as far as it would go before the jeep rattled to pieces. Near the airport, we veered off to the right, taking a paved but generously potholed road through the center of Alajuela. Edgar was not following any signs or looking for particular landmarks. He just seemed to know where to turn onto yet another nameless side street, as we crisscrossed our way

An outdoor marketplace for fresh farm produce in a San José suburb, Zapote, on a Sunday morning.

through this peaceful city, so clean and gleaming. I would learn from Edgar and others that Costa Ricans do not find their way around the country by using road signs or street addresses. Everyone simply learns where to go and remembers how to do it.

Edgar opened the engine to a full throttle, shifted gears madly, and pushed ahead with great effort, up the gradual but steady climb through coffee *fincas* and sugar cane fields. Country folk smiled at us along the way, walking along the edges of the road carrying firewood, generously sized trunks of heart-of-palm, and other produce, usually on their backs. This gateway to Sarapiquí was filled with clean, humble dwellings with gardens full of many kinds of flowers, both ornamentals and native species. Poinsettia trees, three or four meters tall, graced many homes. Chickens scooted away in front of the jeep, missing certain death by microseconds, or so it seems. Frantic dogs barked and jumped up at the sides of the jeep, while little children in clean school uniforms of blue and white laughed and waved at us, with us.

Each time I pass through these hamlets that the rest of the world seems to have forgotten, I find myself contrasting this natural warmth and openness to the restless streets of America's big cities and suburbs. I always feel refreshed by this infectious spirit of friendliness here near the leeward slopes of the Poás Volcano.

I heard the steady buzz of cicadas in the *Inga* trees shading the coffee bushes as we continued our journey. We rounded a sharp turn and I looked back to a breathtaking panoramic view of the Central Valley far below. The landscape was broken and the vegetation low and uneven for as far as I could see. Over the years, I became familiar

Picking the coffee harvest in the Meseta Central. Costa Rican school children sometimes are excused from classes to help with the coffee harvest.

with how the landscape and plant life change traveling into the slopes and across the valley into Sarapiquí. Coffee *fincas* have replaced much of the ground cover below a thousand meters elevation. In the hills above Alajuela and neighboring Heredia to the south, patches and strips of moist forest still cling to the steep sides of little streams (*quebradas*). *Madero negro* (black wood) trees *(Gliricidia sepium)* and a different species of *Erythrina* are planted here in neat, even single-file rows to make living fenceposts. The roadside and the interior boundaries of dairy farms, higher up the slopes, are marked off similarly. Many of these trees are planted, I learned, by simply cutting a sturdy branch with a machete and shoving the cut-off end, with its freshly exposed cambium layer, into the damp soil.

We were still climbing, on broken asphalt, as the coffee belt gave way to a damp lushness and eerie overcast, even in the morning. Looking out of the back windows again, I saw that the Central Valley was rapidly fading into a mist of vivid blue haze. But up here, a light drizzle coated the windshield and tickled the skin on my forearm, which was draped over the rolled-down side window in the front seat next to Edgar. I got goose-marks from the chill in the air. The bright red roofs of dairy farmhouses dotted the lush grassy fields, their sealike uniformity broken only by the thin lines of the living fenceposts, creating a patchwork of squared-off parcels of pasture. Thin wisps of bluish smoke trailed off from the houses. Near Los Cartagos, the jeep lurched around a hairpin turn putting us face to face with a troop of dairy cattle blocking the road and surrounding us. Two boys, maybe sixteen or seventeen years old, and a thin, wiry man perhaps in his sixties, all three with rosy cheeks, appeared and disappeared as they weaved among the twenty-odd cows. All three cowherds were wearing little white canvas hats with the brim pulled down and black rubber boots. Their shirts and pants were muddy and streaked. Brandishing long, willowy sticks, they gently guided the clumsy herd around our jeep. The smell of fresh cow dung wafted through the air. On a flat stretch of road a few more kilometers from this point, we pulled over to one side and got out.

Sprawling dairy farm on the leeward slope of the Poás Volcano, near Vara Blanca. Fences between pastures are frequently created by "living fenceposts," when cut-off branches of *Erythrina* and other trees are pushed into the soft earth and allowed to resprout.

What a peaceful silence there is up here. Against a slight rustling of water-soaked leaves in the cold winds and the distant sounds of birds, I heard little else. Tiny beads of water encased the long blades of grass overflowing from the pastures onto the asphalt. I stepped into the grass and lost my footing. My field boots sank down nearly a foot into the grass. I had not expected this. My feet slipped away and my shirt was caught on a piece of old barbed wire stretched between two trees. Edgar and Monte were some distance away, so I pulled myself up to the road. My pants were wet and muddy. This fragment of my initiation into the tropics was not over yet. I quickly felt a rush of needlelike pain on one of my ankles. My foot was covered with tiny reddish ants, perhaps thousands of them. The skin of lush grass concealed their nest where I had fallen through moments before. But the discomfort quickly subsided and I wandered down the road. The mist-slicked asphalt was decorated here and there with fresh, glossy olive-green cowpats, still steamy and perhaps only minutes old. Flies belonging to perhaps a score of species clustered on one of these, as if appearing out of nowhere. I had never seen cow dung before, nor these kinds of insects fervently drawn to it.

In a thicket of yellow bamboo jutting out from a stuccolike wall of rocks with cascading rivulets, small brownish butterflies, satyrids (wood nymphs), fluttered within inches of the puddled ground among the stems. A few of these butterflies perched on a moist spot on the rock ledge behind the bamboo. Overhead, I occasionally made out the silhouettes of small, brownish birds, perhaps warblers or wrens, as they flew out of bamboo thickets and brush higher up the cliff on the inside of the road. As it is here most of the time, the sky was leaden with the threat of rain. But when the sun did occasionally peak through the clouds, orange butterflies, akin to our fritillaries in North America, flitted across the road. Low-lying weedy flowers near the roadside reminded me of species I had seen in the U.S., especially in the Northeast. This entire area, above the coffee *fincas* and below the peak of the Poás Volcano high above us, had a surprisingly north-temperate complexion to it. What few glimpses I had of the animal life here confirmed this, as did the general appearance of the roadside flora. Certainly little here appeared tropical of the kind I had expected. Roadside flowers, including foxglove, were biological links between the American tropics and North America. Here I was, some eight degrees north of the equator, immersed in a chilly temperate mountainside.

The milk cows looked so clean and well kept up here. Many years later, I would learn from José Giralt, a friend of mine on the administrative staff of LACSA, that he coordinated the shipment of dairy cattle from Madison, Wisconsin, in the 1960s as part of an effort to "seed" these hills with milk producers. In those days, LACSA used the World War II workhorse aircraft, the DC6B, a four-engine propeller plane, to haul this living cargo from Wisconsin to Costa Rica. Farmers today in and around the Madison area still remember this bond of cooperation with Costa Rica far away. Though I didn't know the story in 1968, those milk cows were another sort of link to a north-temperate countryside.

As we continued on, I became less interested in the ramblings of affable Edgar and the factual treatises of Monte on various points of interest, and more affixed to the scenes unfolding around me. When the wheezing jeep found its way to a gentle straight grade along a ridge, I could see now the lofty peak of Poás off to the right, through the windshield. Something curious caught my eye. I noticed that on the neighboring peaks that were part of the bulky mass of Poás itself, lips of dense, dark green forest, seemingly uniform in appearance from this great distance, cascaded over the mountain crest, presumably from the eastern (windward) or Caribbean side still hidden from my view. These irregular slabs of forest, peaking through the dense, white clouds, stood out from the agriculturalized vegetation below, on the western slopes of Poás and nearby peaks for as far as I could see.

Closer at hand, little hamlets, slightly more than clusters of white houses and farm buildings with red roofs, stood out boldly against the crisp, green lushness of the sprawling pastures that fell away from either side of the road. Around each bend in the arduous winding road, as the jeep chugged harder and harder in the frosty air that condensed on the windshield, there was a new pleasant surprise. And through it all, what impressed me was the tranquility on these slopes, places where things wild, rugged climate, and people seemed harmonious and closely interwoven.

One particular spot that comes to mind in this regard is the bend in the road at Los Cartagos. Over the years, Los Cartagos became a landmark for my journeys to and from Sarapiquí. There are features about this spot that I think are very special, even today. Near here, the road dips down through a series of steep curves, crossing little creeks and streams bathed in dense shade from overhanging trees and woody vines. Like islands, small strips of ancient forest trees line the sides of these waterways, right up to where the road cuts across the water on narrow cement bridges encased in mosses and lichens. Some of these trees, both near and away from the road, are very old, the lone survivors of an original, long-extinguished cover of cloud forest. Agriculture, dating back thousands of years, has pushed aside much of the primeval forest. Great volcanic eruptions of past years must have shaped this place, with its webwork of little waterways and steep rolling hills. I have stopped at these little bridges many times over the years to see, close up, these trees and the life they support. Nowhere else in Costa Rica as in these mountain passes of the Cordillera Central does the theme of life building upon life become so readily apparent, even to the casual glance.

At Los Cartagos, the air is chilly with mist, drizzle, and rain. Milk farms are a dominant presence. Along the road, on the hill above Los Cartagos, there sits the withering estate of former Costa Rican president León Cortés, who ran the country from 1936 to 1940. Immediately to the upper side of the road, the fading yellow and red Cortés farmhouse still stands, a reminder of how this stretch of road came into being. In twentieth-century Costa Rica, it is more or less tradition that bridges in the countryside are named after the governing administrations that built them. Each administration took the opportunity to improve roads and build new bridges. Perhaps nowhere else in the countryside is this phenomenon more evident than in the upper slopes of the Cordillera Central.

To increase tourism to the Poás Volcano, the Cortés administration decided to build a new gravel road between the city of Alajuela and Vara Blanca. Rather than taking the most direct route between these points, the road deviates to swing by Los Cartagos and the Cortés farm. By the time the road was built, oxcart trails had already been established on the steep slopes of Poás and Barba, the wheels easily sinking into the volcanic ash soil, creating steep gulleys that defined the placement of future roads. The vast majority of these fledgling roads crisscrossed the western flanks of Poás and Barba, usually up to no more than 1,500 meters (about 5,000 feet), the upper boundary of coffee plantations in Costa Rica. Thus today, the town of Carrizal on the slope of Barba is the end of the road linking this *pueblo* to Heredia, the nearest big city farther down the mountainside. Between Carrizal and Heredia, there are many bridges crossing streams and gulleys, bearing the names of various Costa Rican presidents in whose administrations they were built. Much of this was in direct response to the expanding human population of Costa Rica in the late 1930s. People moved into the coffee and dairy farms of the slopes of Barba and Poás to find work. Los Cartagos is so named because the people who settled it came from the city of Cartago, the old capital of Costa Rica. Until the advent of World War II, the "modern" gravel road through the mountains and into Sarapiquí in the northeast did not extend beyond Vara Blanca. Before this, the road was little more than a footpath or horse trail linking the hinterlands of the *tierra caliente* to the Central Valley, a route dating from pre-Columbian times and the colonial era. It is in the hills around Heredia that many of Costa Rica's oldest, well-established coffee-growing families settled, including that of Julio Sánchez Lepis, whose *fincas* today are still recognized by their iron gates bearing the initials "J.S.L." Sánchez Lepis was the grandfather of Oscar Arias Sánchez, the president of Costa Rica from 1986 to 1990 who received the Nobel Peace Prize in 1987.

With just the sounds of the gurgling water and an occasional yelp of a dog off in the distance, I find great solitude standing near the foot of one of these big trees at Los Cartagos. Mist often swirls around its highest branches, and when it clears away, blown off by strong gusts rippling off the volcano above me, I see that virtually every spot on the branches is occupied by many kinds of epiphytic plant life. The spikelike, stout leaves of thousands of reddish green bromeliads give a rosy hue to the tree against the mist and drizzle all around. Stringy laces of pale green lichens resemble an ethereal maze of tiny roadways among the bromeliads. I am surprised to find ferns and even small trees and vines rooted to the branches. Centuries of the accumulation of airborne dust, fusing with the silt and ash of volcanic eruptions long ago, establish an aerial nursery for plant life here, secure within the incredible, rough-hewn tapestry of gnarled branches on these huge oaks. With my binoculars I make out the bulbous nodules of orchids out of bloom and nestled among the other epiphytes. Perhaps next week, next month, or a year or two from now, these orchids will send forth their inflorescences, some gaudy and big, but most subdued and inconspicuous to the human observer standing in this mist. But the pollinating insects will find them as they have for eons. At certain times of the year, I'd see the pendant red inflorescences dangling from the largest of the bromeliads. The incessant moisture of this place clearly encourages the growth of epiphytes everywhere, even on fenceposts, barbed wired, and electrical lines!

Once a group of students and myself collected a sample of water-filled bromeliads near here to see what kinds of animal life dwelled in them. Scattering ourselves over a large area so as not to overcollect on a few trees, we culled a few dozen bromeliads, the epiphytic wild cousin to the cultivated pineapple, and emptied their contents into white enamel pans to see what crawled away.

Through the light drizzle and grayness of that day, our fingers numbed by the chill and wetness, we shook the bromeliads, upside down, over the pans, shaking free creatures that scurried and scratched on the metal's slick surface. First came predatory arthropods such as spiders and scorpions, and later the more sluggish millipedes, isopods, and insect larvae, wrestled out of their tiny piles of plant debris wedged in and about the bromeliad's rigid leaves. These creatures are the decomposers, nature's recycling machines, breaking down organic debris into smaller pieces only then to be taken up by the bromeliad's tissue for its own nourishment. Mosquito larvae and an occasional immature dragonfly nymph, brown and subdued, slid down the concave wet surfaces of the bromeliad leaves into our pans. A couple of the bromeliads even yielded tiny tree frogs.

The food chain seemed complete for the miniature cycle of life that was sheltered in the dark recesses of the bromeliads thriving in the rugged slopes below Poás. Mosquito larvae fed upon bacteria

Tank bromeliads, often filled with gathering
rainwater along with many other kinds of
epiphytes, festoon trees in pockets of cloud forest
on the leeward slope of the Poás Volcano.

and other microorganisms collecting in the pool of rainwater at the
base of each bromeliad, and these insects became food for other
animals such as dragonfly nymphs and tadpoles. Once at a later date,
when the rain forest in Sarapiquí was being felled at one particular
locality, I found snakes such as the little docile *Imantodes* and its eggs
in some bromeliads.

The bromeliads sold in florist shops in the United States, with their leaves perfect and polished to a shine, their interiors swept clean of life with soapy water, mirror very little of what is truly special about these organisms in their natural habitats. Living water-filled bromeliads, and their companion epiphytes encrusting the primary branches of the few remaining ancient trees dotting the landscape, are microcosms of the bigger picture of biological diversity blanketing the American tropics. Organic debris accumulating in the cavity of a water-filled bromeliad establishes a highly organized food chain involving microorganisms, insect larvae, tadpoles, snakes, and other organisms—depending in some measure upon the size of the bromeliad and its lifespan. Other kinds of epiphytes harbor knots of wedged soil and plant debris that supports arboreal assemblages of litter organisms. Over the years, I sometimes found myself thinking, especially near Los Cartagos, that if we could understand the dynamics of life contained in a bromeliad in relation to its existence on the tree, we would have advanced greatly in our understanding of how tropical nature is structured overall.

But here below the shadow of Poás, which still loomed ahead of us, there were few other signs that we were in the tropics, apart from the epiphytes. The curious *Gunnera* plant fell into the same category of mystique at this time. As we advanced along the ridge just above Los Cartagos, the giant leaves of *Gunnera*, some close to a meter and a half across, hugged the steep cliff on the right side of the road. Within a year of my first time in Costa Rica, I would become close friends with Jorge Walter Coto, a successful studio photographer in San José who had spent a good part of his childhood at Los Cartagos. From him I learned about the attachment the people of this and other hamlets along the road had to the *Gunnera*. The flattened, fanlike leaves of the *Gunnera* were used as "poor man's umbrellas" by the country folk. The first time I saw these plants I was startled by the immense size of their leaves, the biggest I had ever seen anywhere. At certain times of the year, reddish spikelike inflorescences sprang up from the base of the stubby herb, barely peeking through the carpet of big leaves that formed a loose, shinglelike network of green over the steep side of the roadcut.

Under the very low intensities of sunlight characteristic of this cloud forest region, the large surfaces of the *Gunnera*'s leaves may help to trap what little light there is to fuel the metabolic machinery of this creature. Because of this, its very existence must be precarious. Embedded inside the thick stem of the *Gunnera* are evenly spaced packets of blue-green algae that seem to have no connection to the outside of the plant. How do these tiny, hidden partners of the *Gunnera* function? No one really knows. One intriguing thought is that these algae are symbionts, providing the *Gunnera* with some essential nutrients, while the *Gunnera* somehow feeds the algae with its metabolic waste products. Can the big, leafy *Gunnera*, certainly a very successful and abundant denizen of the roadcut through the

The giant leaves of the *Gunnera* plant are easily spotted along the winding road on the leeward slopes of the Cordillera Central, leading toward Sarapiquí. The leaves are often more than a meter in diameter.

cloud forest here, survive without these entombed partners? Again, no one seems to know.

Questions such as these, and many others, have been the grist of tropical natural history and biology studies for many years. Why is it that we find so many examples of unusual partnerships and associations between different kinds of living organisms in the American tropics? How have such interactions contributed to the development and maintenance of the immense biological diversity of the tropics? From the cloud forest embracing the slopes of Poás to the steamy *tierra caliente* of Sarapiquí farther to the northeast, each foray into the bush reveals a new partnership, a new interaction, waiting to be studied.

Today, we have yet to truly understand the workings of the *Gunnera*, a plant that has hugged the rugged terrain of the Cordillera Central for thousands of years. We have yet to understand the totality of any single kind of organism, for that matter. Yet the approach and the challenge bear verdant shade of optimism for those who choose to study tropical nature. In much of my own work, I have opted to study the natural history of individual species, for such basic facts are needed to build a comprehensive view of how tropical forests are structured and the ever-changing assemblages of life forms they support.

Here and there, during the dry season, I find only the skeletonized outlines of the *Gunnera's* big leaves. Hordes of shiny metallic-blue beetles clustering on the plant's thick stems tell the story. These leaf beetles, belonging to the huge beetle family Chrysomelidae which reaches its own zenith of diversity in the American tropics, are probably host-specific herbivores on the *Gunnera*. This fact, coupled with these insects' habit of affixing large numbers of their eggs on the leaves of this plant, ensure what I see before me on these roads when the *verano* is at its highest point. Near the end of the dry season, when the *Gunnera* sends forth tender, reddish young leaves, these too become the food of beetles. Possibly these insects have few enemies in nature, as reflected in the huge buildup of their populations—but who knows? During the long rainy season, the beetles are subdued, almost vanishing into the backdrop of plant life upon the high slopes. Perhaps it is seasonally related changes in the leaf tissue chemistry and the plant's own special means of anticipating the rainy season, as the summer wanes and it sends forth new shoots and leaves, that trigger the proliferation of the beetle population? I do not know the answer, but the question seems justified by the clockwork events of tropical nature that unfold in the leeward slopes of these mountains.

What I see along this road, what I get from a fleeting glimpse of the *Gunnera*, the epiphytes, and the occasional hummingbird appearing for a split second or two at a pale yellow-green inflorescence of a *Heliconia* plant hanging precariously from a cranny on a fern-choked cliff, are fragmented insights into the soul of tropical nature. I will never fully understand, nor will anyone else, the entirety of any of these parcels of hidden knowledge about the physical beauty of this world, but I am always awed and inspired to probe further.

As part of my cumulative Sarapiquí experience, I have also come to appreciate the whimsical facets of tropical nature that expose themselves only occasionally. Take, for example, tarantulas. On many of my passages through the mountains into Sarapiquí in the early morning hours, when the sun is strong and little columns of steam dissipate off the slippery asphalt, a lone voyager appears, slowly, carefully emerging from a roadside tangle of plants. A big black tarantula with vivid orange legs slowly inches its way through the wisps of vapor, crossing the road and silently disappearing into the cover of herbaceous vegetation. I am too enthralled with the magic of such a special moment to collect the big spider, a most magnificent creature. Its deliberate but fleeting debut and exodus remind me of the broader, unseen tapestry of wildlife that abounds in these hills—in places that know no roads. If I had searched all day for one of those tarantulas, a species that appears to be endemic to certain mountainous regions in Central America (whereas the more familiar brown species are common in the tropical lowlands), I am sure that I would not have found one. For me there is an unexpected element to the study of tropical nature; I can merely appreciate and be cognizant of its hidden elements.

It is a beautiful scene out here, but a mixed blessing in some ways. In a sense, the opening of the cloud forests here by the early settlers in the sixteenth and seventeenth centuries, and the explosive development of highland farming in the eighteenth and nineteenth centuries, established this patchwork of forest remnants and lush pasturelands in the Cordillera Central. In the highlands of Central America we do not find native grasses being used as fodder for dairy livestock. On these foggy slopes in the shadow of Poás, Kikuyu grass, *Penacitum clandestrum*, originally from Kenya, is the dominant fodder. The grass gets its species name from its habit of intense proliferation, namely, by underground rhizomes, which makes it a very productive, easy to introduce fodder. It is this spongy mass of rhizomes, hidden beneath the narrow leaf blades, that causes a person to sink quickly into the ground after taking a few steps on the grass, as I had done on my first trip. The native grass of this region in Costa Rica, as throughout Central America, is the bamboo, along with a handful of related, broad-leafed grasses that do not proliferate quickly.

Today, ninety percent of the highlands of Central America are covered with exotic grasses, the native species pushed aside by the insatiable tenacity of interloper species that spread quickly and expansively. The British naturalist Thomas Belt, in his *The Naturalist in Nicaragua*, a now-classic nineteenth-century account of natural history in Costa Rica's northern neighbor, discusses the clearing away of the highland rain forests and the introduction of exotic species of grasses for cattle. We know that many of the introduced grasses came in from Africa, principally through Brazil and Argentina. Much of this activity occurred in the last century. Today, most of the native flora of Argentina has been largely displaced by the several species of grasses, including the Kikuyu, that crossed the ocean from Africa.

The road connecting the Central Valley and San José with the Sarapiquí hinterland to the northeast was only recently completed (about 1960), becoming an entryway for the development of lowland farming, as settlers made their arduous way toward Puerto Viejo in the east from more upland points along the Cordillera Central. At Vara Blanca they crossed the Continental Divide. Today, on one side of the road at Vara Blanca the streams and creeks flow westward toward the Pacific, and on the other side of the same road they flow east to the Caribbean Sea. Along the road it is west of here that the land, with its uncanny alpinelike complexion, most closely resembles what it must have been like at the time when the region's first farmers, humble hard-working people from Spain—not the militia —cleared this land and built their first *fincas*. Today's Costa Rica is much altered, of course, from what it was like in those early times. Even in the eighteenth and nineteenth centuries, much of the Cordillera Central and mountainous zones south of there were largely blanketed in a fairly continuous forest.

It was after World War II that the road linking the Central Valley with Panama to the south was opened, paving the way for the development of highland agriculture in the southern portion of the country. The Cordillera's first introduced settlers, the Spanish farmers, probably did not bring with them the seeds of fodder for their farms-to-be. The deliberate introduction of exotic grasses such as the Kikuyu was most likely a product of the last century, although nobody knows for sure. It might even have been a matter of someone's cousin in Europe getting some seeds of this fast-growing grass from a friend or relative farming in the highlands of Argentina. Most likely the Kikuyu's arrival was an unplanned, unstructured "happening" with a tremendous impact upon the native flora of the highlands under the gaze of the Poás Volcano.

On my first visit to the region in 1968, I had no idea that the beautiful vistas of pastoral lands in these hills represented a story of ecological upset and change, in which native plant species and the animal life they support, the organisms that evolved in this once-vast forested land over millions of years, were pushed back into the steep cliffs and inaccessible crevices gouged out by little creeks and streams since the last cycle of glaciation tens of thousands of years ago. What the forces of nature had shaped and reshaped, in response to broad, sweeping changes in the natural environment over very long periods of time, would be pushed aside in incredibly short time through the advent of European colonialism since the sixteenth and seventeeth centuries. But I would come to appreciate this fact more and more, seeing firsthand the quickly changing face of forest in the lowlands of Sarapiquí over the next decade and beyond. This is what was really represented in my very first view of the logging truck, ever so slowly making its way down the winding road to the Central Valley from Vara Blanca and points farther northeast.

There it was, coming head-on around one of the many hairpin turns in the road, wide enough for only one vehicle, a big blue machine straining under a load of immense logs, each one five or six meters in girth, tacked down most precariously by a webwork of loose chains. The driver waved to us enthusiastically and friendly, as many would do over the years. It did not sink in right away that I was seeing but a very tiny part of an immense environmental dilemma, the clearing away of the lowland tropical rain forests of Sarapiquí. I did not connect those enormous logs with the trunks of giant trees several centuries in age, seedlings when Columbus had first set foot on what became Costa Rica.

Only later did I realize that each one of these huge logs going by us on the road had once supported thousands of generations of orchids and bromeliads down in the *tierra caliente*, and together all of these once-living plant tissues had supported tens of thousands of generations of butterflies, beetles, and other insects, not to mention providing both food and shelter for many species of birds, reptiles, and mammals. But on this first occasion I was more concerned about whether we would make it around the curve in the jeep, which was being quickly squeezed over to the inward edge (and not the drop-off side, thank goodness) of the asphalt. It did not take me too long to appreciate for the first time in my life the often fine line that separates life and death. Edgar, correctly sensing my anxiety over this situation, quickly volunteered a bit of logistical advice since he knew that I would be making this same journey many times on my own in the next twelve months. In his rapid-fire broken English, he implored me not to travel this road at night, since it was often foggy and dangerous. I would come to understand his concern.

Just beyond Los Cartagos we passed a steep rocky outcrop to the right, with little rivulets of water cascading under and occasionally over a mat of what appeared to be a morning glory vine. I was impressed by the immense size of the vine as it draped itself down the cliff, smothering the massive rock. Old rotting tree stumps jutted out from the mat where the rock gave way to earth, and in some places the trunks were completely encased in vine. At the very bottom of the cliff, a meter or two in from the road, *Gunnera* plants shaded and concealed little pools of water. Farther down the road there was a patch of *Gunnera* growing right up to the asphalt. Here, too, were crystalline pools of water, but not waterfalls or creeks. Rainwater dribbled off the big leaves and collected beneath the plants.

Not long ago, and after many years, I stopped to examine these pools of water that seemed to be there every time I passed through. In fact, along many places in the road, pools of rainwater gathered in the depressions to the inward side, before the terrain rises abruptly toward the clouds. This time, I noticed the cast cuticles (skins) of a very large-sized species of dragonfly. Several of the skins, caked with mud, were clinging to the undersides of the *Gunnera* leaves, and I almost missed seeing them. But my usual habit of always gently lifting up the leaves of tropical plants, especially when I see telltale signs of leaf-chewing damage from insects, ensured my unexpected discovery of the cast-off skins of this insect. Nearby I noticed a freshly eclosed adult dragonfly still clinging to its cast skin. It had apparently emerged only an hour or so before, just after sunrise on this sunny morning. Its big wings, a good six inches from tip to tip, still shimmered with that patina of newness so characteristic of freshly hatched insects. Its cast-off nymphal skin was just under the edge of a leaf, and the adult insect was illuminated in the glare of the sun.

Primary colors danced off its glistening wings and its big green compound eyes shone as if molded from polished metal. It seemed as if I was seeing a tiny rainbow issuing from the dragonfly. The creature's long body was ringed in shades of green, blue, and black. Only the day before, even the night before, the dragonfly had been a nymph crawling through the slick muck in the little pool beneath the *Gunnera*. There it had lived for at least several months, perhaps a year, feeding upon other living animal life sharing its aquatic existence. Even before its mother dropped an egg into this pool, this

A newly eclosed adult dragonfly clinging to the edge of a freshly unfurling *Gunnera* leaf along the roadside near Los Cartagos, early in the morning, a favored hatching time for many dragonflies. The mature naiad or nymph of this insect crawled up the *Gunnera* plant from a muddied puddle; the cast skin of the dragonfly appears as a dark smudge behind the insect.

baby was ensured by the fusion of two parents through sexual reproduction. Its parents lived long enough to fend independently for themselves, to secure enough energy in the form of flying insects snared
on the wing, to find each other and unite.

The dragonflies, one of the most ancient groups of insects or of
terrestrial animal life (which secondarily returned to the water for
development), have always been, for me, one of the most fascinating
examples of three-stage metamorphosis. The dragonfly nymph was
able to mobilize enough food in this small pool of water, a
microhabitat subject to periodic drying up and therefore temporary.
I peered into the water, scooped some up in my hand, and found
lots of mosquito wrigglers and other kinds of fly larvae. As the mud
and insects slipped through my fingers, I saw tiny strands of algae.
The mud was dark and rich with the stains of rotting plant debris.
The *Gunnera*, the mud pool, and the dragonfly were thus all closely
connected in this roadside vignette of nature. The big leaves of the
plant shaded the water once it ran off the leaves and road. The pool
became an incubator for life, its warmth encouraging the growth
of algae and other tiny plants.

Dying tissues sloughed off the *Gunnera* and other plant life embracing the little pool, with nutrients for yet new life to come. A settling
film of rotting debris on the mud became the host for a multitude
of microorganisms and protozoans, the baby dragonfly's first meals.
In the course of weeks and months, this nutrient bath became food
for herbivorous and scavenging insect larvae, these organisms being
the staple diet of the dragonfly nymphs as they grew.

During my years of study in the tropical rain forests of Sarapiquí,
I would come to appreciate too a similar example of how some dragonflies adapt to breeding in small pools of rainwater collecting high
above ground, not on it. The noted entomologist Philip J. Calvert
reported in the early part of this century that giant damselflies, close
cousins to the dragonflies and sharing the same ecological habits,
of the genera *Megaloprepus* and *Meceistogaster*, with wingspans of fifteen or eighteen centimeters from tip to tip, undergo their life cycles

in tank bromeliads where rainwater gathers. The adult stage of these enormous insects inhabits the sun-flecked openings in tropical rain forests, such as the places where a giant tree has fallen over and a "hole" of sunlight streaks down from the canopy break high above. Costa Ricans call the insects *helicópteros* because of their gyratory appearance in flight. Their gauzelike wings have bands of blue and white, giving the illusion of rotating blades.

I have had many long hours watching the *helicópteros* pluck tiny flies and other struggling insects snared in the tough, gooey webs of the golden orb weaver spider in the Sarapiquí forests. The big insects appear awkward in flight, as if very easy to catch with an insect net. But like the swift-moving dragonflies, they are very difficult to snare. Once a *helicóptero* perceives danger, it exhibits the motions of a real helicopter, making right-angle dips and dives just beyond the reach of the insect net, and then darting off swiftly to the higher reaches of the forest. But they seem to do a lot of foraging near the ground. The long, slender nymphs of the *helicóptero* curl themselves up in the debris at the bottom of a tank bromeliad, or lie outstretched along a submerged leaf blade of the epiphyte.

Although I have never found the nymphs in the bromeliads in the cloud forests near Poás, I have discovered them in the lowlands of Sarapiquí. Here, they devour the larvae of other insects and even the small tadpoles of tree frogs, such as the arrow poison frogs of the genus *Dendrobates*, which breed in the water-filled tank bromeliads high above the forest floor. Organic debris is continually raining down through the forest, lodging on branches, rotting there, falling into the cuplike central cavities of bromeliads, and becoming a nutrient-dense substrate for new life. High in the cloud-forested mountain near Poás and in the rain forests of Sarapiquí farther east, winds and rain unite to carry plant debris, to break it free, and establish an organic layer above the ground.

Most of the organic breakdown of plant debris in the cloud forest or rain forest stays well above the ground, never reaching the earth. For this reason, tropical forests support a wealth of plant species high above the forest floor. It seems as if every square inch of branch is used as an anchorage for some epiphytic plant life. The tank bromeliad, like the roadside pools under the *Gunnera* leaves, is a living trap that collects nutrients on which other forms of life depend for sustenance and shelter. By and large, this pathway of energy production and release, derived from the sun and fixed through photosynthesis into living plant tissues, which in turn become debris and living animal tissues, is absent from the temperate zone. Even under the cooler conditions of the slopes of Poás and the rest of the Cordillera Central, there is an element of environmental constancy, the year-round availability of moisture and the absence of freezing temperatures, that promotes the proliferation of nature into many life forms, one building upon another, some becoming a resource base for many others.

At Vara Blanca, where the Continental Divide marks the end of the leeward side of the mountains and the Central Valley, we stopped on that first journey at a little country restaurant, El Checo, at the fork in the road. Straight ahead, the road branches off to the volcano, which is now very close at hand. In forty minutes' time, we could be standing at the steamy crater or walking through the stubby forest to the lake crater. To the right, the road continues on, now windward, with a lot more winding as it gradually slopes down into the *tierra caliente* two more hours away. But for now, as I would come to do for many years, we chose to pause for a rest stop at the restaurant.

For several years following, the same short, chubby fellow behind the bar counter always greeted me with a big smile. Fernando was perhaps in his early twenties when I first met him. His thick black hair was neatly combed to one side, in a sort of modified 1950s style, shiny and slick. The most striking thing about him was his friendly demeanor, set off and enhanced by the ruddy hues of porcelain skin on his roundish face.

Fernando exuded an instinctive kindness, even to strangers like myself. He was the one in charge of the little roadside restaurant, the meeting place for farmers, log truckers, and the U.S. biologists in need of coffee and *bocas* (snacks). That first time, Edgar ordered *café con leche* for us. Imagine my surprise when the coffee was served in a regular drinking glass! Monte explained that the warmed milk or cream was poured into the glass first, followed by the hot, thick brew itself. Costa Ricans have perfected the way to pick up a piping hot glass filled almost to the brim with *café con leche*. I fumbled a lot, with burnt fingertips, the first couple of times.

It was not customary here to drink coffee alone, without a snack. Monte ordered *queso blanco frito con tortilla*, something famous in these parts of the *cordillera*. A locally made white cheese, dry and crumbly at room temperature, became satiny smooth when melted over a kitchen stove between a couple of tortillas. A few dashes of thick red tabasco sauce, aimed at the thin wedge of puffy cheese between the tortillas, was the finishing touch to our morning snack. The flavor was delectable and we ordered a second round. In subsequent years, good friend and Sarapiquí companion J. Robert (Bob) Hunter and I would enjoy these and other *gallos* here on many occasions. It was here, in the chilly recesses of this country inn at Vara Blanca, that I began learning some of those delightful *tico* (Costa Rican) expressions such as "*Regalame un cafecito, por favor*" (Give me a coffee, please).

This first time, Edgar, Monte, and I sat at a rough-hewn table in the darkened interior of the restaurant. A clean red and white checkered tablecloth partly covered the table. The stool was a bit small and low for me. A mural of a cruise ship, crudely done, was painted on one wall of the room. An old jukebox stood in the corner, one that accepted Costa Rican coins called *colones* and offered a strange mix of Latin tunes and then-current U.S. rock hits like Joe Cocker's "A Little Help from My Friends." The smell of dampness filled my nostrils, competing with the occasional smoke that seeped out from the kitchen. As I ate I could look in, through a little window in the wall separating the dining area from the kitchen, and see two young women as ruddy and well-scrubbed as Fernando preparing food for the few other patrons. Every once in a while, one of the girls would peek out and stare at us, curiously.

Fernando knew Edgar from before, and he asked what we were up to. When Fernando learned about my interest in insects, he took me over to the windows along the front side of the building. He had something to show me. Eagerly he pointed to several sphinx moths perched motionlessly beneath the window frames on the outside of the building. Looking closer, I noticed an assortment of scarab beetles perched on the window sills. Most of these beetles were about the size of the familiar grapevine chafer found in the northeastern United States, but a few of them were gold in color. I had never seen a gold-colored living insect before. I went to the jeep and fished out a killing jar from my gear and started to collect the beetles, after being coached by Edgar on how to ask permission to do so in Spanish. At that point I did not know any Spanish, but the language would come to me fairly easily over the next couple of years. Fernando chuckled his agreement, *"sí, sí, con mucho gusto!"* The moths were next, including a big wild silk moth (Saturniidae). Fernando told me, in his broken English, about the big *cornizuelo* beetles that came to the lighted windows at night, crashing and banging into them with such force that you could not miss them. These creatures, he said, were the size of a man's hand. I knew then he was talking about the biggest of the scarab beetles of Central and South America, *Dynastes* and *Megasoma*. I had only seen these huge beetles in museum collections or in natural history picture books. At Vara Blanca, according to Fernando, May was the big month for them.

The Vara Blanca stop impressed me with the high species richness of sphinx moths, beetles, and dragonflies I had seen at the inn's windows—less than forty-eight hours after arriving in the tropics for the first time in my life! Detecting my interest and elation, Fernando volunteered to become an insect collector of sorts for me. He would save moths and beetles in old cardboard boxes until I passed Vara Blanca the next time. And so it was, for several years. He saved many specimens for me, which eventually were deposited in the permanent collections of the Milwaukee Public Museum.

Two things I found particularly interesting about the moths he and I collected at the restaurant's windows over several years. First, many of the species were ones I had not seen at lower elevations in Sarapiquí. Second, we rarely came up with several individuals of a single species. Here, at the Continental Divide, almost 3,000 meters (about 9,000 feet) above sea level, the moth fauna was both biologically rich and unique to the area.

Sometimes on the road, especially between Los Cartagos and Vara Blanca, the fog is so thick that visibility is near zero. At such times I cannot see the asphalt, and stepping out of the jeep I cannot see my feet. But I can hear the winds and the patter of light rain on leaves. This is an eerie sort of silence, one broken by the occasional chirp of a bird off in the distance, perhaps at a spot where the clouds have whimsically opened, letting in the sun, ever so briefly. But it is surely not where I stand or drive, for everything is ghostly white at such times of the *temporal*. Now the rain forest is the cloud and the cloud is this forest and the land. I have been out here at night too when the fog is this way. Before coming to these mountains and Sarapiquí I had never experienced such a sense of being alone, of being lifted from the earth, into the mist and fog that surely gives this land its special life.

Seeing all of this, I had hoped one day to spend some time walking through these misty slopes of the Cordillera Central's volcanoes. That opportunity would not come for several years after my first visit. In 1975, I brought a group of thirty undergraduate students from Lawrence University to Costa Rica for a three-month course in tropical biology. One of our stops for field work was a small patch of mixed primary and secondary-growth cloud forest near San José de la Montaña on the slopes of the Barba Volcano not far from the Poás Volcano. The forest was a little dell, with steep sloping sides and several small, deep creeks. It was surrounded on all sides by rolling dairy pasture dotted with pine trees. Like long, gray beards, tangles of mosses and lichens dangled several meters down from the branches of tall trees within this forest. Squirrels darted among the branches, our fascination with their acrobatics broken only by the chatter of unseen birds high above.

Dangling from several big trees, clusters of the bat-pollinated flowers of a legume vine, *Mucuna*, swayed in the gentle breeze a meter or two above our heads, just out of reach. From the road, the forest appeared as little more than a wall of trees, blocking our view almost totally from its interior. A small gully, perhaps a meter wide and twice as deep, separated the beginning of this forest from the road. At first, I had barely noticed this menacing crevice, because the gully was covered by a thin mat of branches and herbs growing right over the open space. We found a place where we could cross it on the trunk of a small, fallen tree. The hard soles of our field boots skidded against the wet wood and the rock-hard soil where the log touched both sides of the gully. But all of us managed to cross over the abyss several times without mishap. Not only did I fear broken ankles way out here, I was petrified that the dreaded pit viper, the fer-de-lance, *Bothrops atrox*, might have taken refuge in the moist, dark bottom of the ditch. In many places, we could see the bottom of the dark recesses here and at other gulleys within the forest. Our field boots only covered our ankles, leaving plenty of room for snakebite.

Entering this little alpine forest was like walking into a large airy room filled with dancing shadows. The border wall of trees gave way to a rugged terrain with many scattered tall trees. A low cover, less than two meters tall, of tree saplings and bushes covered much of the ground. Except for the occasional pendant *Mucuna* cascading down from the big trees, whose canopies were a good twenty-five meters above our heads, and the strands of moss, the space between the forest canopy and the shrub layer was fairly open. Streaks of sunlight shot down through the canopy, highlighting tiny patches of the forest floor, like spotlights on a stage at night, and everything else was bathed in deep shade.

I felt as if we had entered a strange new world, as if we were suddenly quite far away from the broken asphalt road nearby. Standing still, I craned my head slowly in different directions, up and down, sideways, to detect signs of movement. I braced myself on my insect net. Through the tissue fabric of my cotton work shirt, bisected transversely by the thick cloth strap of my field pack, I felt the coldness of the drizzle that had somehow, incredibly, penetrated the leafy boughs high above and reached me. Sudden eddies of breeze acted in concert with the slow movement of an arm or leg to adhere the rain-soaked fabric to skin. Trickles of water fell from the tip of my nose. My Costa Rican *campesino* hat shielded my brow from the drizzle. My reward for such times was to see narrow-winged butterflies flutter slowly through the underbrush, the silent gliders over dark green leaves made shiny with the slick of mist and drizzle. Some of these butterflies, of the family Ithomiidae, or nymphalid subfamily Ithomiinae, had transparent wings, while others had wings decorated in tiger stripes of alternating lines of yellow, orange, white, and black. They perched on the leaves, their long, slender legs seemingly weak and fragile but capable of keeping the insect in place when assertive breezes suddenly rocked the understory.

Although I was to learn many landmarks along this road through and across the great *cordillera* over many years of traveling to and from Sarapiquí, I smelled my first volcano on that first trip with Edgar and Monte. One particular spot along the road became a landmark since, invariably, the peculiar smell of Poás was always there, waiting to engulf even a swiftly passing jeep. As we pulled away from Vara Blanca, I stuck my head out the window and sniffed the air. Just as we started our descent along a ridge, now to the left of us, the air was saturated with the horrific fumes of hydrogen sulfide or something very similar. A fissure near this point emitted fumes from the Poás Volcano whose cone was high above us.

Not long after this, I had an opportunity actually to visit the volcano. On my first trip to Sarapiquí I was to meet Gordon Frankie, an entomologist who was studying the phenology of flowering and fruiting of trees in Costa Rica as part of the Comparative Ecosystem Study, particularly at La Selva and in the northwesterly province of

Guanacaste. Subsequently, Gordon and I would travel to San José together from La Selva. On one of these trips, we decided to take a side visit to the Poás Volcano. It was the first time I had ever seen a volcano crater. But even more interesting to me was the distinctive vegetation we saw on the way to the two craters of Poás. As we came closer, distant forests, eerie smudges of dark green suspended in clouds and sentinels to a very different world behind the volcano, became clearer and easier to discern. With the exception of an occasional dairy *finca* that wedged its way into the edge of the forest, this belt of greenery in the immediate shadows of Poás seemed largely devoid of human habitation.

Bordering the craters of Poás, one of which last erupted in 1957 and the other a pristine lake, there is a dense forest of dwarf, gnarled trees. These trees are filled with many epiphytes, some of them bromeliads but many others not. Small orange butterflies weave their way through the flecks of sun dabbling across the leathery leaves of the trees. In such a place, insects are truly at the mercy of the weather. I have come across bees and butterflies perched comatose on leaves and branches poking through the perpetual mist of Poás. There they sit, motionless, waiting for a beam of heat from the sun to break through and tune up their metabolic machinery. Much more than in the lowlands, insects are held prisoner at these heights by the persistent cold and dampness. Only when the clouds are burnt off by the sun does the Poás forest come alive with the drone of bees, the flashing colors of butterflies, and even the throbbing darts of hummingbirds. Close to the seemingly lifeless crater of the volcano, this mountaintop is alive with many kinds of plants and animals, but one must search intently for them. Places like Poás remind me of the tenacity of nature, the way it comes back following a volcanic eruption. True, within the fury of the eruption much life is scoured away. But life does return, even within the scope of a few decades.

Some very special moments have come to me standing at the crater's lip on its westward side, gazing out toward the east. On a clear day, the *tierra caliente* can be seen from the Poás crater, giving a telescoped perspective on what is really a very rugged terrain between here and there, though a mere fifty kilometers or so as the crow (vulture) flies. Through strata of clouds at 3,000 meters above sea level, I could spot ridges of primeval forest beyond the mountain. It is this way each time I come here, yet slightly different too— one does not get bored with the magnificence of Poás! Off in the distance, when the weather was clear, I could see vultures high in the sky. At such moments I wished I had a vulture's-eye view of those inaccessible windward slopes of Poás. From our perch on the crater, I could only surmise what was out there, beyond where the ashen cone falls away into rain forest. I am sure I would have seen the mighty waterfall and the headwaters of the Sarapiquí River, appearing as a ribbon of whiteness against the gullied, forested slope of this mountain. Although very different, the forests of the windward and leeward slopes of Poás and the gray zenith of the volcano shared the same time and space. The seemingly dead opening in the earth where geysers of steam sallied forth now and then, the mirrorlike blue crater lake off to one side of this scar, these had shaped this place, setting the stage for the evolution of nature's symphony in the forest that closed in upon it.

If I could look west beyond the mountains from here, I would see an even greater piece to the complex landscape of Costa Rica, the expansive tropical dry zone in Guanacaste Province, once covered with dry forest centuries ago. Yet, too, when I look beyond the crater to the patchwork of *bosque* (forest) and *fincas* below the crater's edge, I am reminded that nature does not always make such a dramatic comeback, restoring life to a patch of scarred earth. What a vivid and tragic contrast it is to see the lushness of the tropical rain forest, with its complex layers of plant life and the fabric of animal life supported within it, side by side with a sun-baked deforested area where little can return to flourish again. Every year, I have seen more and more of this environmental scale-tipping in Sarapiquí. When great expanses of forest are cleared by machete, chainsaw, and bulldozer, the biological complexity of the original forest cannot return. For gone with it are the animals that pollinated the flowers of the plant life and other animals that dispersed seeds and fruit to replenish life.

At the hamlet of Vara Blanca and at the Poás Volcano looming above, I saw that nature, when left alone, moved slowly up here. Insects were incessantly at the mercy of the weather, unable to crawl or fly when it was cold and rainy. Near the top of the volcano pockets of pine trees dotted the land, before the dairy *fincas* gave way to the holdout vestiges of cloud forest even closer to the top of the cone. Above Vara Blanca the pine trees, introduced from northern Central America, replaced living fenceposts as the predominant borders to grazing pastures. At a few points along the road continuing to Sarapiquí on a ridge near the foot of this mountain, big iron gates, some with fancy emblems bearing family crests, now rusted and faded, decorated the entrances to dairy *fincas*.

WINDWARD ACROSS A MOUNTAIN RIDGE AND INTO SARAPIQUI

2

We had crossed the Continental Divide. Gradually we left the *cordillera* as the road, now very broken and filled with gravel and larger stones, hugged the ridge across the mountains. Up and down we went, passing many pasturelands to the right at first and then entering an area of steep, wooded ravines. For close to three quarters of an hour we followed the gravel road along a steep ridge, and here and there I caught fleeting glimpses of the churning, white waters of the Sarapiquí River far below. Now the clouds seemed to streak by us, and rain pelted the windshield with a force I did not experience on the leeward side of this mountain. Although we basically followed a ridge along one side of the Sarapiquí River gorge, our journey was not without its tumultuous ups and downs. Incredible hairpin turns where the road went steeply up or down (one in particular) seemed to defy the invention of jeeps, especially ones on the muddied gravel. Coming down one of the few grades in the road, we came upon the wonderful Catarata de le Paz waterfall near Cuesta Angel and La Cinchona. Today this spot is a regular stop for tourism buses from San José, because it is now very accessible with the newly paved road. But when I first started traveling to Costa Rica, the waterfall was a hidden jewel of nature tucked away in the windward slopes of the Cordillera Central.

Largely undiscovered at the time, it was best known to the loggers, local farmers, and OTS biologists on their way to and from La Selva.

Before reaching this mighty waterfall, we passed abandoned pastures and low-lying marshy fields. From the dirt cliff to the left, thick bands of *Epidendron*, a genus of orchid that roots itself in the ground, unlike most others which are epiphytic, was quickly noticed by the brilliant red and orange color of its flowers. Unlike many others of the estimated twelve hundred species of orchids native to Costa Rica (an incredible statistic considering that the country is about the size of West Virginia), *Epidendron* seems to prefer growing out in the open, with full exposure to the sun. Its very conspicuous flowers are certainly easy to notice against the grassy brown debris and herbaceous cover of the roadcut.

What is particularly striking about the orchid here is its dense popu-

A distant waterfall, El Angel, as seen from the ridge at La Cinchona, close to the headwaters of the Río Sarapiquí.

lations, a condition fairly uncharacteristic of many kinds of arboreal orchids. *Epidendron radicans*, this particular species, flourishes as a direct result of a mutualistic association between its roots and a certain kind of fungus. This fungus aids the orchid, its biological partner, by breaking down complex sugars, nutrients otherwise unavailable to the orchid for growth. In turn, the fungus receives nourishment from the orchid. Seeds of *Epidendron* germinating in close proximity to already established plants come into contact with this fungus, thus promoting the proliferation of the orchid as a locally dense population.

One of the first things I was told in Costa Rica was that this insect-pollinated orchid uses deception to attract bees, mimicking the floral colors and flowering habits of *Lantana*, a weedy herb in the mint family (Verbenaceae), which readily attracts all kinds of insects, including wild bees. *Lantana* flowers are rich in both fragrance and nectar, two things insects really go for but which are largely lacking in roadside populations of *Epidendron* throughout Sarapiquí and elsewhere. In order for this pollination-by-deception to work, the rewardless *Epidendron* must grow within close proximity to the insectophilic *Lantana*. I have not seen many insects on the exquisite blooms of this orchid, and I have not seen *Lantana* growing side by side with *Epidendron*. The idea certainly makes good sense, especially when throwing in the third floral partner in this three-way ring of deceitful mimicry, the familiar, roadside milkweed of Sarapiquí, *Asclepias curissavaca* Linnaeus. Mature plants of all three species are about the same height and often grow in the same kinds of habitats. *Asclepias* skillfully attracts hordes of insects to its fragrant, nectar-rich blossoms.

Yet along this particular stretch of road just beyond the Continental Divide, the orchid stands alone and seems to be doing very well for itself, given that I have seen it there for twenty years. I have not studied its methods of propagation, but I hold some skepticism about the workings of deceptive pollination in this particular population. Mustn't pollinating insects like wild bees rely upon multiple cues, over short distances, to confuse the orchid for an *Asclepias* or

Lantana inflorescence? Do the bees move great distances, say between separate populations of these three plant species, within the sufficiently short amount of time required to associate the similar floral color patterns between the reward-rich "models" and deceptive "mimic"? These questions have intrigued me every time I drive by this area in Sarapiquí, but I have not found time to study them. Much farther down the road, where the floodplain is just beginning and gentle rolling hills come off of the great ridges of the *cordillera*, at the hamlet of La Virgen de Socorro, there is a field filled with *Asclepias* but no *Epidendron*.

A few years after I first saw the waterfall at Cuesta Angel, Bob Hunter explained to me that the sturdy wooden bridge over the roaring water below, not far from the headwaters of the Sarapiquí River, was built by the U.S. Army Corps of Engineers during World War II. When I first saw them with Edgar and Monte, my attention was drawn more to the waterfall than to the bridge, for the latter seemed insignificant at the time. But as he keenly does with many subjects, Bob Hunter brought the bridge to life for me. Farther up the road at La Cinchona, he related, the U.S. government had attempted to develop plantations of quinine trees, a species native to the South Pacific. Quinine, the malaria combatant of those times, was in short supply and Costa Rica's Sarapiquí Valley had been targeted as a place to grow additional supplies of the drug. But the ridge proved too wet for too many months each year, and the project was shut down. But not before the U.S. government did the Costa Ricans a favor by putting in the bridge, which still stands today.

Amazingly, this bridge is built of Douglas fir, precut in the Pacific Northwest of the U.S., and not constructed from local, tropical timber. The engineers and construction crew who built the bridge knew little or nothing about which species of tropical forest trees would be most suitable for bridge construction. In fact, putting in the bridge was part of a deal struck between the U.S. government and that of Costa Rica. In exchange for allowing the U.S. to explore the establishment of quinine farms on the eastern flanks of the Cordillera Central, the U.S. agreed to extend a gravel road from Vara Blanca to La Cinchona and build this bridge. It was also part of the pact that the U.S. would return the land used for quinine to the Costa Ricans once the project (and the war's Pacific campaign) was over. It was not difficult for Costa Rica to enter into this agreement under then-President Rafael Angel Calderón Guardia, since it was the first nation in the hemisphere, even before the U.S., to declare war in 1941 on both Germany and Japan!

A historical footnote to this modernization of the road up to this place during the early 1940s: the U.S. government was then building the Pan-American Highway, since it was deemed important to the war efforts and future U.S.–Central American relations to have access to the Panama Canal, through Costa Rica. Because steel was a limited commodity needed for the war effort, the U.S. opted to build the highway with as few bridges as possible. Douglas fir might suffice for small bridges such as the one at Cuesta Angel in Sarapiquí, but would not be suitable for larger bridges over wide rivers and gorges. Thus between Cartago and San Isidro del General, the highway was built along the Continental Divide, without crossing any bridges. The U.S. company contracted to build the Pan-American Highway through Costa Rica, Mills & Co., set up camp near La Georgina below Cerro de la Muerte, a town known today as Villa Mills.

Even today I still stop at the La Paz falls to take in the view. Ever since I stood there with Edgar years ago, at the base of a very steep mountainside that seemed to go straight up into the clouds, the thing that has impressed me the most is not the waterfall itself but the ways in which the plant life closes in on it. Small broad-leafed trees, intermingled with palms and great ferns, cover the sheer cliffs on both sides of the waterfall. In some areas, there are thickets of the banana leaf–like *Heliconia* plant. This particular species, one of about twenty-five of the genus native to Costa Rica, has pale yellow, pendant floral bracts that, at certain times of the year when the plants are in flower, hang down from the cliff, advertising themselves to the several species of hummingbirds found here. Several hundred feet of space separate me from the *Heliconia* plants, but I can still see the sudden, split-second appearance of a hummingbird, coming out of the thick forest, at the floral bract. And then it is gone. A wisp of a chirp from the swift animal signals me to look over to that spot. It all happens so fast. The forest on the cliff chimes with the activities of insects, birds, and other animals. At dusk, it comes alive with a different cast of characters, as evidenced by the shrill calls of tree frogs and, from below, at the pool's edge, of toads. When the sun comes out, the water sparkles as the thick sprays cascade down over a series of rock tiers from high above.

Usually when I pass by this place, the air is filled with light drizzle or grayness from mist higher up the slopes. But occasionally I get lucky long enough to see the brilliant, electric-blue flashing of a *Morpho* butterfly as it meanders along the riverbed to the other side of the road from the waterfall. For years I would pursue the study of the life cycles of *Morpho* in Sarapiquí, and would soon come to recognize this particular species as *Morpho peleides*, a "blue morpho."

The wall of forest climbing up the cliff, jutting out from the cliffs, bordering the waterfall is like a thick, haphazard wire mesh holding back a pile of rocks. The intertangled carpet of tree roots, vines, and plant debris has formed a brace to hold the terrain from falling down. Most of the time, it works just fine. But over the years, I came to learn that landslides were a very common occurrence in these mountain passes.

On one occasion about eight years ago, I was driving to Sarapiquí with Bob Hunter's wife, Nancy. En route, there had been a mudslide just before one of the several very sharp curves in the road. The reddish brown claylike earth formed a thick sheet across the road almost at the point where the road curves downward. A steep drop-off of about fifteen meters separated the upper half of the turn in the road from the bottom half. A big logging truck, attempting to cross the mud coming up the hill, was stuck, jackknifed, in the middle of the earthen mess. Traffic had accumulated on both sides of the impasse. Nancy pulled out a cigarette and sighed something to the effect that we would be here for a long while. A lot of advice was being exchanged among the occupants of the stranded vehicles about what to do to move the truck and clear away the fallen earth. Where the earth had broken away there was a thick strip of brown cutting through the forested cliff above the road, as if the rugged rain forest had been bisected by a huge orange-red ribbon of earth.

After several hours of waiting, when it was obvious that little was being done to rectify our problem, a few of us decided to slowly maneuver our jeeps across the muddy sheath. I opted to work my way around the outer side of the truck, where there was slightly more room to maneuver. The danger was slipping off the mud and tumbling down the incline to the road far below us. As a light drizzle filled the afternoon sky, I gave it my best, and just barely got us across the landslide. It made me wonder why we had waited so long! But judging from the numerous death markers along this road, especially at curves like this one, patience was the best option under these circumstances.

When Edgar pulled me away from the waterfall on my first visit, we drove off and I looked back over my shoulder as the jeep chugged up the long grade carrying us closer to the *tierra caliente*. I could still feel the cool freshness of these mountains tingling my arm as it jutted out over the door frame. I could see the full height of the waterfall as the jeep made it to the crest. There were three tiers or ledges, and near the top everything faded into the white mist. This must be one of the most beautiful sights in the world, for there was something both idyllic and tantalizing about the wall of dark green cloud forest and the eddies of mist spiraling off of the tall, thin trees on this windward waterfall.

I was always very impressed by the quietness of Sarapiquí. It was refreshing to shut out the noise and pressures of technological living in the city. But it was different from escaping to northern Wisconsin for a break. At times I needed the exotic element, the total submersion in the tropical setting. My nostrils needed to be filled with the perpetual fragrance of the damp, moldy earth of Sarapiquí. My eyes needed to see the shimmers of a *Morpho* butterfly captured momentarily in a shaft of sunlight along a creek bed. My ears were attuned to the sounds of the cicadas, katydids, and tree frogs of the tropical rain forests, and my fingers became accustomed to the slippery feel of rain-soaked leaves, lateritic mud, and my soaked field boots. Because of the enormous separation from life in the U.S. that I felt during my first two years in the tropics, I would not have guessed I would end up feeling a need for such things. But this is the way it turned out.

People certainly made a big difference. In Sarapiquí, I have been very fortunate to interact with local folks who shared my enthusiasm for nature in a casual way and were always willing to help me out. The closeness I felt with the people in Sarapiquí is part of my personal experience with tropical nature. I could not readily separate my interest in exploring the natural history of insects from my associations with the Costa Rican people and others who took an interest in me and my studies.

On the road, the Costa Ricans were always willing to give assistance when my jeep broke down. Usually I had to deal with minor repairs that I could do, such as flat tires, but on other occasions the assistance of others was most welcome. Many times I have felt the queasiness of despair when my jeep "died" on a steep grade in the middle of the countryside. I had not grown up a handy person, a tinkerer, with automobiles. The simplest of tasks initially proved difficult when my jeep failed. But someone always came along to help out. Guests I have taken with me into Sarapiquí have never failed to be utterly amazed with the willingness of strangers to help fix my jeep. Although I offered money in exchange, it was seldom accepted. Usually the reply was "*Somos amigos*" (we're friends), and a comment to the effect that one day perhaps I could return the favor out here. At these times I could not help thinking that this spirit of unconditional cooperation out on the open road must have been characteristic of colonial and pioneer eras in the U.S.

But I was not always cognizant of the unconditional friendliness of the Costa Ricans. It took me a while to appreciate that their friendly, spontaneous smiles were not mere politeness but were completely sincere, and were backed by a willingness to be of practical assistance. This was a very gratifying feeling, one that made me want to keep returning to their country to pursue my studies. It would have been easy to turn away and quit after two years, but, in part because of certain people who came along the way, I developed a special bond to Costa Rica. I have come to appreciate the Costa Ricans' realistic sense of caring for others, reflected in large measure at the societal level by an equally marvelous sense of balance, politically, socially, and economically, in the affairs of living. A tremendous encouragement for education for all, employment laws reflecting a socialistic sensitivity, socialized medicine for all, and a vigorous individualism and independence in financial success comprise this sense of balance. And yet the rest of the world does not really know much about this aspect of Costa Rican life.

Minutes after leaving Vara Blanca, while the road is still hugging the back side of Poás and before it teeters on the apex of the very narrow ridge into Cuesta Angel, there is a *pulpería* (little general store) set off to the left. The tiny wooden structure, painted in time-stained hues of blue and red, is nestled in a recess cut into the earthen road bank. From here, it is not very far down a steep, winding grade to the La Paz waterfall. I have passed the little store many times, although I hadn't noticed it on my first time through here with Edgar. I have seen the *pulpería* flourish with the vibrant smiles of country folk on a Sunday afternoon, and I have seen it on the wane as a dying ember of the colonial-era ways of life for the several families of *campesinos* who live close by.

It was here I had first stopped to inspect the huge, bell-shaped blossoms of the *Datura* shrub (*Reina de la Noche*, "Queen of the Night"). In many places along this ridge and farther on, the pendant flowers stand out all year long, attracting bats that pollinate them at night and all sorts of small insects by day. People here plant the

A *pulpería-cantina* near La Cinchona, on the windward slope of the Cordillera Central along the road to Sarapiquí, as the road appeared before it was paved a few years ago.

shrub as an ornamental next to their houses. Sometimes the flowers are greenish white while other times they are pink. Before this, I had never seen flowers so large in size. The shrub belongs to the huge Neotropical family Solanaceae, the group to which cultivars such as tomatoes, eggplant, potatoes, and tobacco belong as well. In the forest of Costa Rica there are hundreds of species of "solanums." The first time I saw the *Datura* blossoms here, I thought they had come very close to my expectation of strange, tropical plants —the same way I felt about the *Gunnera*.

Many times I did not see anyone behind the open counter of the *pulpería*. Its square, darkened interior seemed devoid of life. But a few times I noticed a young girl, perhaps sixteen years old, with bright reddish hair and a face full of freckles, peering over the counter, which appeared to be too high for her. The first time I stopped, she wore a tattered old sweater, and her body trembled in the damp chill of this day. She was small and frail against the drizzle of that afternoon, but she smiled and asked me what I needed. "I'd like a cold Coke," I asked. "*No hay hielo*" (we do not have ice), she sighed. I accepted a warm Coke. I had not expected to discover a freckled, red-haired Costa Rican out here on this desolate ridge on the windward slope of Poás. Cans of sardines, tuna fish, peas, and other foods lined the crude wooden shelves at the rear of the store. Behind that wall there appeared to be family living quarters. A baby wailed and a puppy scurried about the girl's feet, both largely hidden in the shadows of the floor.

I inquired if she had seen many butterflies here, to which she responded in the negative. After paying the few *colones* for the Coke, I was on the road. Just down from the *pulpería* there were a couple of small houses along the road. Tin cans of many sizes were filled with flowering plants of several kinds, adding a festive appearance to these modest dwellings. Throughout the valley, flowers adorned the houses. Potted plants festooned the wooden railings of porches and bordered the pathway from the road to the house. Before venturing into Sarapiquí, I had never seen so many flowers around a house, anywhere. But here in this valley it was not always easy to separate nature from the people who lived in these little houses.

A few kilometers beyond the *pulpería* the road swings very abruptly around, in what must be one of the tightest hairpin turns anywhere in the world, and off to one side a generous slice of rain forest blankets the windward side of an extinct volcano. From the road to the beginning of this forest is only a few hundred meters, and thus the forest stands out boldly against the pastures closer at hand. I did not realize it on this first trip to the region, but several years later I was told by the residents of Cariblanco about *el tigre* (the jaguar) that thrived in this rain forest. How very close to civilization the majestic beast of the rain forest was at this place! Sometimes, on my later trips when I became familiar with the region, I'd pull over on this crest and gaze out at the rain forest. The marvel of the human eye permits taking in the breadth of nature at such moments. I scanned from the bottom of the forest, where the pasture and little creeks gave way to thickets and later the rain forest, to the high slopes of the volcano and the clouds. This was the home of the jaguar, for I knew that *campesinos* understood this land. I have not seen *el tigre* here, but I know it thrives there. Its presence is as assured here as the rain forest itself, the cry of the toucan, and the din of the winds brushing across this land. Whenever I drive by this spot, I think about *el tigre*, even many years later. Another facet in the charm that defines this mountain ridge.

Along the bumpy stretch of road as it comes off the hills is the pastoral setting of the Echandi farm. Below the mountain the expansive *finca* stands out boldly, the red metal roofs of the buildings all huddled together beneath a cluster of big trees. The lemon-green carpet of rolling pastures, fusing upland with the cloud forest beneath a volcano, resembles the scenes on the way up the mountain to Vara Blanca on the other side. Edgar and knowledgeable others I came this way with later, such as Bob Hunter, all gave me their versions of the same story, that this farm was one of the most successful in the Sarapiquí Valley, and that it was owned by Alfredo Echandi, brother of a former president of Costa Rica. The white wooden walls of the main house, with its huge enclosed front porch, breathe an element of importance. On the fairly flat expanse of land around the dwellings, there is little evidence of the forest that once grew here, as ranch hands, on horseback, go about their work.

Prior to World War II, Sarapiquí's landscape between Cariblanco and La Virgen farther east was made up of German- and British-owned dairy farms and coffee plantations. In the early 1900s the site of the Echandi farm was the German-British Sarapiquí Coffee Estates. Between 1946 and 1947, Alberto Echandi Montero rented a tractor and plowed a road between the farm Isla La Bonita, owned by Fernando Alvarado Chacón, situated at La Cinchona where the quinine farms had been unsuccessfully planted several years earlier, and this farm near Cariblanco, farther east. The task was completed in 1949, a year after Costa Rica's famed revolution, led by the popular José ("Don Pepe") Figueres (who later went on to become president three times), which abolished the military. Echandi needed a road link to La Cinchona, Vara Blanca, and into the Meseta Central to haul milk from his farm to San José. In this manner, the gravel road I first encountered in 1968 was extended to Cariblanco.

During the 1940s, Fernando Guardia Montealegre, a cousin of Dr. Calderón Guardia, then president of Costa Rica, purchased thousands of acres of previously owned German dairy farms at La Virgen, for about 40,000 *colones* (about U.S. $8,000 at that time; $5,000 today). One of these farms even had an airstrip, and today the *pulpería* El Aeropuerto still stands on the east side of La Virgen. This land purchase prompted an extension of the modern gravel road from Cariblanco through San Miguel to La Virgen, which was accomplished between 1950 and 1954. Between 1955 and 1956, then-President Mario Echandi, a son of Don Alberto Echandi, pushed to have the new road extended from La Virgen to the end of the line, Puerto Viejo; this was completed by 1959. Prior to the road, the population of Sarapiquí was very small, with many of the inhabitants making a living with bananas and balsa wood trees along the rivers. A retired World War II boat was used, in the pre-road days, to haul these commodities down the rivers to the coast, from where they were taken to Puerto Limón. Because of the region's inherent inaccessibility, Sarapiquí was not opened up to Costa Rica's central population until long after the lowlands of the Limón area (which was connected to the Central Valley by a railway).

Several years after my first journey in, I came to appreciate the thirst-quenching taste of the "water apple" (*manzana de agua*) from the stand of trees along one side of the road near the Echandi farm headquarters. My first encounter with this exotic fruit is still vivid. The jeep had stopped very abruptly that morning, and Bob Hunter, who was driving, didn't tell me why. He just got out of the jeep and poked around with his machete at the lower branches of the trees. At first I did not see what he was looking for. Many times before I had come by this spot on my own but not noticed the pinkish fruit hidden in the foliage. All I could see from the jeep were the thick clusters of shiny, dark green leaves of these tall, stately trees, all lined up in a neat row parallel to the road. "Here, try one of these, Young," he mused, as he tossed a peach-size, oblong pink fruit toward me. My teeth sank quickly through the succulent white pulp of the water apple, which is not an apple at all. The bland taste of the fruit did not impress me, but I could feel my dry, parched mouth swelling back to life. I wondered if this tree grew naturally in the forests around here? As if reading my thought, Bob offered a bit of history on the water apple, which, as I learned that day, was introduced from the Orient. Since that day in 1972, I have stopped here many times to fetch my own treat.

Even though much of these hills and ridges along the Sarapiquí Valley is close to a thousand meters above sea level and the air is cool and fresh, I often felt hot and thirsty while country folk bundled up against the weather, exclaiming, "*qué frio!*" Many times, little boys, outfitted with long bamboo poles, knocked down the water apples, while others climbed into the trees to fetch the fruit. Crushed fruit spotted the dense ground cover of dry leaves with splashing of red and white mash, the handiwork of human feet and the hoofs of cattle and horses. Tiny flies, representing many species, buzzed around the exposed pulp fermenting in the dry morning air. I had hoped to find butterflies feeding on the fruit too, but seldom did. The crushed fruit, even after rotting for a day or two, did not have much of an alluring fragrance.

As if this road heading northeast into the *tierra caliente* of Sarapiquí was a corridor through a vast outdoor theater and the plants along its sides the principal players, over the years I found myself anticipating what I would find at the next turn. Would things change dramatically from the last time I was here? Consider the beautiful Bengal clock vine for instance. Just beyond the stand of *manzana de agua* trees, the huge leafy mass of the Bengal clock vine completely covers a cluster of small trees. Its shiny, dark green, ivylike leaves are hardly discernible against the other foliage that forms a low-slung wall concealing from view the rolling pastures beyond the road. But at certain times of the year, this latticework of solid green comes alive with the large, lavender blooms of the vine.

I had seen this vine growing in gardens in San José and other cities in the Central Valley, where its profuse and large flowers make it stand out from everything else. But something was distinctive about seeing the vine out here in a dense patch of brush along the road to Sarapiquí. For one thing, the vine, even though a massive tangle, did not seem very conspicuous here, even when in bloom. Out here, it appeared more like a part of nature, even though an exotic species, rather than an adornment for a city garden. Still, I found myself drawn to the flowers when they were present on this vine. At such times I paused here to watch them for hours. Even in the shaded recesses of this spot along the road, the flattened, platelike petals of the flowers stand out, with an almost ghostlike appearance. Suddenly, on this morning, the clouds break apart and ribbons of sun reveal this patch of beauty, rising up three or four meters above me, exposing it to the rest of nature. *Thunbergia grandiflora* (family Acanthaceae) springs to life as scores of stingless bees (*Trigona*) descend upon its flowers peeking out of the foliage. Solid black bees, amber bees, and bees of both colors move silently, separately, from one flower to the next. Here and there, a tubular, wrinkled drying flower drops on the leaves, ignored by the bees. Even from where I stand, a good meter away from the closest blooms, the creamy white clots of pollen in the pollen baskets (corbicula) of the bees are easy to spot against the darkness of their bodies and the backdrop of the foliage. The sun goes away as quickly as it came, and that ethereal patina of moments before has returned, as if the flowers were bioluminescent. But the bees carry on, seemingly oblivious to the dimming of the sun as the clouds fuse together overhead.

I begin to notice a pattern to the antics of these bees, which must have included at least three distinct species. Sometimes an individual bee ignores the trumpet-shaped central core of the flower, shunning the yellowish inner walls of the corolla and the cluster of mustache-like anthers huddled inside. Instead, the insect hovers momentarily on the outside of the flower, near the base, before alighting there. Slowly I approach the flower. The bee is chewing its way into the turgid tissue of the corolla, bypassing the opening in the flower and making its own entryway into the inner depth of the flower. Why not go the easy way? Why bother with all of this biting and chewing through floral tissue when access is already there? Once the perforation is made, the bee dips its head inside and appears to be lapping up a clear, watery liquid.

Later, I take a micropipette, the mini-straw of field biologists interested in collecting small amounts of freestanding floral fluids, and ease it gently down through the corolla opening to the bottom of the flower. Twisting the syringe cap impaled on the pipette, I draw up a few drops of the fluid. A simple field test, using a diagnostic chemical, can tell me whether or not the fluid contains sugar. The bees are going after nectar from the Bengal clock vine in a most unusual manner. Other bees crawl down the slippery corolla, tumbling along part of the way and grasping at the tubular stalks of the pollen-engorged anthers. Peering into the flower, I can easily see that the bee is chewing into the anthers and collecting the creamy white pollen grains.

These industrious stingless bees are getting pollen and nectar from the *Thunbergia*'s flowers without tripping the mechanism of pollination. I have never seen any fruit on this vine or on several others in the area. Based upon a lot of field studies in Costa Rica and elsewhere in the American tropics by many biologists over the years, it appears that such opportunistic "pollen-thieving" and "nectar-thieving" behavior by these bees and other floral visitors occurs quite frequently. Flowers are targets for insects because both pollen and nectar are rich in nutrients, especially proteins and carbohydrates. In each species of plant, floral physiological traits, such as the amount of nectar and its nutritive composition (even though it is largely water) and the amount and nutritive make-up of pollen, have evolved to accommodate the food needs of specific animals that pollinate the flowers in the wild; they also are exploited by maverick opportunists.

Especially in the American tropics, these interrelationships between plants and their pollinators reach a zenith of specialization and intricacy. The timing of flowering, the intensity of flowering, and whether or not both male and female reproductive organs are contained within the same flower (hermaphroditic, as in the case of *Thunbergia)* or held separately in different flowers on the same individual plant or on different plants within the population, are additional behavioral traits of each plant species that shape its relationship with its floral visitors and its principal pollinating agents. More than anywhere else on the Earth, the tropics support the greatest diversity of animal-mediated pollination systems in plants. Through the detailed field study of animals such as bats, hummingbirds, bees, flies, and others in relation to plant biology, tropical biologists have built on the foundation laid by Charles Darwin, Thomas Belt, and other early naturalists in elucidating the close interdependence of plants and animals in promoting each other's survival.

Because geographical regions and even local habitats vary greatly in the kinds of ecological factors present and in past evolutionary history, it is logical that intimately intertwined ecological associations between plants and animals, well documented for the American tropics, differ also from region to region. The Bengal clock vine, I learned later from Luis Diego Gómez Pignatario, a renowned Costa Rican botanist, is native to India, where its flowers are presumably pollinated by certain species of large-bodied bees endemic to that region of the world. Stingless bees, native to the American tropics, are not a "good fit" for *Thunbergia* flowers, I surmised.

Even in the hundred or more years since the *Bounty* commanded by Captain Bligh, and under the guidance of chief botanist Christopher Smith, brought to the Caribbean islands an assortment of Pacific and Asian exotic plants, including *Thunbergia* and *Bougainvillea* (which also does not set seed in the New World tropics), bees and other insects native to the region have not adapted to these plants as pollinators. Such plants are propagated by cuttings. Thus all of the Bengal clock vines and *Bougainvillea* bushes (the Costa Ricans call it the *veranera* or "banner of summer," since *Bougainvillea* blooms chiefly in the dry season) I see today in Sarapiquí and elsewhere in the country are direct descendants of the original material brought over by the British in the last century. Aside from unusual somatic mutations, these plants are presumably all genetically identical with the plants originally brought over. From my encounters with the beautiful Bengal clock vine, an exotic misfit in the already species-saturated countryside of Sarapiquí, I thought it was also possible that all of the vines were genetically self-incompatible, that is, the pollen from their flowers was not capable of successfully fertilizing the egg cells (ovules) of the same flowers, even though the reproductive structures of both sexes occur together in the same flowers.

Bob and I mused that we had the Caribbean island British governors of the last century to thank for many of the exotics, such as *Thunbergia*, that have made their way into mainland Central America from the islands. The governors wanted these plants as attractive ornamentals for their palatial gardens, and along with spices, such as nutmeg and pepper, these became a regular part of Captain Bligh's cargo brought over from the Old World tropics. Scattered down the Caribbean coast of Central America, from Belize to Costa Rica, are settlements of former West Indian blacks, whose history in these parts dates back to the last century. In the era of British pirates, these populations blossomed.

When Minor C. Keith, an engineer and a founder of the United Fruit Company in Boston, decided that a railroad should be built from the Caribbean port city of Limón to San José, blacks were brought in to form part of the labor force needed to build the railroad, which was completed in 1890, thirteen years after it was begun. Keith's dream was to ship bananas from Limón to Boston and New York, but he needed a means to get the fruit to the coast from the plantations in the steamy coastal interior of the floodplain. Even today, when I visit Limón, I admire the ways the blacks there decorate their homes with flowers. Costa Ricans, I am convinced, and particularly the communities on the windward side of the Cordillera Central, are diehard lovers of nature. Their humble dwellings glow with many species of ornamental plants. And here in the tropics, it is a year-round love affair, unencumbered with the necessity of hothouses. By and large, I cannot find exotic plants growing in the wild habitats of Sarapiquí; these plants live on the margins of tropical nature. Because many exotic plants are highly inbred and have been artificially selected for certain characteristics having little or nothing to do with survival in nature, they generally lack the ecological traits necessary for competing in the wild with endemic plant species.

Yet they serve to remind me of a basic axiom about tropical nature. The tropical forests are filled with hundreds of species of plants (some biologists estimate as many as three or four hundred species of plants per acre of lowland tropical rain forest in Sarapiquí, an astonishing figure). In the north-temperate zone of our hemisphere, perhaps there are a mere dozen or so species per acre. In the species-dense forests of Sarapiquí and elsewhere in Central America, each plant species is acutely adapted to the prevailing physical environment and the multitude of other species of creatures found here, from microorganisms, living squashed down in a thin film on leaves, stems, and roots and in the dense rotting litter on the ground and trapped high above in epiphytes, to the insects converting plant tissues into their babies, to the birds and mammals that feed on them or disperse their seeds and fruit.

What all of this tells me is that there is no place for exotics in tropical forests. In the north-temperate zone, each summer people concern themselves about invasions of weedy species into native habitats, from the purple loosestrife across the northern states to water hyacinths in Florida mangrove swamps. Such events, in which an exotic plant species takes over a habitat, are far less likely in the species-saturated tropical forest. Even if *Thunbergia* and *Bougainvillea* could set seed, they would most likely stay at the margins of nature. In Sarapiquí, plantations of black pepper and cacao are favorite feeding places for certain species of birds, which very likely disperse some seeds from these cultivated, but sexually reproducing, plants into the surrounding rain forest. I have walked through these forests for many years and see no signs of black pepper or cacao taking over. Nor do bananas, which originated in the Indo-Malayan region, take over the forest. It is usually the other way around. But I must admit that I am enthralled, each time anew, by the lovely colors of the potted flowers decorating the homes in the Sarapiquí Valley, knowing that many of these are exotics introduced as ornamentals from faraway lands, through a circuitous route brimming with world history.

I hadn't seen Alvaro Wille in many years when I stopped by to ask him to identify the species of *Trigona* specimens I had collected from the flowers of two Bengal clock vines, one in Sarapiquí, the other in San José. He used to have an office in the old School of Agronomy building on the University of Costa Rica campus when I first met him in my days with OTS. But this was 1979 and he reacted as if I had dropped out of the sky, a ghost from ten years ago. Back then, Alvaro was still fairly fresh on the heels of having received his doctorate from the University of Kansas, where he studied bee systematics under Charles D. Michener. Since then, he had become the leading authority on stingless bees in Central America and Mexico. When I finally found him, in his basement office in the Fine Arts Building, he gave a loud, hearty laugh as I closed the door behind me. After an *abrazo* (hug), we sat down and closed the gap of years in a matter of minutes. He kept pushing back his thick gray hair and his sentences ended with mirth and laughter. The same Alvaro I had known before.

The bees were quickly identified. He swung his chair around to a table with a dissecting microscope and emptied my three vials into a dish. He talked away about lots of different things as he peered intently through the eyepieces. Business out of the way, Alvaro told me he was going to the newly created Corcovado National Park to camp out for six months with some students. This would be some adventure, for sure. Corcovado is situated on the Osa Peninsula in the southwestern corner of the country, and its area includes a magnificent stand of tropical rain forest. He invited me to come along. I felt honored, but I could not get away for that length of time. Knowing Alvaro's intense love of nature and his ability to rough it in the wild, I suggested to him that he write a book about his Corcovado experience. He liked the idea.

"I'll tell you something, Allen, about stingless bees," Alvaro offered. "I believe that they are responsible for most of the pollination of tree species in the tropical rain forests here." Over the years in Sarapiquí I had come across these bees on many plant species, and what Alvaro said made sense to me. I offered back, "These bees certainly seem to be very versatile in what they do, where they feed, that sort of thing." They were certainly opportunistic, even in terms of floral robbing. Virtually every blossom on the *Thunbergia* I had been studying had been perforated with the telltale damage of *Trigona*. I was confident that these bees would have little difficulty visiting the blossoms of native species in Sarapiquí's forests.

Later, when Alvaro's award-winning book *Corcovado—Meditaciones de un Biólogo* (EUNED, Costa Rica, 1983) came out, he discussed his own observations on these bees in Corcovado, and the evidence for their ubiquitous role as pollinators. I saw Alvaro Wille again in 1983, after his book was published. The Corcovado experience had been rough on him, and he had been ill for some time afterward. Teasingly, he chided me, "Allen, the book was all your fault!" We were both glad that he did the book. It articulates how he felt immersed in the rain forest of Corcovado, the almost spiritual experience of being there. More than the book, I enjoyed Alvaro's enthusiasm for Costa Rican nature when we talked in his cluttered office.

Looking back over the years, I believe that one of the most enjoyable aspects of studying tropical nature was returning to San José to share my discoveries with Costa Rican biologists and ask for their input. Luis Diego Gómez, a wiry man with a thick black mustache and wire-rimmed glasses, a most serious student of tropical nature, never turned me away. He never minded my coming around the museum to ask questions, to ask for assistance in identifying food plant species of the butterflies and other insects I was studying in Sarapiquí.

Like the open spontaneity of Alvaro, the kindnesses of Luis reflected, I believe, his perception that I was serious and persistent in my pursuits of descriptive natural history in his country. I felt deeply honored when Luis had me appointed as an "honorary curator" in entomology at the National Museum in 1974. There were the special quiet moments when we sipped wine in the den of his home, listening to classical music and discussing the philosophical side of natural history and biologists. But now, back to my first foray into Sarapiquí.

Edgar pushed on, undoubtedly tired from the rough road we had come through up to this point, and a silent calm penetrated the jeep, even though the vehicle still jumped up and down over the gravel and very deep potholes and my ears rang from the incessant rattling. Bad road has a mean way of wearing you down, and this one was no exception, especially after three hours of hard driving. Soon, however, I detected a very distinctive change in the terrain. We started plunging down hillsides more than we went up, a half an hour or so east of Cariblanco. The tropics had arrived! The jeep very quickly became hot and stuffy as we descended more and more, leaving behind the refreshing coolness of the highlands and the mountain ridge. I would come to know this transition in climate many more times. Great clouds of dust engulfed the jeep and a thick sweat coated my forehead as we rocked all over the road, one side to the other.

This is the threshold of Sarapiquí's steamy hot lowlands, the *tierra caliente*. The change in air temperature is phenomenal coming down out of the mist and mountains behind me. The green lushness of the cloud forest gives way to the yellow hues of tall grasses blanketing the sides of the roadcut and the rolling hills dropping away from the road. The steep ridges and crests of the mountains seem light-years away, even though they are less than an hour's drive. Off in the distance, through the blue haze of sunny days, unfolds the pano-

Potholes in the Sarapiquí road during the rainy season near La Virgen, about 1979.

rama of the sprawling tropical lowlands. This is really the arrival into the region called Sarapiquí.

This is about the point in the journey where my cotton work shirt begins to stick to the cracked vinyl of the jeep's seat, as if the rough ride has fused my body with the machine itself. Not far before La Virgen de Socorro, a dense stand of natural rubber trees, *Hevea brasiliensis* (Para rubber), borders the left side of the road for a few hundred meters. The bark of these trees is crusted with several kinds of lichens, and small bromeliads sprout from the thin branches beneath the canopy. The rubber gives way to a field of dark shiny-leaved bushes, coffee plants, when the road curves around sharply to the right. The *finca* belongs to a Costa Rican named José Heinrich von

Storen. During the rainy season the bushes are filled with the white blossoms of the *robusta* variety of coffee. Whereas most coffee, especially the flavor-rich varieties, is grown in the highlands, *robusta* is a base-bean coffee that can be grown at the lower humid elevations of the Caribbean watershed. At the bottom of this hill, two large trees to the right side of the road, behind the large main house of this *finca*, have been nesting sites for the oropendula for many years. The big, teardrop-shaped nests, consisting of tightly thatched vines, grass, and twigs, hang down from the top branches of these trees, easily spotted from the road. The large crow-size birds, dark maroon with yellow tail feathers, can be seen flying in and out of the cluster of nests. It was the strange call of the oropendula, a series of deep gurgles followed by a crackling sound, that really convinced me I was in the tropics.

Leaving La Virgen, the road cuts through a flattened area of the floodplain planted a long time ago in African oil palm, once a major

Nests of the oropendula.

source of the principal oil used in the making of margarine. What must it have been like for those first *gringos* from the United Fruit Company and other companies to come down here and clear this land before there were bulldozers? What tremendous amount of sheer manpower had it taken to convert the cover of tropical rain forest that once blanketed this region into the monotony of African oil palm? Surely it all must have started with a road of some sort into new reaches of the terrain and the rain forest it once supported. But before the road there must have been something more modest, an opening picked apart by human beings thrashing machetes to and fro.

It is because of these things that the main road into Costa Rica's northeasterly wilds, the road across the mountains and through Sarapiquí, has a special complexion for all to deal with and recognize as such. This man-made entity really slices through a time dimension as well as the rugged landscape of this green-embossed isthmus. What sort of history was buried in these winds, what events in the lives of people happened in the shade of that enormous *Ceiba pentandra* tree that still ushers the traveler into the outskirts of Puerto Viejo, the last stop on this road? It is the giant tree that no one who passes by can help seeing. The tree's huge main branches form a candelabra effect against the sky, and great throngs of epiphytes reach down toward the earth from their anchorage points fifty meters high. Did the toucans, parrots, and morphoes once glide through its leafy boughs during ancient times when the rain forest stood here and this stately tree was one ecological minutia in a tapestry of many? What the tropical rain forest was like here long ago we must now appreciate in the isolated, scattered survivors, such as this giant *Ceiba* with its rich assemblage of piggyback creatures, and the creatures that disperse its seeds and feed on its leaves and roots. For isolated survivors like this add to the store of knowledge to be reaped from what little intact rain forest still exists out here on this plain. But today, as it was in 1968, the rest of the fauna has been pushed back to the other side of the Sarapiquí River, within easy eyesight of the big tree.

As we came over a small crest, I thought Edgar was heading straight for the Puerto Viejo River looming straight ahead! Instead, he came to a screeching halt at a gas pump, making a swift ninety-degree turn on the soft gravel, but hardly raising an eyebrow of the fellows standing around. For many years, and still today, the same fellow came out to service the jeep, now caked with mud below and a coat of red dust above. Poker-faced then and always, his conversation was minimal at best. Just below this gas station, the typical scene at the river bank also hasn't changed much over twenty years.

Slender dugout canoes with outboard motors, painted in pastels, sit idle in the mirrorlike pools of brownish water on the Puerto Viejo side of the river. Sometimes another pulls up, brimming over with bananas. Small pickup trucks slowly back their way, as far as they can, down the bank to within fifteen meters or so of the water. Young boys silently pick up the heavy bunches of green bananas, loading the trucks which take the produce to the Central Market in San José. These modest shipments of fruit are the toils of little banana farms farther downstream, well out of sight from here beyond the wall of rain forest that blocks our view. Not too far below here, the Puerto Viejo River flows into the San Juan at the border between Costa Rica and Nicaragua to the north. I seldom thought much about the physical closeness of Nicaragua in the sixty or more visits I have made to this spot to gas up and gaze down at the river. But today I feel that closeness, reaffirming that this region, Belt's "Seripiqui," is indeed one of change, reflective of the times.

A few years ago, as I sipped a cold Coke while waiting for gas, a dugout canoe pulled up with three young men, each one of them no more than twenty years old. Silently, they tied up their boat and walked up the slippery patch to the gas station. All wore tattered tee-shirts and shorts and each carried a military-style automatic rifle. The sweat-stained shirt of one of them was emblazoned with *"Viva la democracia."* They wanted cold Cokes too. I surmised that these fellows must be patrolling the river farther downstream and the Costa Rica side of the San Juan.

Seeing these young fellows was a sobering experience, bringing into focus the reality of human strife not far from where I stood. I could not help thinking about how different it was when I would visit Puerto Viejo while studying at La Selva. Puerto Viejo back then was a refreshing respite for myself and Gordon Frankie from La Selva. Our priorities tended more toward ice-cold Cokes, cookies, or cold *cervezas* (beers), and exploring *almacenes* (all-purpose hardware stores) for things like rope needed in research projects. I thought too about Edgar taking me to my first *almacén* in Puerto Viejo on that first trip to Sarapiquí.

Looking down the hill from the gas pump at the end of the road in Puerto Viejo, as I have done many times while waiting for my turn at the busy pump, and seeing the dugout canoes coming and going, I consider what it must have been like here centuries ago. During colonial times, ships docked at Greytown at the mouth of the San Juan River northeast of here. Merchandise and people were hauled from Greytown up the San Juan to the Puerto Viejo River, and unloaded at Puerto Viejo. This was in the time of Belt's "Seripiqui." Dugouts could go little farther upstream due to rapids, so the rest of the journey into the interior had to be overland. It was a one-day trek on horseback or foot from Puerto Viejo to La Virgen, another day to San Miguel, and so forth. What became established as a footpath and horse trail in Sarapiquí in these times was the forerunner of the modern gravel road. Because of the arduous nature of the overland journey to the interior of Costa Rica, the Central Valley with its flourishing farms, in the eighteenth and nineteenth centuries, it was not uncommon for some Spanish seagoing ships to journey up the San Juan River to Lake Nicaragua and seek overland passage for people and cargo using a Pacific coastal route. Access into Costa Rica through the expansive plains of Guanacaste Province, especially during the lengthy dry season, was considered an easier task than through the mountains of Sarapiquí.

History just didn't seem to leave Puerto Viejo alone. Way out here, where the tropical rain forest once covered the land, where a mighty river system soon meets the tropical sea, I feel the legacy of a history spanning four centuries, from the early Spanish settlers to the political strifes of modern-day Central America. Even so, on my early visits to the region, I could not help being enchanted with the frontier ambience of places like Puerto Viejo. The ferry crossing on the Río Puerto Viejo is a good example of what I remember most about the human history of Sarapiquí.

The engine-driven ferry launch, guided on a steel cable and pulley, shuttled jeeps, trucks, buses, people, and horses across the river where the old road continued on to Las Horquetas and Río Frio. This ferry was owned and operated by a Lebanese–Costa Rican named Antonio Sauma, who put it there to provide access from Puerto Viejo to and from his farm on the opposite side of the Río Puerto Viejo. Today, his son Jorge Sauma is the executive director of a new agricultural university located near Siquirres in the Atlantic Zone, and called "E.A.R.T.H." (Escuela Agrícola Regional Tropical Humedo). Today the ferry across the Río Puerto Viejo operates no more, having been replaced by a modern concrete bridge at a different place near the town. But in the old days, the ferry added a special frontier touch to the area. In those times, virtually the whole region depended upon the ferry and the ferryman. The generator-operated ferry's giant pulley-and-cable system kept it on course and prevented the structure from being swept downstream, especially during the torrential floodings that came in the latter half of Sarapiquí's long rainy season. The ferry itself did not appear terribly assuring as its rusted steel and wooden body was well worn by its many years of service. And there was no protective superstructure to escape from the rain. I also remember that there could be very long waits for service. If the ferryman was out sick, or if the little gas station (*bomba*) ran out of gasoline, or if the cable system broke down, it could be hours or days before service was resumed.

It was here, on the Puerto Viejo side of the river, that we waited for the La Selva boatman, Rafael Chavarría, to take us to Finca La Selva, a twenty-five-minute boat ride upstream. This first time and

The ferry on the Río Puerto Viejo at the village of Puerto Viejo, in the 1965 rainy season. This ferry operation, once the vital transportation link between Sarapiquí and Las Horquetas, Río Frío, and other places in the *Vertiente Atlantico*, no longer exists, having been replaced by a bridge not far from this site. Photo courtesy of Gerald R. Noonan.

many other ones tended to have the same ritual. We'd unpack all of our gear from the jeep and stack it near the water. Rain or shine, we'd wait there for Rafael who, uncharacteristically for Costa Ricans, would show up precisely on the schedule he agreed to with the OTS office in San José. Rafael did not display much of the *mas o menos* (more or less) philosophy about schedules typical of the city folk, who had their own customs of *hora tica* (Costa Rican time), which generally meant being fashionably twenty or thirty minutes late to an appointment. When we arrived at the river in time for the noon trip to La Selva, sometimes we'd occupy ourselves by skipping stones over the water. Here is where I learned about the big green *Basiliscus* lizards, dubbed the "Jesus Christ lizard" because of their habit of scooting quickly across the water when frightened. The creatures would dart out from the edges of the water, from some unseen spot, at what seemed to be the slightest provocation.

Rafael's boat, appearing around the curve in the river, would break my folly with the lizards and stones. He always stood erect and proud as he docked his dugout canoe on the gravel. Tight-lipped and serious, he skillfully put the boat in its place with a long stick. Rafael was a man of few words who required a bit of work to open up. But once he did, he was a very friendly and helpful man. For many years, he was the boatman hired by OTS to ferry people, lumber, and supplies to and from the field station that many years later would be dubbed Estación Biológica La Selva, but to us back then was just Finca La Selva or La Selva. He sat at the back of the canoe, weaving the boat through the knots of rocks, tree stumps, and logs that formed an obstacle course on the river. Swiftly we passed through a zone of rocks, the water alive with a white froth. Then we were in a world of mirrorlike water, with the tropical rain forest closing in above our heads as we pushed against the river's strong currents to La Selva.

Not far upstream from the ferry landing, the Sarapiquí River fuses with the Puerto Viejo River. The Las Vegas farm, consisting largely of pejeballe palms and cacao, covers the tip of this confluence between these two great rivers of Sarapiquí. Up until a few years ago, it was owned chiefly by Robert Hunter, who also managed the La Tirimbina farm near La Virgen. Today it is part of La Selva.

We continued up the Puerto Viejo for perhaps another ten minutes beyond this point, and I could see a two-story wood-frame building perched on a hill high above the river to my right. Amazingly, at first I missed it, even though the building stood out prominently on the hill. Edgar told me to look again. It was just that there was so much new to see, especially the wildlife along the river, such as the caimans sunning themselves on patches of dried mud where the water had receded. Going up this river was leaving behind most of what civilization was about, an adventure into a special world where nature was evident in what appeared to be an infinite number of ways.

This was La Selva in 1968. When it was purchased by OTS from tropical forester Leslie Holdridge in that year, La Selva consisted of about sixteen hundred acres of tropical rain forest and the two-story wood-frame "field station" built by its previous owner. La Selva became the first field station of its kind to be owned and operated by the Organization for Tropical Studies.

Rafael shut down the motor a few feet from the river bank and skillfully maneuvered his boat to a small slab of concrete. Here we got out and unloaded our gear and climbed up the steep set of earthen steps to the building, a good thirty meters over us. The rain forest came right down to the water to the left of this little, twisted path. To the right was an open grassy area for another fifty meters or so, before the rain forest continued beyond a tiny creek flowing into the Puerto Viejo.

The mess hall was full of conversation and commotion as I sought a niche in the long table for my first lunch at La Selva. Les Holdridge was giving a course on tropical rain forest trees, and Dan Janzen had arranged for me to sit in on the end of the course. The lunch, rice and beans, salad and meat, was great after the long trip from San José that first time, and for many other times too. The La Selva cooks, Oscar and Chico, went out of their way to please.

The building was constructed of *laurel (Cordia alliodora)*, a high-density, apparently termite-proof hardwood native to the rain forest. There was a dining room, kitchen, and equipment storage–work area downstairs, and sleeping quarters upstairs outfitted with cots. The shower was outside, fed by a big square tank that held rainwater. A second tank supplied the kitchen and our drinking water. The small, wooden outhouse stood alongside the footpath leading from the building into the rain forest, about ten meters away. This was to be home for two years. During my stay there I witnessed the construction of additional space. Jorge Campabadal, then the resident director of OTS, together with Rafael Chavarría, coordinated the physically very difficult task of hauling sand and gravel upstream from the ferry landing at Puerto Viejo in Rafael's dugout boat, as well as lumber and other supplies needed for the construction work at La Selva. Never before had I seen building construction done under such difficult conditions.

What I liked most about this building were the big, screened-in walls upstairs and down. At night, the screens filled up with a great assortment of sphinx moths, beetles, and huge katydids, lured in from the forest by the electric lights powered by a generator. Inside, we were pretty much bug-free. Part of this had to do, I am certain, with the great numbers of golden orb weaver spiders that made huge webs on the outsides of the screens. These webs formed an irregular layer of sticky, yellow silk from the roof of the building to part-way down the screens, a virtual bug trap.

In the daytime, hummingbirds darted out from the wall of forest nearby and plucked strands of silk and insects from these enormous webs. The spiders were well out of reach. A year after I arrived here, a La Selva committee appointed a fellow to "clean up" the place. Much to my distress at the time, he rigged himself up on a ladder one day and swept away all of the spiders and their bug-proofing webs. The mosquitoes and other flies would have their field day with us after all!

The close proximity of the building to the rain forest provided an incredible backdrop of the calls of night creatures. Even on the rainiest of nights, these melodies of nature, far more intense and vivacious than I had ever experienced in the U.S. summer night, came through the deluge striking the metal roof and the monotonous sputter of the generator. And if you listened closely, you'd hear a broad mix of sounds, some muted and soft, others very loud and bold. The soul of the rain forest spoke to us every night this way. We were the benevolent trespassers on this cornucopia of nature's ingenious ways.

Thanks to Jack Ewel, I gleaned some interesting concepts in forestry from the few remaining days of the Holdridge field dendrology course. Jack was a forestry student from Duke University. He was willing to share with me what he had learned in the course. Les Holdridge took us out on the trails of La Selva, pointing out the distinguishing attributes of some of the canopy tree species. Physically, he looked like a resurrection of Don Quixote. During the course, this tall, thin man with silvery hair and mustache raised his arm and pointed into the top of this rain forest. I knew that he was pointing to a specific leaf shape high above our heads, but all I could see was an interlocking mass of many leaf sizes and shapes, all black against the afternoon sky. I felt as if I had an awful lot of learning to do and fast.

Rafael, the venerable and dependable boatman, our life line to the outside world, lived very close to La Selva. His house was a ten-minute walk along a footpath through the rain forest, near the river. Rafael lived there with his wife, son, and daughter. In addition to being the boatman, he was also in charge of the field station and its premises. He coordinated a small contingent of workers to clear paths and clean the building. Rafael himself turned on and off the generator each night. Sometimes he lingered after tending to the generator, chatting with Gordon and myself into the night.

Sometimes Rafael would bring us back in his boat from Puerto Viejo at night, often in the pouring rain and pitch-black darkness of the rainy season. With one hand on the steering lever of the boat and the other holding an ordinary flashlight, he never failed to pass through the obstacles of the river on such nights. He knew just how to wave the light to catch, in its beams, the next set of rocks or tree stumps. We never capsized. Sometimes, especially when he turned off his flashlight, I caught a glimpse of his cigarette, its tip glowing in the dark, and from it I could tell Rafael's movements at the rear of the dugout boat as he stood up or squatted in maneuvering us toward home.

From Rafael we learned of life in Puerto Viejo, like the once a week killing of a cow for fresh meat, a scarce commodity in these parts. When the gas engine generator went out, Rafael was there to fix it. He and Campa worked together, in those days, to set La

Selva on its now well-known course to being one of the world's premier field stations in the tropics. But back then, La Selva was little more than Les Holdridge's vision of a little cacao in the tropical rain forest of Sarapiquí. Today it is vastly different, a large complex of several buildings, air-conditioned laboratory, new dormitories, and other facilities. Now there is a footbridge across the river where the groves of old, abandoned cacao used to be, and where Tobías Artavia used to live. But long ago, when I wandered along the river here for the first time, through the old cacao with Dan Janzen, we came across a bare-breasted woman standing in the doorway of a little shed, nursing her baby. I had never seen such a sight before. This incident and others at La Selva made me realize that I had a lot to learn about life in the tropics and under the circumstances of *el campo* (the countryside). Looking back on La Selva, I can say that it was a period of long, sometimes difficult adjustment for me.

Before La Selva, I now believe I had lived a fairly sheltered life, even with four years in Chicago under my belt. Things happened at La Selva that I hadn't experienced before, catching me off guard in more than one way. La Selva and Costa Rica came up in my life very quickly. When I was finishing my Ph.D. thesis under Thomas Park at Chicago and looking for employment, Monte told me about a brilliant young biologist, Dan Janzen, at the University of Kansas, who was looking for someone to assume a postdoctoral position in the tropics. Interested, I wrote Janzen inquiring about the position. One day, months later, Janzen poked his head into the lab where I was working and called over to me, "You're Allen Young, I'm Dan Janzen, and you have the job. . . . I'll be in touch, see you in Costa Rica in September." Without much more exchange, he was gone. I was thrilled at this opportunity. But was I ready for it? I didn't know, but I went ahead. Janzen's zest for field biology was very contagious, even in the few brief moments we met.

La Selva was the end of one road for me; a new world opened up new challenges. The happiest moments were when I immersed myself in the beauty of the rain forest. The fledgling system of forest footpaths became a threshold in my life, shaping my destiny in more ways than I knew at the time. Through these portals I became lost. Losing a flashlight in the middle of night way off in the forest, alone, or even walking just a few meters off a trail in the daytime, were symbolic measures of life's challenges to me at the time.

One of my favorite places at La Selva was not at all far from the field station, a place I still recollect vividly. Just beyond the entrance into the rain forest, the terrain dipped slightly, stepping out of the sunlight into the forest understory. From here, the terrain then angled down more sharply and suddenly into a sun-drenched opening in the forest. Thick walls of dense vegetation lined both sides of this path, which led into the darkness of the forest again across a little bridge. Flowering *Hamelia patens* trees added vivid splashes of red to the astounding rich greenness of this place, as did the pendant inflorescences of *Heliconia* plants. Particularly during the morning hours, when the sky was vivid blue, butterflies of many sizes and colors flitted through this patch of life. Most impressive were tailless swallowtail butterflies, with the upper sides of their broad wings colored in a striking patchwork of black, red, and metallic green. These silent creatures wove their way artfully in and out of the dense knots of vines that formed an almost impenetrable barrier into the vegetation on both sides of the footpath. Other butterflies with delicately clear wings meandered about my feet, across the path, disappearing into the cool depths of the brush. To a large degree, I had little or no idea what I was looking at. Probably for three-fourths to ninety-five percent of the organisms I could see by just standing in one spot on the path, there was little or no natural history information available. This impression would come up over and over as I ventured into the wilds of Sarapiquí in the years since La Selva.

Looking at life in the rain forest this way convinced me early on that what was direly needed in the tropics was basic descriptive studies on the natural history of organisms, with an emphasis on what other species they interact with. Only later did I come to realize the need to structure a field research program in such a way as to combine long-term experimental field studies on certain groups of organisms with descriptive natural history studies on a few species along the way. Yet I must credit La Selva with my beginning to study tropical nature. It was here that I first became cognizant of butterflies, cicadas, and much more, all setting a stage for many years to follow.

I left La Selva and Sarapiquí in 1970, after two years of postdoctoral research. When I boarded a LACSA cargo plane with my boxes of insects (Jorge Campabadal had arranged for me to hitch a ride on this cargo flight to Miami, at a time when LACSA owned one *carguero*, a DC6B piston engine plane), I did not know when or if I would return. But leaving turned out to be a new start. My journey in the tropics and self-discovery was just beginning; I would have the good fortune to come back to Sarapiquí for many more years. The first step was rooted to the thickets along the Sarapiquí River, just across from the Las Vegas farm at the confluence of two great rivers flowing down to the sea from the Cordillera Central.

"Oh, you say that you're an entomologist. Well, what can you tell me about leaf-cutter ants?" the tall, lanky man shouted as he came toward me through the brush. "Hi, I'm Bob Hunter," and he extended his hand. "Oh, you're the owner of Las Vegas," I volunteered. "You bet," he shot back. Hunter, a Ph.D. agronomist, was a part-time farmer in Sarapiquí and the field studies director for the Costa Rican Program of the Associated Colleges of the Midwest headquartered in Chicago. He stayed in the two-story farmhouse at Las Vegas and also at Finca La Tirimbina, his other farm near La Virgen. We stood there in the hot afternoon sun that day and chatted back and forth about insects. "These leaf-cutter ants are stripping away the new flushes of leaves on my cacao trees," he sighed. I couldn't offer him much practical advice on the matter, but we became acquaintances.

Across the water the pejeballe palms rose like awkward spindly creatures above the reddish-leafed tops of the cacao. The blue outlines of the volcanoes stood out in the distance, the cones of Barba and Poás seeming far away. Here, where we first chatted and got to know each other a bit, I did not feel as if we were in a valley. The land was flat here, and the valley must have ended before Puerto Viejo, I thought. But here was the big river, now wide and shallow, just a few feet away from us. This had been the first time in my life that I had followed the course of a river, from near its headwaters on the windward slope of Poás to the floodplains of the *tierra caliente*. What a beautiful landscape this is, I thought, between the mountains and here. As we parted that day, after talking for twenty minutes, Bob called out, "I hope to see you again, Allen, real soon." Then the man in the stained khaki pants and plaid shirt vanished through the brush. "I hope so, too," I called out to the tall grasses and tangle of vines.

NATURAL HISTORY STUDIES OF MORPHO BUTTERFLIES

3

"Hay mariposas azules aquí?" I asked the friendly man busily washing shot glasses in the raucous *cantina* at the González inn in Cariblanco. *"Bueno, sí, hay muchas ahí abajo"* (well, yes, there are a lot of them down in the ravine), Challa replied softly. In June 1971 I stopped at the inn, a two-story wooden building painted blue and pink and set off to one side of the Sarapiquí road. I was hoping to locate here, as the little town was only a few kilometers from the Cuesta Angel ravine, at the point where the Sarapiquí River begins its way down from nearby cloud-covered mountains to the sprawling floodplains of the *tierra caliente* to the east. I asked Challa, the oldest son of Gonzalo González Baquero who owned the inn, if I could stay here. His broad grin, exposing flashes of silver, signaled his approval. Cariblanco would be one of my two homes in Sarapiquí for several months each year from 1971 through 1976. One of my interests here, a thousand meters above sea level, and at La Tirimbina, farther east and about two hundred meters above sea level, was to study the habits of *Morpho* butterflies, especially *Morpho peleides*.

Upon joining the faculty of Lawrence University in Wisconsin as an assistant professor of biology in the summer of 1970, I was able to obtain very helpful logistical support for field work in Costa Rica through the Associated Colleges of the Midwest, since Lawrence was a member of this consortium of undergraduate liberal arts colleges. I had received a small grant from the Bache Fund of the National Academy of Sciences in Washington, D.C., to study the behavior of *Morpho* caterpillars in Sarapiquí during 1971. At this time I also prepared a successful multi-year research grant application to the National Science Foundation to study the ecology of Costa Rican cicadas, which provided the funds necessary for me to return to Sarapiquí twice a year, for two or three months each time, between 1972 and 1976. Because of this funding for a principal research project, I was able to pursue adjunct field projects, such as studying butterflies, while meeting the goals of the cicada research as well. From 1971 through 1976, I used ACM facilities and rented a jeep from them to conduct my field studies in Sarapiquí and elsewhere in Costa Rica. Until 1975, Bob Hunter was the director of the Costa Rican Field Studies program of the ACM, and he helped me to establish research field sites at Cariblanco and La Tirimbina. When I first started studying morphoes in 1971, Bob's secretary was Dorothy Lankester, one of two daughters of Charles Lankester, the famous British botanist who was a specialist on the Costa Rican flora. Lankester's other daughter, Pamela, married the well-known ornithologist Alexander Skutch, who lives in Costa Rica. Later, María Schlicker became secretary. Darién Zuñiga, whose family operated a log-hauling business between Sarapiquí and San José, was a young Costa Rican employed at the ACM office who gave me a great deal of assistance with jeep problems during this period. My reputation as the "destroyer of Landrovers" followed me from my OTS days to the years of my association with ACM.

In 1975, Ridgway Satterthwaite became the director of the ACM program in Costa Rica, giving me further logistical assistance for the remaining months I would be associated with Lawrence. Following this period, during the transitions, Bob Hunter, who went on to devote full time to the management of the La Tirimbina and Las Vegas farms in Sarapiquí, continued to be supportive of my research studies, allowing me to continue using La Tirimbina as my major research site beyond my experiences at Cariblanco in the earlier years.

Leaving Lawrence University in the early autumn of 1975, I became the Curator of Invertebrate Zoology at the Milwaukee Public Museum, a position I still hold at the time of this writing. When my NSF grant expired in 1976, the then director of the Milwaukee Public Museum, M. Kenneth Starr, had provided funds, through the Friends of the Museum, Inc., that allowed me to continue my Sarapiquí studies in 1977. At this time, and with the encouragement and endorsement of Bob Hunter, I started on a long-term field project on the insect-mediated pollination of cacao in Sarapiquí and elsewhere in the Atlantic or Caribbean lowlands, with funding from the American Cocoa Research Institute, beginning in 1978 and lasting until the present. Over these years of different funding sources and research priorities, I continued to find time to observe morphoes. But aside from La Selva, it really all started at Cariblanco in 1971. Without the connection to ACM, beginning in 1977 I began renting a field jeep from the ADA Rent-A-Car Agency in San José, whose owner, Andrés Montalto, was enthusiastically interested in my studies in Sarapiquí. I spent time explaining the nature of my work to him and his staff, including the mechanics, forging a wonderful relationship with ADA lasting many years, up to the present. It was Jorge Campabadal who initially suggested I check out ADA for renting a four-wheel-drive jeep.

Ever since seeing morphoes for the first time at La Selva two years before, I had been intrigued, virtually transfixed, by the unsurmountable beauty of these large butterflies with iridescent blue upper wing surfaces. I had noticed that the dazzling solid-blue-winged males of *Morpho amathonte* flew through the same openings in the rain forest day after day, as if they had regular routes. As soon as the first rays of morning sun hit the vegetation along a forest opening, such as a path or creekside, the big butterflies began to appear, first one and then another, until several males undulated in broad swooping motions through the opening. Suddenly they appeared and suddenly they

The butterfly *Morpho peleides*. Unlike in this photograph, the alighted butterfly usually conceals the iridescent blue upper surfaces of its wings, holding the wings tightly closed, revealing only the earthtone-shaded undersides.

were gone. By eleven in the morning, with the approaching noonday heat, this splendid daily display was over.

I was determined to study morphoes. But wanting to study them without first choosing a conceptual research question and then selecting an appropriate species to approach it with did not seem very scientific at all. Other biologists teased me, joked with me. "Why study morphoes when there are so many small, inconspicuous butterflies in dire need of study?" "We know, you like morphoes because

of their size and beauty—the 'Oh my!' insects of the American tropics!" Well, there was some truth to this. The beauty and size of the
morphoes enthralled me. But outward beauty, I believe, heightens
one's interest in exploring creatures' hidden, inner beauty, the unseen,
yet to be discovered subtleties of their natural history. I viewed it
as a real challenge to study morphoes, these outstanding symbols of
tropical nature. And I was in good company. Naturalists of an earlier
generation like Miles Moss in South America, and contemporaries
such as F. W. Urich and Malcolm Barcant in Trinidad and Luis Otero
in Brazil, devoted many years to the study of morphoes. All species
possess an intricate hidden story, the real beauty of nature, and it
is the biologist's task to explore and expose this core. I liked the
idea of exploring a creature of obvious outward beauty, for in doing
so I had, in my opinion, the very best of both worlds—the objectivity
of science and the emotion-laden beauty of tropical nature.

Mine was a simple approach. I set out to discover some basic facts
of the natural history of *Morpho* in Sarapiquí. My overall plan was
to do as many field projects with *Morpho* as I could, hoping that
each one would help to explain the total relationship of these butterflies to the tropical rain forest. My initial goals were to determine
the food plants of the caterpillars of each species I could observe,
describe the early stages of each species, observe habits of the adult
butterflies in the wild, and initiate population studies of a particularly
common species, *Morpho peleides*. These interconnected objectives
seemed straightforward enough, and certainly a far cry from a
concept-based research project involving experiments aimed at understanding a particular process in tropical nature. But as I would
soon find out, particularly with a challenge lasting several years, the
simplicity of my *Morpho* projects proved anything but easy and
straightforward, and my original objectives would lead me to begin
to think conceptually about how these creatures of great beauty actually interact with other organisms of the rain forest.

Initially I decided to concentrate my study in the Sarapiquí River
ravine near the little town of Cariblanco. I had noticed an abundance

of *Morpho peleides* along the riverside at the bottom of the ravine, and, even more intriguing, the presence of a rare, elusive species, *Morpho theseus*, a most ethereal creature of this rain forest, with expansive, pale greenish white wings, lacking entirely the bluish iridescence common to most other species of the genus. I enjoyed the notion of cohabiting in this forest with the seldom-seen *theseus*, a creature that flicked its wings and drifted on the eddies of air that swirled around the treetops, seldom coming down to earth, or so it seemed. This species would prove to be one of my greatest field work frustrations, one still unsettled. Beneath my vigor to elucidate the natural history of *peleides* was the nagging desire to stumble upon some facets of the very secretive life of *Morpho theseus*.

Little more than a week was needed at Cariblanco to feel like a part of the González family. I settled into one of the upstairs rooms.

The village of Cariblanco during the 1982 *verano* season.

Patrick (Patricio) Eagan, one of the first Lawrence University students I brought to Costa Rica as a field assistant, had a room across the narrow hall. Together our two rooms provided a cramped "laboratory," storage area for research supplies, and butterfly nursery.

One end of the building, closest to the filling station shed, was a combination *pulpería* and *cantina*. The middle section was a dining area filled with several small wooden tables and chairs. The other end was the kitchen, separated from the dining area by a clapboard wall with a serving window through which plates of food were passed. A tiny wooden staircase, which twisted once in the middle more than ninety degrees, provided access to the upstairs. At the foot of these stairs, which opened into the dining area, there was a small, unisex bathroom. Upstairs, four little rooms were located on either side of a narrow, dark hall, about four feet wide with a couple of overhead light bulbs. The women used one of these rooms, at one end of this hall, for ironing and sewing. The González family lived in a house attached to the inn. My room was on the back side of the building, and its single tiny window faced an embankment covered with mosses and vines. Straining to look up from the window, I just barely made out an incredible flower garden Doña Virginia, Challa's mother, had planted where the embankment leveled. Little sunlight came into my room, as attested by the mildew and dampness clinging to everything in it all of the time. Whenever a big logging truck roared by, which happened both day and night, the whole building rocked, as if lifted off the ground by some hidden lever beneath the road! Because of the curve in the road as the big trucks approached out of the east, their lights shone right into the rooms at the front of the building. Dogs yelping in the dark, the old jukebox blaring rough-hewn *salsa* and *ranchero* in the *cantina* below, and the roaring trucks, shifting gears, infiltrated our nights with a constant turmoil that many times exceeded the rapid-fire chatter of people so easily heard through the thin wooden floor of our rooms.

There seemed to be little or no grace period in getting to know one another. The Gonzálezes were naturally friendly, jumping right in with lots of questions about our work. Breakfast was usually *gallo pinto con tortillas*, a mixture of refried beans, onions, and scrambled eggs, with fresh home-baked tortillas on the side. When we were there for lunch, they served us *casados*. Dinner was a large bowl of soup with chicken or beefsteak on the side. At Cariblanco I had my first tripe soup. The thick broth was delicious but I had trouble, at first, figuring out what the little squares of rubbery meat were in the bottom of the bowl.

Yet there were moments when the inn at Cariblanco tested our fortitude. Soon after arriving there, I discovered bedbugs or some such critter that gave me very itchy welts each night. The bed was an elbowed metal frame with very old, rusty coil springs, overlaid with a thin mattress stuffed with straw. It was the skinniest mattress I had ever seen, and the whole bed sagged at the middle. Every time I stretched out, in a fetal position only, since the bed was too short for my six-foot-two height, the odor of mildew from the mattress and the rest of the room became omnipresent. But we were optimists, always hoping for a streak of dry weather to bake off the tenacious mold from our rooms.

Patricio and I woke up many mornings itching terribly, our skins crawling with an awful, irritable sensation unlike any we had ever experienced before. The bedbugs! Nothing seemed to deter their nightly feasting on our tired, sweaty bodies. But I found a way, perhaps the first of its kind. What if we put plastic bags under our sheets? Could this stop the bedbugs from reaching us, since presumably they were in the straw of the mattresses? I sliced open twenty or so of our not yet used butterfly nursery bags and carefully sandwiched these in between the sheet and the mattress, being sure the little bags overlapped, like shingles on a roof. What great relief the following nights! My method worked and our bites cleared up! Improvisation of this sort, we soon learned, was the key to high spirits and success in tropical field studies. Sometimes I slept with one of my work shirts over my head, with the buttons fastened and my nose and mouth poking through. It was a somewhat helpful way of warding off mosquitoes, especially when the shirt was well ripened with a week's worth of sweat from scaling the ridge of Cuesta Angel.

Dampness and mold were a real problem in another way. It was really tough to dry out our clothes because of the incessant rain and humidity. The nights up here are chilly and we soon discovered just how uncomfortable it was to put on damp, dirty clothes in the morning, especially after a chilly shower. But soon we became numbed to our clothes, or just learned to accept them. Out here, there was no such thing as a hot shower. But a cold shower at the end of the day, rather than in the morning, gave great relief to the sweat, insect bites, and muscle soreness of field work.

The first time I scouted the Cuesta Angel ravine, on an unusually clear, sunny day in late June of 1971, I was impressed by the abundance of *Morpho peleides* I saw frequenting the strip of rain forest bordering the Sarapiquí River. Accessibility was another factor in choosing to study morphoes here. A few weeks before, I had inadvertently discovered *Morpho peleides* ovipositing on a large vine at a less accessible, rugged ravine southeast of here. But what I had observed there provided clues needed to get started with the research at Cuesta Angel. In early June I had taken a broken asphalt road from San José to the mountains above Coronado, then descended into the thick mist of Bajo La Hondura. I could take the jeep only part way. I walked down a tiny footpath to the river far below. This place is only an hour's drive from San José, but it seems like a different world. Mosses and bromeliads give the forest a pall of gloom, shielding out the sunlight that strains to poke its way through.

I stumbled and fell on the rocky path. Strange big ink-blue blister beetles scurried across the slippery, moss-covered stones in this forest where it always seems to rain. As I made my way along the narrow trail, I heard the river raging far below. I looked behind me at the towering wall of darkness, the dense tangle of trees, vines, and fallen debris, feeling a bit uneasy. Would I ever make it back up to the high ridge where I had parked the jeep? It was so dark here, even

Bajo La Hondura in Braulio Carillo National Park.

at eleven o'clock in the morning this particular day, and a light drizzle sprinkled my forehead, feeling like a ticklish powder being tossed in the wind against my skin. The vegetation was silver and slick with wetness. Finally approaching the bottom of the big ravine, I walked through bands of dense fog.

The forest ended just a few meters from the foaming river, the Río La Hondura. A mammoth volcano not far from here had most certainly blown its top a long time ago, peppering this gorge with the huge boulders I saw all around me. I slowly made my way across a thin strip of sand and smaller rocks, through the brush. On the other side of the river, about fifty meters away, I could barely see where this tiny foot trail continued through bamboo and dense brush, disappearing into another mountain that loomed in front of me. Later on, I returned to this place several times, an endpoint where, in those days, few other biologists ever ventured. Over a couple of years, I met only one other biologist here, William Burger, a botanist from the Field Museum of Natural History. Bill appeared with his wife one day on the path. He was coming up from the river, I was on my way down to it. There were only a few other people experiences I had in this crevice of primeval cloud forest. One day, as I sat on a rock looking across the water, a little man with bright red hair suddenly appeared from the brush and made his way pensively across the river. He was preoccupied and hunched over with a large bulging sack on his back. Reaching my side of the river, he didn't see me until he almost bumped into me. A toothless smile spread across his freckled face, as he untied his sack and showed me the *yuca* (manihot or tapioca) he was taking to town to sell. We chatted in the drizzle for a few moments and he suddenly was gone, up the hill behind me. But before he left, I learned from him that this riverbed was a good spot for *mariposas azules*.

On several different visits, I did not see many butterflies at all. But one morning the sun broke through the mist, a rare event here, and the riverbank buzzed with the sounds of insect life. When the mist finally lifted and the sun came out, the place came alive. Nature had been waiting to wake up, taking a cue from the sun's warmth. Then the morphoes appeared, flying up and down the edges of the river. I could tell that the species was *peleides* by the broad black borders on the upper sides of their blue wings. Most of those I saw that morning of sunshine were males, their wings smaller than the females' and their flight more direct and feverish.

Then one day it happened. Poised with my net, I spotted a female heading up the river, behaving differently from the other morphoes I had seen that day. She stopped and fluttered close to some plants along the river bank, opposite where I was standing. I suspected she was searching for a plant on which to lay eggs. Excited and nervous, I entered the water and stalked after the big butterfly. She was still in sight, just barely, as I rounded a bend in the river, following her.

Suddenly I was up to my waist in water. The thought of the deadly fer-de-lance streaked across my mind as I held on to rocks for support, just inches away from the dark, shaded riverbank, now a small cliff. A perfect nook for vipers, I lamented to no one. But I was too close to my goal of discovering the caterpillar food plant of *Morpho* to desist now. I pushed on, tripping over submerged logs as I fought to steady myself against the swift current. I was getting awfully cold, too. "Will she ever stop and lay an egg?" I felt like shouting. But rationality prevailed and I was soon rewarded.

I froze to the spot, almost to my armpits in water now. The butterfly had alighted on a large vine hanging down over the water from the low cliff. Then she fluttered and landed again, and repeated this behavior several times. Even from a distance of fifteen meters or so, I felt sure the *Morpho* was placing eggs on the shiny, dark green leaves of the vine!

I can never forget this moment! After almost a year of searching for eggs of *Morpho* I had succeeded in witnessing oviposition. When she flew off a few moments later, I hurriedly plowed through the water to the vine, forgetting about snakes, and cut off a large piece with my machete. There they were! The eggs, each about two millimeters across (which is big for a butterfly egg), were scattered on several leaves. At first I did not see the eggs at all; their greenish color made them very difficult to spot as I inspected the leaves. But inadvertently I turned a leaf sideways and the profile of the egg, a tiny bump on the leaf, jumped out at me. I collected eight eggs that day. Holding the cut vine in one hand, I pulled a plastic bag out of the pocket of my corduroy jeans with the other and dropped the vine into it. With the bag tucked under my pants belt, I made my way victoriously downstream to the path.

At the herbarium of the Costa Rican National Museum, which was being modernized by Luis Diego Gómez, at the time the acting museum director, with collaboration from the Field Museum in Chicago and the Missouri Botanical Garden in St. Louis, I was able to identify the vine as *Mucuna urens* (Leguminosae). Luis had encouraged me to consider Bajo La Hondura for studying morphoes; he and his staff were always willing to sort through the plant specimens I brought from the field as part of my butterfly studies. We shared in the perennial frustration that most of what I brought in for determinations lacked flowers and fruit, the principal structures used in identifying plant genera and species. Even so, for some plants such as *Mucuna* with its distinctive leaf arrangement, it was possible to obtain determinations to at least genus. Digging into Standley's *Flora of Costa Rica* in Luis's office, I found out that *Mucuna* was a genus of legume vine widely distributed throughout much of Costa Rica, and this particular species was abundant in the mountain forests of the Cordillera Central, especially in the Sarapiquí region.

Studying the life cycles of butterflies and other insects, I soon discovered, was like unraveling a mystery. The biologist is the detective, working with little pieces of information, such as the name of a caterpillar food plant, to eventually piece together a reliable picture of the insect's natural history in a particular place. In order to understand the insect's habits, one had to learn about botany and the habits of the insect's food plants, and the other way around. The webs of ecological interdependence between insects and plants were especially tight in the tropics.

In the years that followed my discovery of *Morpho* oviposition, and as I became more familiar with Bajo La Hondura and Cuesta Angel, I recognized that these rugged ravines were home to very distinctive assemblages of butterflies, many species of which I did not see anywhere else in Costa Rica. Wedged in between my studies of *Morpho* and of cicadas, I studied the life cycles of several other butterfly species at both localities. The butterfly nursery at the Cariblanco inn filled up quickly with bags of caterpillars, and our almost daily ritual of photographing our fledglings on the road outside the inn became a village event, drawing people to watch and wonder. Using pieces of stiff cardboard, I fashioned a crude plant press to preserve voucher specimens of caterpillar food plants, which were either identified at the *museo* in San José or taken back with me to the U.S. for identifications at the Field Museum or Smithsonian Institution. Systematic botanists at these museums, like Bill Burger, Velva Rudd, and Dieter Wasshausen, were very helpful in my exuberance of requests for plant identifications.

I ended up carrying my baby morphoes from Bajo La Hondura to Cariblanco and La Tirimbina. Soon I was able to spot the telltale triplet leaves of the *Mucuna* vine along the road between Vara Blanca and Cuesta Angel. First Patricio and later John Thomason, who joined me in 1972, became my "co-directors" of the morpho nursery as I learned how to obtain more eggs, and our charge of baby butter-flies grew.

Because of the dismal lighting upstairs at the inn, we often checked our cultures of butterflies in the better-lit dining room area during the daytime. Our rooms were soon taken over by the butterfly nur-sery, filled with plastic bags containing cuttings of food plants and caterpillars in various stages of development. Every day we needed to check these cultures, cleaning out the droppings and rotting plant debris, taking notes, and photographing eggs and caterpillars to doc-ument their life cycle. We also recorded how the caterpillars fed on the plants and their other habits.

I developed a simple technique for obtaining eggs from *Morpho peleides*. A female butterfly, caught in the wild, was confined to a large clear-plastic bag containing a cutting of the caterpillar food plant. These bags of butterflies were strung up along the windows, since sunlight often is the cue to induce butterflies to move about, encouraging oviposition. Once a day I checked the bags for eggs, which were then transferred to other bags for rearing the caterpillars when they hatched about ten days later. Then I gently removed the adult butterfly and placed her on a small dish containing a pile of mashed, rotting bananas. Most of the time she sat quietly, uncoiling the proboscis to feed on the juices for several minutes and occasionally for as long as an hour. Seldom would the butterfly fly off, even though she was not confined to her bag during these meals.

Occasionally the Sarapiquí bus caught us off guard. There we were in the dining room downstairs, with our butterfly cultures open and spread out, checking the caterpillars or feeding the female morphoes. As soon as I heard the screech of brakes in dire need of lubricant, it was too late. In seconds we were surrounded by a crowd of tired, thirsty travelers who seemed to perk up at the odd sight of us with our bags of butterflies. Little was spoken but there was a lot of very curious looking-on. Only Fanny, one of Challa's sisters, with her booming shouts, snapped them out of their trance, as they gazed upon these *gringos locos* doing something they had never seen before. She called them for their snacks and coffee before the bus reloaded and scooted away, over the hills. We did not mind these intrusions, but we were a bit fearful of losing a few eggs or caterpillars underfoot, or of a few morphoes, intently feeding away on the bananas, getting spooked and finding one of the several doorways to the outside.

Sometimes I heard a faint *"Por qué?"* from the folks huddled around me. I gave them a brief discourse on who we were and why we were studying the butterflies, complimenting the people on their wonderful country and its very interesting flora and fauna. Amidst lots of smiles, I sensed genuine interest by the people to know more about natural history, including the insect life, *los bichos*. Invariably one or more of my listeners had a story to tell me, of a special *finca* in Sarapiquí where we could find lots of these *mariposas azules* and the other butterflies we were studying. We even had a few volunteers to keep an eye out for us.

Unexpectedly, *"el gringo mariposero,"* as I became known, became a curiosity of sorts out here in the hills of Sarapiquí. Word spread rapidly up and down the valley and people recognized me by the ever-present insect net and field pack. Challa and other members of the González clan were thrilled at this fame, and they were glad to have me come back each time I left for the States.

Taking advantage of a well-known habit of morphoes, that is, their attraction to rotting, sweet-smelling fruit as a source of food and perhaps other resources, I set out fruit baits in the Cuesta Angel forest to collect gravid female butterflies to obtain even more eggs for studying the life cycle of *peleides* and other species. At both Bajo La

Hondura and Cuesta Angel, I successfully baited morphoes by placing rotten bananas along footpaths in the rain forest. We saw lots of males show up at our baits, especially in the morning hours, and very few females. Females showed up on rare occasion in the early afternoon and only when the bait had rotted even more, turning the mashed fruit into a blackened, vinegary paste unattractive to most other insects.

I was by no means an artisan when it came to making bait. We would go to the marketplace in San José and ask fruit vendors for the most putrified bananas they had on hand. Outfitted with fruit-stained cloth sacks, we dug through the fruit, pushing aside the fresh, ripe bananas and taking only the most crushed, smelly ones at the bottom of the storage bins. Housemaids and vendors gathered around in poker-faced silence to watch this show.

Our sacks bulging with fruit and juices seeping through the coarse fabric, we struggled through the crowd on the city streets back to the jeep. Going to the market for rotting fruit became a standard part of the "leaving town" ritual when heading to Cariblanco or La Tirimbina. Then, of course, the ride to Sarapiquí added its own special touch to the soupy froth of stinky fruit filling the back of the jeep. Our jeep was a sort of fermentation vat, the combination of rough road, high temperature, and the closed quarters of its boxlike carriage hastening the processes of decay.

Together with the morphoes, several other kinds of butterflies came to the rotting bananas, indicating that these species too fed on similar food in the rain forest. Our baits were visited by satyrid butterflies with bright reddish or blue patches of scales on their otherwise transparent wings. These butterflies, with a wingspan of about five centimeters, flitted just above the forest floor, almost invisible as they weaved and bobbed around the stems of small palms and fallen branches. In the woodlands of Wisconsin and New York I had seen only a few species of butterflies, such as the familiar mourning cloak and question mark, come to fermenting crushed fruit and moldy sap wounds in trees. But in Sarapiquí, I was very surprised to see firsthand as many as twenty species exhibiting this sort of feeding behavior, not only at the banana baits but also at fungus-encrusted sap flows on trees and various rotting fruits of tree species native to the rain forest.

Some of the satyrids at the baits were brownish with white markings on their wings. The big "owl" butterflies, with conspicuous eyelike markings on the ventral sides of their hindwings, came to the baits early in the morning, well before eight o'clock, and again in the late afternoon until dusk. We observed at least two species of owl butterflies on our putrid bananas, the more abundant *Caligo memnon*, well known in Central America because its big, brown-striped caterpillar feeds on the leaves of the banana plant, and *Caligo atreus*, whose caterpillar feeds on the leaves of *Heliconia* and *Calathea* along the shaded borders of rain forest in Sarapiquí. During the sunniest hours of the morning at Cuesta Angel, an occasional *Prepona*, a large, swift-flying butterfly (Nymphalidae) with bands of blue iridescence on the upper sides of its brownish wings, fed on the bait along with *Morpho peleides*. At the slightest noise, like the sudden snapping of a dry twig or crunch of leaves, the *Prepona* shot off like a rocket, barely perceptible at its remarkably high speed.

What intrigues me about the butterflies that feed on rotting fruit on the floor of the rain forest is that they always hold their wings firmly closed up over their bodies. Only the undersides of their wings, usually colored in earthtones and with or without eyespot markings, are exposed as they feed. Their crypsis against the forest ground cover is really incredible. The brighter colors of their wings are confined to the upper sides, concealed as they sip on the juices of decay. Two different aspects of coping with survival are encoded in the wings. The undersides give the insect protection from lizards and other insect-eating vertebrates as it feeds on the forest floor, and the vivid hues of the upper surfaces communicate a signal of recognition among individuals of the same and opposite sex. As Lincoln Pierson Brower once stated, "The wings of the butterfly represent a paintbrush of natural selection," for in them we learn the challenge to survive and to reproduce, the crux of evolutionary adaptation confronting all species.

Netting butterflies for the purpose of marking and releasing them provided me with an opportunity to inventory each one as to types of wing damage, a common occurrence in all species of butterflies. In *peleides* I soon began to notice a high frequency of butterflies with symmetrical portions missing on each hindwing, alerting me to consider what kinds of animals in the rain forest might be predators on these insects. Although some species of *Morpho*, especially *peleides*, possess large eyespot markings on the undersides of their wings, predators such as lizards may not see these vertebrate-eye patterns when approaching a feeding butterfly from directly behind. These eyespot markings might be effective in frightening off predators when perceived fully, and to the human observer they also enhance the general crypsis of the feeding insect, muting its profile into the shadows of the forest floor.

I found morphoes to be exceedingly skittish insects, prone to fly off at the slightest noise, such as the snap of a twig, or sudden motion. Did these insects have lots of predators? At La Selva I discovered little piles of the wings of morphoes on the forest floor, presumably beneath perches used by birds to feed on insects snatched from the air. Alexander Skutch told me that jacamars snare morphoes on the wing. I noticed that most of the wings I found were those of the more subdued species, like *peleides*, and not of the brightly iridescent ones such as *amathonte* and *cypris*. After reading about how a certain species of deer in South America uses a white rump patch to distract predators, I reasoned that perhaps something similar occurs in morphoes.

The dazzling colors of some species, coupled with a confusing pattern of flight involving lots of bobbing up and down, helps to foil predators like jacamars. With the earthtones of the undersides of the wings displayed in the upstroke of each wingbeat, the *Morpho* seems to disappear against the backdrop of the forest, just for a split second, but long enough perhaps to confuse a bird on the wing as to its

exact location in flight. The effect is strongest in the dazzlingly iridescent species, since the contrast between conspicuousness and camouflage, switching back and forth in very rapid succession with the
beat of the butterfly's wings, is greatly enhanced. Certainly the more
dazzling species seem to be less successfully captured by birds.

Visual perception in butterflies plays another key role in their survival. I was surprised to observe that female morphoes selected the
dark green, tough, older leaves of *Mucuna* on which to place eggs,
ignoring the pale green, succulent young (meristem) leaves of the
vine. I had observed that in many other Costa Rican butterflies, the
opposite is true. In the citrus swallowtail, *Papilio anchisiades*, at La
Selva and La Tirimbina, for example, eggs are placed on the freshest
leaves, easily spotted from a distance by the human observer (and
presumably by the butterflies as well) by their yellowish green color
against the dark green older leaves.

I have since watched the morphoes at Cuesta Angel and La
Tirimbina, noting that often a female searching for food plants actually touches a leaf and flies on. Such "drumming" of leaves, which
is displayed in many butterflies, allows the female to smell the plant
before deciding to place an egg or not. Color perception and smell,
the latter a very specific cue among plant species, guide the egg-laden
butterfly to place her eggs on the correct food plant for the caterpillars, ensuring the perpetuation of the species. Through highly sophisticated sensory equipment, registered through tiny hairs strategically
placed around the mouthparts and legs, the caterpillar of each species
of butterfly or moth "knows" whether or not to feed on the plant.

I didn't know what to expect when those first eggs of *Morpho
peleides* from Bajo La Hondura began to hatch. I didn't have a solid
clue because I could not find any reliable published works on the
early stages of morphoes. The photocopied pages on the morphoes
from the famous Seitz volume, which I carried with me, were stained
and tattered from use by the time the eggs started to hatch. I read
and reread the few scattered descriptions of caterpillars, yet still was
not able to come up with a good idea of what to expect from my

brood. Daniel Janzen once told me that he had heard a talk at the Field Museum given by Luis Otero from Brazil, who had been rearing local species of *Morpho*. Janzen recalled from this lecture that the caterpillars had a patchwork of colors and somewhat fuzzy heads. In November of 1971 I began to correspond with Otero, who generously shared with me his very insightful firsthand observations on the life cycles of Brazilian species of *Morpho*. Although his studies of *Morpho* remain unpublished, I am sure Otero has very important observations on the life cycles of several species.

A few days after I collected the eggs, each developed a jagged, reddish brown ring, as if dividing the top of the egg from its sides. A day before hatching, the egg was very dark and the caterpillar pushed its head through the top, the eggshell opening like a lid on a can. Then it was out. The caterpillar, about four millimeters long, had a dark red head covered with long, bushy black hairs. Its body was a patchwork of red and yellow markings and had scattered hairs. It was a very strange-looking creature, with an enormous head and slender body. Each caterpillar immediately ate its eggshell as a first meal.

I discovered that the caterpillar requires close to a hundred days to mature, during which time it moves about on a thin trail of silk that it puts down as it crawls along leaves. A caterpillar stage of more than three months was the longest I observed in the tropics for any species. During the first three instars (growth periods), our young morphoes remained pretty much the same, with the body thickening and the color pattern becoming slightly more variegated but not losing the vivid yellow patches set off with darker markings. But the final two instars brought about a dramatic change. The caterpillars were now mottled and streaked in a complex network of lengthwise lines, a mix of earthtones making them appear very camouflaged against a dark background. This pattern of color was even more pronounced in the fifth instar, the mature caterpillar.

Later, at La Tirimbina, I managed to study the life cycle of *Morpho granadensis*, a much less abundant species in Costa Rica but one very similar in appearance to *peleides*. Its early stages were almost indistinguishable from those of *peleides*. The plump, green chrysalis of both species is very similar, but that of a third species, *Morpho amathonte*, I discovered at La Tirimbina, has a thick white band forming a conspicuous ring about the body.

During 1971–73, I scoured the ravine at Cuesta Angel for eggs and caterpillars of morphoes. Besides *peleides*, we had other *Morpho* butterflies come to our baits in the forest, even more elusive species. While most were *peleides*, a few *theseus*, the very elusive canopy species, turned up on occasion, apparently lured down by the rancid fragrance drifting into the forest.

At Cuesta Angel, I was determined to discover the caterpillar food plants of *Morpho peleides*. Would it be possible to study the habits of *Morpho* caterpillars in the wild? I knew this would not be an easy task since the caterpillars most likely were sparsely distributed in the rain forest. It had been no problem to obtain fertile ova in the butterfly nursery at Cariblanco. But finding caterpillars in the wild was an entirely different challenge.

Because of what I had discovered at Bajo La Hondura earlier, I was not surprised to discover *Mucuna* as a caterpillar food plant of *peleides* at Cuesta Angel, even though doing so took quite a bit of effort. After all, *Mucuna* vines were abundant along the roadcut through the Sarapiquí gorge, especially between Vara Blanca and Cariblanco. I came across a big section of the vine intertwined with other species of vines on a mammoth tree branch that had fallen down on the road leading to the bottom of the ravine. I found a partly grown *Morpho* caterpillar on this vine. But was *Mucuna* the sole food plant of *Morpho peleides*, or did its caterpillars also feed on other legumes? Shortly thereafter, I found a *peleides* caterpillar feeding on an *Inga* sapling, giving me two solid food plant records. Were there others? I decided to try tracking female butterflies as much as possible, a very difficult task on this terrain.

Where the Sarapiquí road straightens out along the ridge high above the raging river at Cuesta Angel, there is a steep embankment covered

Life cycle of *Morpho peleides*. Several eggs, each one about two millimeters in diameter, oviposited on a *Machaerium* leaf in the "nursery" at Cariblanco. Typically in the wild only one egg is placed on a food plant leaf, so that the female butterfly distributes her offspring over large areas of habitat.

Life cycle of *Morpho peleides*. Newly hatched first-instar caterpillar (larva) eating its eggshell. Two other eggs, about to hatch, can be seen to the right.

Life cycle of *Morpho peleides*. First-instar caterpillar on a *Mucuna* leaf.

Life cycle of *Morpho peleides*. Half-grown caterpillar in its typical resting position on the underside of a leaf of its food plant. Caterpillars feed for about fifteen minutes at dusk and dawn and are inactive most of the rest of the twenty-four-hour day-night cycle.

Life cycle of *Morpho peleides*. The chrysalis.

with a thick bamboolike grass and many small ferns. At one spot along the hillside rising sharply above the road, before the crest and drop-off down the opposite slope of the ridge, there had been a mudslide, perhaps a year or two before I first arrived here. I could clearly see where tiny channels of water had gouged steep grooves within the reddish brown clay, which was now almost rocklike and very slippery. In a sense, these tiny grooves symbolize the forming of the entire Sarapiquí Valley. Water, too, in all its force and glory, had carved out the gorge from sheer rock, running together into the

Sarapiquí River making its long way down off the ribs of the Cordillera Central to the Caribbean coastal floodplains, the *tierra caliente*. What I saw before me, gazing up the steep slope at the streaked surface of the mudslide where a wedge of tropical vegetation had sloughed off into the road, was the sculpting water does in a matter of years.

Suddenly, a big female *Morpho peleides* swooped down off the crest above the scarred hillside. She hovered over the exposed area of mud, now thinly covered with an occasional vine. She fluttered above some plants growing in the tangle of grass and ferns bordering this open area. From where I stood, perhaps ten meters below, I could barely see the lemon-yellow small leaves of a vine. Suckers of this vine popped out of the sun-hardened mud. The leaves of the vine were different from those of *Mucuna* and *Inga*. Seconds later, this butterfly, intensely interested in this smudge of scoured earth, alighted on some leaves of a tiny vine and appeared to be placing an egg on it. Another food plant!

The butterfly made more touchdowns on several small vines in the clearing before darting out over my head and down into the forest canopy on the opposite side of the road. Grabbing the thickened stems of some tall grass, I started up the embankment, my eyes glued as much as possible to the clumps of vines hidden in the brush where the butterfly had been just moments before. I didn't mind at all the steady drizzle that now turned the clearing into a slippery, icelike sheet of hard ground. At such victorious moments, very little seemed to help my footing. The leather soles and heels of my field boots were no match for the slick clay as I inched my way up the mudslide toward the vines bearing, I hoped, eggs of *Morpho*. Slipping several times and sliding back down the hill, I wouldn't give up. I have fallen down a lot of embankments since, even a few times when I least expected it to happen.

I reached a place in the clearing where the terrain leveled off slightly, allowing me to pin myself down in the grooves of earth where water flowed down to the road. In fact, I followed some of those grooves as I continued upward. I discovered that I could anchor my boots more securely in the grooves than on the smoother, higher ground. Finally I saw my quarry. The little vines, probably suckers off of a large vine that had died, looked very much like legumes. Some sets of leaves were pale lemon-yellow while older, mature leaves were dark green and very shiny. There were several eggs of *Morpho peleides* on these vines, and to my surprise and delight also several caterpillars of this species in various stages of growth. A real bonanza! No eggs or caterpillars were found on the fresh, light green meristem leaves; all were on the older leaves, confirming for this food plant what I had observed previously for *Mucuna*. I decided not to collect any of the eggs and caterpillars. This spot became my study area for learning something about the habits of caterpillars in the wild. Later, again with assistance of the National Museum's herbarium in San José and further consultation with the Botany Department at the Smithsonian Institution, this food plant of *Morpho* was identified as *Machaerium seemannii*, another leguminous woody vine that, at the genus level, is widely distributed in Central America.

One peculiar thing I noticed in discovering *Morpho* caterpillars in the wild, this time and others, was that I did not find them feeding, corroborating what I had also observed in our nursery cultures. They always seemed to perch, without movements. This made me wonder if they were nocturnal feeders. I set out to watch their habits at night. In 1971, Patricio shared this experience with me, staking out caterpillars and snoozing in the jeep between observations.

I was barely awake. Lucky for me that Patricio had the foresight to bring along his little cassette player and a tasteful assortment of tapes of balladeer Gordon Lightfoot and classical music. The cassette kept us awake for several nights as we rested between observations inside the jeep. I had parked the jeep on the side of the road opposite the mudslide on the embankment.

Our mission was simple but strenuous, namely, to observe the caterpillars on several of the *Machaerium seemannii* vines up the embankment once every hour around the clock for several days and

Searching for the caterpillar food plant of *Morpho peleides* above the roadcut
at the La Cinchona ridge, 1971. The tip of the machete is pointing to
Machaerium seemannii on the steep incline. Photo by Patrick Eagan,
student assistant.

nights, and to quantify the daily and nightly pattern of feeding activity in the caterpillars. Doing so would perhaps shed some light on
the adaptive role of the bright red and yellow color patterns of caterpillars of *Morpho peleides*. Usually such colors in insects are reserved
for species that taste very bitter (or for their mimics), bright colors
serving as a warning coloration or aposematism to advertise their
noxiousness to their predators. But if this is the case with morphoes,
why would their caterpillars feed at night, a time when the colors
would be least effective in advertising their presumed noxiousness?
I needed to determine if indeed the caterpillars fed at night.

It was at times like these that I envied the field biologists who
chose to study vertebrates, large-bodied creatures like frogs, lizards,
snakes, monkeys, and birds. Finding the caterpillars in the vine

patches while positioning ourselves precariously on the mountainside was difficult enough in the day, and much more so, and more danger-ous, in the pitch-black darkness of Sarapiquí's nights in the rainy season. To help matters, I tagged several vines with *Morpho* caterpil-lars in that small clearing, and some of the vines had as many as four caterpillars scattered among their leaves. Never again would I discover such a high density of *Morpho* caterpillars in one small area.

Fanny, Challa, and *el patrón* Gonzalo worried out loud about us being out in *la montaña* all night. Weren't we afraid of snakes and *el tigre* (the jaguar) that roamed the rugged slopes of Cuesta Angel? What if one of us, or both of us, broke a leg? They even related to me a couple of legends about people disappearing at night out there, the handiwork of a *hombre loco* who walked the gorge in search of victims, even in the rain! Fanny pulled me aside one evening after dinner, coaching me, "*pobrecito Patricio*" (poor Patrick), feeling sorry for this young college student with the eyeglasses that always fogged up in the forest. Truth is, there were evenings when neither Patricio nor I relished the thought of spending another night out on the ridge in the jeep, especially when the bone-chilling *temporales* closed in on the ravine.

But we did it, on schedule. Listening to the classical music tapes while staring out at the pitch blackness of the ridge helped a great deal, especially in the early morning hours when even the caterpillars weren't doing very much. There is something oddly special, even a bit surreal, about listening to Mozart and Beethoven at night in a tropical rain forest, far removed, otherwise, from any hints of human existence. I feel as if the exquisite epitome of human genius, the works of the great composers, fuse with one of nature's greatest achieve-ments, the tropical rain forest—a rare, special moment when marvels of human creativity blend with that other creativity expressed through the forces of nature.

Sometimes, a truck or jeep slowed as it passed us, especially when Patricio or I was up on the hill, aiming the red-cellophane-covered flashlight at the *Machaerium* vines to watch the caterpillars for a few minutes. But no one stopped, rightfully assuming that it must just be those two *gringos locos* at it again in the night and drizzle! Challa glazed over in total disbelief when I told him what we were up to, but he was too polite to laugh or pass judgment in front of us.

After a couple of weeks at this, Patricio eagerly agreed with me that we had enough data on when *Morpho* caterpillars feed in the wild. Why they feed when they do is another matter. The caterpillars appear to have a definite daily feeding rhythm, one that is not always timed precisely the same from day to day, suggesting to me that it may be externally controlled. Perhaps slight differences in cloud cover and air temperature determine the onset of feeding, while digestion of the ingested plant material "tells" the caterpillar to feed again roughly twelve hours later.

Between climbing the hillside to inspect the caterpillars and filling the time in between with music in the muggy confines of the jeep, our "field sanctuary," I had little problem passing the night on the Cuesta Angel ridge. We survived and the caterpillars told me an interesting detail of their lives. We discovered that they feed briefly only twice each day, for about twenty minutes just after dark and again near dawn. Had we not stayed out there and checked on them every hour throughout the night, we might have erroneously assumed that they were nocturnal feeders when, in fact, they are strongly crepuscular.

From an evolutionary standpoint, this feeding rhythm allows *Morpho* caterpillars to feed at times of the day-night cycle when many kinds of predatory animals searching for insects are least active, that is, during the two transitional periods near dusk and dawn. These are times when diurnal predators (such as birds and many lizards) are either winding down (just after dusk) or starting up (near dawn), with the reverse true for nocturnal predators such as many reptiles and frogs. It seems less likely that such feeding is a means of circumventing attacks from parasitic flies and wasps, since I have come across several caterpillars in the wild that eventually died in captivity from these parasites. Curiously, even though the younger stages of

the caterpillars are brightly colored, they are nevertheless extremely difficult to detect among the foliage. The leaves of *Mucuna*
and *Machaerium* possess many small rust-red lesions, presumably
from bacterium and mold pathogens, giving the leaves a spotted or
marbled appearance.

Encouraged by what I had witnessed, I pressed the search for other
eggs and caterpillars of *Morpho* on other *Machaerium* vinelets along
the edges of this clearing. Poking into the thick, damp carpet of
grasses and ferns to one side of the clearing with my machete, I
could barely see an occasional cluster of the vine's telltale shiny leaves.
Quickly I found myself in a prickly mess of dried plant debris,
swarming with millions of tiny, biting ants. The living vegetation
was just a thin crust overlying a network of dried stems from grasses,
ferns, and other plants. I was doing my best to trace each vine to
its base, inspecting its leaves as I crawled along. My efforts paid off
in a special way. Not only did I find more caterpillars, I discovered
that some of these that were half-grown or larger perched off of the
vines entirely, usually on a dead grass stem adjacent to the vine.

I first noticed this behavior of *Morpho* when I found a bright yellow
and red caterpillar, about five centimeters long, on a dried grass stem
that was entirely hidden by the dense vegetation until I cleared away
a small opening around a vine. Now I paid close attention to the
stems of plants around a vine rather than the vine itself, finding very
small caterpillars on the leaves of the vines, and only an occasional
larger caterpillar at the base of a vine.

It was even tougher to find the mottled brownish mature caterpillar
in this morass of dead plant debris, but I did manage to find one.
What gave it away was a speckling of several tiny white dots near
its head where no such markings are usually found. Upon closer inspection with a hand lens, the little ovoid dots turned out to be the
eggs of a parasitic fly. I was amazed that the fly manages to find
the big caterpillar nestled deep in the darkened, damp debris beneath
the vegetation.

We tagged grass stems and other plants where caterpillars were found perched in the daytime, to facilitate tracing their movements to and from the food plants. In every case, the caterpillar returned to the exact same spot after each feeding! Do the caterpillars use a chemical scent to relocate their perches between feeding bouts? In some instances, we found strands of fine silk on the leaves and stems, perhaps providing a physical road map to and from the leaves of the vines. But in other cases, we did not find the silken walkways. Perhaps a combination of physical and chemical markers allow *Morpho* caterpillars to behave in this manner?

I have a clue that *Morpho* caterpillars are capable of exuding a pungent fragrance. I had discovered a tiny, eversible gland slightly in front of the first pair of true legs, which is everted when the caterpillar is picked up with forceps. When everted, an odor, reminiscent of rancid butter, is very noticeable, very likely produced by the tiny pocket gland. We had hoped to determine if this odor is a repellent against attacks by predators or serves some other adaptive function, such as providing a chemical walkway through the undergrowth. Following the guidance of Dr. Thomas Eisner of Cornell University and "milking" the caterpillars for samples of the substance, we anticipated that a chemical analysis might help to solve this riddle of the morphoes. But in *Morpho* caterpillars, unlike many other butterfly caterpillars, this particular gland gives off only trace quantities of the mysterious substance, and I was unable to rear sufficient quantities of *Morpho* caterpillars to obtain enough for an analysis.

Although the caterpillars behave cryptically, I am not sure that they are entirely free of chemical defenses derived from their food plants. Many species of tropical plants are notorious for their insecticidal properties. Daniel H. Janzen and his collaborators have shown that the seeds of *Mucuna* vines, for example, are terribly noxious, brimming with naturally produced plant toxins that deter herbivory by certain kinds of weevils. The leaves and flowers of many plants often contain plant toxins as well. Could it be that the leaves of *Mucuna* also possess insecticidal properties? If so, clearly some insects, such as *Morpho peleides*, have overcome this natural plant resistance and feed successfully on these species. Do other legume food plants of morphoes, such as *Machaerium*, possess this built-in resistance to insect attack? These are intriguing questions, especially considering the conspicuous metallic wing colors of the adult butterflies, hardly a form of crypsis.

At Cuesta Angel and Bajo La Hondura, I have found the large, yellow-spotted, dark red caterpillars of *Astraptes* skipper butterflies feeding on *Mucuna* vines. The adult skippers are large with streaks of blue iridescence and white spots on their chocolate-brown wings. During the daytime, the caterpillars stay concealed inside silken tents made by anchoring down the edge of a leaf against the other side of the leaf, completely shielding the insect from the rest of the world. But at night the caterpillars leave their shelters to feed.

I find it striking that in these two unrelated groups of butterflies the caterpillar stages are red and yellow, the adults possess blue iridescence on their wings, and both groups feed on *Mucuna* vines. But the story of the tropical rain forest includes many such associations between animals and plants. These patterns of life are driven by nature's chemical intermediaries, cementing some relationships and blocking others from taking hold. Each species of plant is a library of chemical resistance, an ecological filter of sorts, screening out some species of insects while others penetrate it. The chemical diversity of the rain forest is a basis for its organismic diversity. It is a matter of very fine-tuned biological engineering and design.

The leaves, flowers, and fruits of each plant species possess diversified sets of chemical weaponry and attractants, the whole integrated system the product of a single genetic map of that organism. Yet this adaptive guidance system varies greatly from one plant species to the next, with different chemicals involved among the thousands of species in the rain forest. And because of this, each plant is a crucial, front-stage player in shaping the animal life of the rain forest. The morphoes and the blue skippers of Sarapiquí tell me this is so. For them, the challenge is to harvest the energy stores of the *Mucuna* and *Machaerium*, precisely the opposite of what is most adaptive for the vines to allow. The outcome is determined by the chemical inter-faces between the ovipositing butterfly and the vine, and between the caterpillar and the vine.

I broke away from Cariblanco and La Tirimbina at the peak of my field studies of morphoes to fly up to El Salvador to meet someone who was studying the natural history of morphoes there. Alberto Muyshondt owned and operated an Esso service station in a pleasant suburb of San Salvador, but his first love was butterflies. We had corresponded several times before I decided to visit him. I had learned from him that *Morpho peleides* in El Salvador fed on a species of *Machaerium* sporting stiff, recurved spines on its stems, earning the vine the local title *uña de gato* (cat's claw).

As we made our way in his car through downtown San Salvador, I was caught totally off guard by the amazing press of people every-where, much more dramatic than even in the crowded marketplace in San José. I felt as if I was suddenly thrown into a thick steamy broth of human flesh, perpetually in motion. Alberto picked up on my shock, quickly offering that unlike in Costa Rica, there were so many people in El Salvador that all of the forests, except for a few national parks, have been destroyed. In his excellent English, he commented, "Dr. Young, you've been spoiled by the pristine lux-ury and lushness of Costa Rica!"

We drove straight to his gas station in Lomas Verdes, which, I discovered, seemed to have been converted into a butterfly nursery! Alberto's tiny office, even the grease-stained cement floor, was full of jars and bags containing caterpillars of many species of butterflies. "This is really fantastic," I exclaimed. The mechanics working for Alberto just stood and stared, their boss and this *gringo* peering at caterpillars and leaves, completely absorbed into a world far removed from gas, oil, and auto parts.

Between long draws on several cigarettes, Alberto spoke enthusi-astically of his butterfly accomplishments. He proudly showed me the detailed notes he had taken on the morphology of eggs, caterpil-lars, and chrysalids of many local butterfly species, the pressed specimens of the food plants, and his detailed log book of behavioral observations. Although he did not have a degree from the local university, his experiments were designed correctly and carefully by any scientific standards.

I could quickly see that Alberto viewed the study of butterflies as a very serious endeavor. He also kept preserved specimens of parasitic flies and wasps that had emerged from caterpillars and chrysalids, adding that he thought many of these would be entirely new records for science. I applauded his foresight and tenacity for detail. He was absolutely correct, of course, that, in spite of the tremendous popularity of tropical butterflies to collectors and museums, there were hardly any good natural history data on the life cycles, food plants, and parasites of most species. He and I embarked on a study plan to accomplish such a data base for Costa Rica and El Salvador. Descriptive natural history of this sort, for any group of plants or animals, had to be the first step toward understanding the ecological intricacy of tropical forests, and a basis for eventually evaluating which habitats would receive the highest priority in conservation efforts.

I checked into the Casa Austria, a family-operated little inn not far from the Muyshondt home. Alberto knew the owners, who originally came to San Salvador from Austria. I met Alberto's wonderful family that evening, and learned some fascinating facts about their Flemish roots. The warmth of the Muyshondts' home was evident immediately when I walked into the tasteful split-level ranch house nestled in a stand of trees and vines in the Lomas Verdes suburb. Over dinner, I learned that Alberto, Jr., was aiming to attend college in Florida, hoping to specialize in agriculture, while Rose-Marie pursued zoology at the local university. Pierre, the youngest and still in grade school, was his father's biggest ally in the hunt for butterflies. In my presence, Alberto gave the energetic little boy high marks for discovering caterpillars of some of the more elusive species, in their forays into the brush-lined gullies around San Salvador and above the coffee farms high on the slopes of a nearby volcano.

Next day, Alberto and I headed out to a place where I could possibly collect caterpillars of *Morpho polyphemus*, a very unusual species having semitranslucent white wings. Up to this time, I had not seen this species in Costa Rica.

The rolling hills around San Salvador were dusty and scoured of forest. We swerved onto a little road of broken asphalt, a rough ride in Alberto's automobile. Everything looked so forlorn and desolate. Indeed, I had been spoiled by Costa Rica, and especially Sarapiquí. I yearned to get back to Cariblanco after seeing this. I found it hard to believe that two species of *Morpho, peleides* and *polyphemus*, thrived in the compact, brushy gullies near the city here. We stopped suddenly, without notice, and got out. "Follow me," my companion hailed optimistically.

He slipped away, into a patch of dense brush, and I followed. Alberto had found a tiny crack in the brush that led us down to the cool, shaded creek, about five meters beneath the cliff where we had left the car. "This is where I first discovered the eggs and caterpillars of *polyphemus,*" he offered, as I followed him through the water and up the stream bed. The vegetation closed in over us as we sloshed through the muddy, dirty water. We were not really out in the wilds, something made very apparent to me as we caught glimpses of tiny shacks up on the ridges whenever there was a break in the brush. Everything was covered with a fine, red dust. I stumbled through this crevice, falling over rocks and grasping at overhanging branches. At one point I came face to face, at eye level, with a pair of transparent-wing ithomiid butterflies, perched delicately on a bright red flower, sipping on rainwater freshly collected within the cuplike whorl of the sepals.

Later, Alberto showed me a bush vine with dark, shiny leaves with broadly flattened petioles, *Paullinia pinnata* (Sapindaceae), the caterpillar food plant of the elusive *polyphemus*, the white *Morpho*. I hadn't noticed the distinctive bush at first. "Here at Barranca Colonia Campestre, the *Paullinia* is sometimes covered by a big, sprawling liana, the *uña de gato (Machaerium salvadorensis)*," Alberto called over to me. We continued on, to a spot where the little ravine was deeper and the dense tangle of vines more impenetrable. Still no white *Morpho*. I had to see one before the day was over! "Well, Allen, *polyphemus* is really very common here, even though I've seen it from sea level to about six thousand feet in the Cerro Verde and Sierra Aparneca," Alberto offered, as if reading my thoughts.

We stopped at a *Paullinia* bush partly covered by *Machaerium*. I had high hopes of finding eggs and caterpillars of both *polyphemus* and *peleides* since both of their food plants were here together. As it was the early dry season, everything was coated with dust—not good for finding butterfly eggs and caterpillars. But we found a couple of young *Morpho* caterpillars on the *Paullinia*. They looked very much like *peleides*, but Alberto assured me that they were indeed the fabled white *Morpho*. Although the adult butterflies were active this time of the year at Barranca Colonia Campestre, they were far more numerous at the beginning of the rainy season, still several months away, according to Alberto.

We had no particular explanation as to why the adult white *Morpho* was abundant three times a year at roughly four-month intervals, with the biggest pulse of butterflies with the first rains. We knew that the life cycle required close to four months, so that there could be three nonoverlapping generations of butterflies each year here. Alberto was well on the way to tracking the habits of the white *Morpho*. He discovered that more than half the eggs he came across in the wild were killed by encyrtid wasps, and that tachinid flies destroy half the number of caterpillars. Given these figures, we were lucky to find a few healthy eggs and certainly to spot one butterfly later that morning. We had just reached the crest of the cliff, leaving behind the dense shade of the creek bed and making our way up a dirt path between a couple of houses. I was awestruck by the size and beauty of the pale white creature, another example in the complex, exciting story of tropical natural history that was well worth exploring. Even here, in this desolate spot where the forest had been obliterated long ago, the white *Morpho* still held on, pushed into the crevices of creek beds where *Paullinia* grew tenuously among the crowded overgrowth of vines and trash. All I could think about, in the single instant, too frozen with amazement to wield the net and go after the graceful creature, was what it must have been like here long ago when the forest thrived. Two magnificent morphoes, one blue, the other white, held on because their caterpillar food plants remained in some semblance, albeit remote, of what must once have been.

Alberto's discovery of the sapindaceous caterpillar food plant of the white *Morpho* filled in another piece in the puzzle of how the morphoes meshed with the tropical forests of Central America. In the evolutionary scheme of the flowering plants, of which there are approximately 250,000 described species worldwide with about seventy percent occuring in the tropics, the Leguminosae, which contain the food plants of some morphoes such as *peleides*, *granadensis*, and *amathonte* in Costa Rica, and the Sapindaceae, which include the food plant of *polyphemus* in El Salvador, are not closely related groups. I had also learned from Luis Otero in Brazil that *Morpho* caterpillar food plants there included several other, unrelated families of rain forest plants.

But it seemed consistent that some species, such as the widespread *peleides* in Central America and its cousin species in South America, *achilles*, are legume-feeders as caterpillars. Malcolm Barcant, then an accountant in Port-of-Spain, Trinidad, told me that *peleides* on that island was also a legume-feeder. From these fascinating glimpses of *Morpho* natural history from different parts of the American tropics, it became clear to me that this cluster of butterflies had undergone a tremendous evolutionary diversification to exploit many different families of plants as caterpillar hosts. Such a pattern underscores the close ecological linkage of the morphoes to the floristic composition and diversity of tropical forests in the Americas.

Alberto and I took the naturalist approach to appreciating the high specialization among the morphoes for their caterpillar food plants, an indirect measure, of sorts, of the chemical diversification between groups of plants. Both of us tried feeding *Machaerium* leaves to caterpillars of the white *Morpho* with very little success, and we tried feeding *Paullinia* leaves to a blue *Morpho* (*peleides*) with the same results.

It is of great interest to me that within a single genus of butterflies, in which there are less than two dozen bona fide species, there could be such intense diversification in caterpillar food plant families. Assuming all of the known records of *Morpho* food plants to be correct, one may ask whether there is a common chemical basis for feeding that links these systematically diverse families of plants. A little digging on my part helped to clarify the matter. A distinctive set of naturally occurring chemicals, the saponins, are found in both the Sapindaceae and Leguminosae. These toxic substances even occur in some cultivated legumes such as alfalfa, making the seeds of these and other legumes very toxic to weevil larvae. Could this be the link? Could there be, buried in the evolutionary history of *Morpho*, a saponin-regulated basis for caterpillar feeding? This would help to explain why the white *Morpho* and some blue morphoes, such as *peleides*, feed as caterpillars on unrelated plant groups. Yet it is also known that some sapindaceous plants also possess the very toxic cyanolipids, substances in leaves capable of generating cyanide gas when the tissue is damaged by feeding insects. Could these substances, or other specialized substances including alkaloids, define the apparent specificity of the white *Morpho* for *Paullinia* and its inability to feed on legumes such as *Mucuna* and *Machaerium*, which very likely lack these toxins?

Were the forests of northeastern San Salvador once a home for other species of morphoes, butterflies that disappeared when the forests of centuries ago had vanished? A difficult question to answer, for sure. But it was the kind of thought that raced across my mind as the TACA jetliner skirted a line of volcanoes on the way back to Costa Rica a few days later. What I saw below me through the cloudless sky that morning amplified what I had seen with Alberto on the back roads of San Salvador. Today's Central America is a patchwork of scattered forest remnants, a smudge of the magnificent forests that once blanketed this narrow, mountainous isthmus. Alberto Muyshondt had been a most gracious host, and I hoped to visit him again soon. My visit with him left me with a lesson in ecological contrasts over such short geographical distances in Central America. El Salvador told me in 1973 what Costa Rica could become if the rate of forest losses continued at its present clip. But is was almost unimaginable to me that my favorite place, the Sarapiquí Valley, could ever lose its luster of living green and rich fauna of insect life. I had been spoiled by the lushness of Sarapiquí. I didn't want it to end, even to change a bit.

Arriving back in Cariblanco a few days later, I was able to locate some bushes of *Paullinia pinnata* on the crest of the ridge above the Cuesta Angel ravine. Now that I had seen the plant with Alberto, I had no trouble spotting it. I cherished the two young caterpillars of the white *Morpho* I brought along from the eggs we found at Barranca Colonia Campestre. For several long months I treated these creatures very delicately, giving the plastic bag containing them and *Paullinia* cuttings a special place in my little room at Cariblanco, hoping that tiny ants would not raid them, a perennial problem here, and that the ever-present fumes of diesel and floor wax would not do them in. I was successful and obtained two adult butterflies. During the rearing period I occasionally attempted to induce the caterpillars of the white *Morpho* to nibble on the leaves of *Mucuna* and *Machaerium*, always without success, even though its food plant (though not the white *Morpho* itself) occurs here in the mist-shrouded forest canopy of Sarapiquí.

Once settled again in Cariblanco, I began to reflect on my visit to El Salvador. Something here, in Sarapiquí, made me think about what was so different there. Sure, there was less forest there. But something else was bothering me. Then it hit me. In our few forays into the bush, I did not hear or see any of the larger rain forest birds, such as toucans and oropendulas, when I was in El Salvador. Naturally it all made sense. Less forest means less animal life.

What seemed to make my studies easier to do on a day-to-day

basis in Sarapiquí had been the full experience of nature there. I needed that rich backdrop of life in order to focus on a tiny piece of the picture, as I was doing with the morphoes and other butterflies in Sarapiquí. This heightened my admiration for Alberto Muyshondt and his intense dedication to studying the butterfly fauna of his largely deforested country. The technical publications he prepared from his work have become a main source of accurate knowledge about the natural history of butterflies in Central America.

I received my last letter from Alberto, dated December 24, 1975, wishing that I could visit for Christmas on my way back from Costa Rica to the States. I was not able to do this. A year or so later, I learned that the Muyshondt family had moved to Belgium, a decision made on the basis of ensuing political upheaval in the streets of San Salvador.

The more time I spent at Cuesta Angel and La Tirimbina searching for eggs and caterpillars, the more I became intrigued by the remarkable versatility of *Morpho peleides* to exploit different genera of legume trees and vines as caterpillar food plants. My list of identified plants grew steadily, reinforcing my contention that *peleides*, the most abundant and widespread species of the genus in Central America, is an ecological renegade of sorts, behaving like a weed invading new, marginal habitats, able to feed on a broad range of legume food plants. I do not view the several other species of Costa Rican morphoes in the same light. They seem to be much less numerous, and far more specialized in the ways their populations interface with the rain forests.

In this regard, a glaring contrast to the abundant *peleides* is the much rarer, secretive *Morpho theseus* in Sarapiquí's rain forests. I will always remember the first time I saw the huge *theseus*. I was standing on that crest where Bob Hunter had shown me the splendid distant El Angel waterfall months before. Across the crest came a very large butterfly with pale green, almost white wings. At first I didn't know that it was *theseus*, but it lacked the blue iridescence found in most morphoes. The big creature had a unique flight habit. It flicked its wings momentarily and then floated along for a few more moments, before flicking them again—as if its chalky pale greenish white wings with the russet undersides, and its "snap-and-glide" flight motions, were fragments torn from the whirls of dense, white mist of this great ravine. *Theseus* symbolizes the clouds and rain, while the blue morphoes, like *peleides, amathonte,* and the dazzling *cypris,* are the rain forest's sentinels of sunshine.

And *theseus* proved to be very difficult for me to catch. As it passed almost directly over my head, I could see that the undersides of its wings were reddish brown and studded with small eyespot markings. I knew then it had to be a *Morpho,* but like none of the species I had seen at La Selva. I was riveted to the spot as the butterfly passed over and drifted in the cavernous ravine, just above the dense canopy of the cloud forest below me. A few days later I returned to the crest, hoping for a repeat performance. When I spotted *theseus* coming up one side of the crest, this time I squatted down low with my net poised for action. It floated above and I lunged out with the net and got it. Because this species, unlike *peleides,* seemed to prefer to fly above the canopy of the forest, it would have been impossible for me to net one any other way. So *theseus,* what I call the "green-white *Morpho,*" is strictly a denizen of the forest canopy, thriving high above the ground and far from my gaze, where its caterpillars surely feed on some scarce, patchily dispersed liana. Luis Otero has found the caterpillars of a species closely related to *theseus* on woody vines in the Menispermaceae in Brazil, suggesting a menispermaceous food plant for *theseus* in Sarapiquí. Once only did I come very close to discovering its caterpillar food plant.

It happened on a sunny morning in March 1979 as I walked along a perimeter dirt road at La Tirimbina. As I walked along in the direction of Magsaysay, to my left the forest was no more, reduced to an occasional clump of trees and more often standing trunks, be-headed and covered with vines. Cattle pastures pushed back the rain forest, more and more as the years passed.

As I rounded a bend in the road, a massive vine-covered tree trunk, with a huge butterfly approaching it, caught my eye. The trunk had been lopped off about five meters from the ground, perhaps a year or two before. Low shrubbery and abandoned pasture surrounded this dead tree, which still stood erect, six meters in from the road. The big green-white *Morpho* kept fluttering around and even through the wad of vines that gave the top of the tree stump a mushroom-like profile, as if the tree's own canopy had been replaced, but much closer to the ground than it should have been, with a new, frilly canopy of several species of leafy vines.

I froze to this spot in the road, fifteen meters from the spectacle. I just knew that the butterfly was searching for a spot to lay her eggs. The great size of the insect and its persistent inspection of leaves told me it was a female *theseus* laden with fertile eggs. Had my moment of unheralded joy arrived? Was it all about to happen, to come together? Would I witness what no one else in the world had before me? I didn't think about such things at that moment. I couldn't really say anything or even think much about it.

The butterfly didn't go away. She persisted in her interest in this cluster of vines where a great tree had once stood. My hopes for success escalated! I watched her for several minutes but she still hadn't landed on a leaf. Incredibly, she maneuvered her big wings through the vines, weaving back and forth, doggedly determined to find something. Could there have been some dangling rotting fruit in the hidden recesses of the massive vine, luring her to its scent? I couldn't see any, even with the binoculars. No, this had to be an effort at oviposition. The great butterfly was bound to this spot and I was bound to her.

"Oh, no, this can't happen now, no, please!" I uttered softly to myself in sheer horror. I could hear a tractor coming around the bend in the road opposite me. Heard but yet unseen, the hissing and loud coughing of the machine's engine matched the bellows of blue smoke I could see now rising into the sky above the roadcut. It would all be over in seconds. I tried to warn the driver, busy chatting away with his companion, to stop and shut off the engine, but it was too late. He shut down his engine as fast as he could once he saw me waving at him and pointing to the butterfly. But the green-white *Morpho* soared away toward the forest canopy across the road, and did not return. I stood there for another hour, futilely hoping that the butterfly would come back. The tractor roared past me, the driver with a sheepish apology sweeping across his face as our eyes locked. My eyes followed him as his tractor and flatbed of tree trunks disappeared over the hill behind me.

I was more disappointed than angry. I needed a closer look at the cluster of vines. There must have been at least four species all tangled together. Later that day, I asked my friend Jorge Mejías, the foreman at the La Tirimbina farm, to bring his own tractor and a ladder so that I could have an even closer look. I was clinging to a faint hope that there might have been eggs or caterpillars from a previous time, a situation analogous to what I uncovered for the *Machaerium* vines and *peleides* at Cuesta Angel. I searched and searched while Mejías stood below, stone-faced and serious, surely hoping I would find whatever it was I was looking for. As a last, desperate effort, I hacked off some sections of different vines, tossing them down to Mejías, to take back to the house for a final look. This fanciful fanaticism failed to turn up anything. I had come very close to solving the mystery of what lianas the green-white *Morpho,* elusive *theseus,* fed upon as a caterpillar, and what the egg and caterpillar stages looked like. Although I have not given up the search, *theseus* has eluded me for twenty years.

Happening upon the unexpected is a prevalent phenomenon in tropical field biology. If I had been deliberately searching for *theseus* oviposition sites, most assuredly I would not have encountered this behavior, not in a year, ten years, or a lifetime. I am convinced now that chance plays a very big role in shaping the dynamics of tropical biology research projects. My first encounter with the equally elusive *Morpho cypris* proved to be another fine example of this phenomenon, as were other discoveries of the behavior of *Morpho* butterflies in general that I made in Sarapiquí.

Cuesta Angel is about ten minutes away from Cariblanco by jeep. It is not a difficult hike through the hills to reach it. A small dirt and gravel road follows along a narrow ledge to the bottom of the ravine where the river flows. Near the bottom of the ravine, which is about three hundred meters below the road to Sarapiquí high above, there is a little waterfall, a trickle of water seeping from the rocks to the inward side of the hill. A pool of water collects in the road because it levels off at this point, just enough to allow water to gather. When the sun dries out this spot, on rare occasions, the water ebbs and a veneer of mud is exposed. Many kinds of butterflies, but not morphoes, alight on the mud to imbibe moisture and salts.

Below here, the little road veers sharply to the left and straightens out as it crosses a metal girder bridge spanning the Sarapiquí River. Standing in the middle of this bridge, I can see up and down the river for a considerable distance. The forest comes down to the edge of the river, where huge boulders are strewn. The water is about ten meters below. This is the spot where I caught my one and only specimen of *Morpho cypris,* which frequents the canopy of the rain forests in Sarapiquí. Although somewhat smaller than other morphoes, the male has incredibly iridescent wings. The female of the species, unlike most morphoes, is very different, its wings being brown and yellow and altogether lacking blue iridescence.

One sunny morning I was standing on this bridge with my net. Looking upstream, a distant spark of blue caught my eye. The *Morpho,* I calculated, was about two hundred meters away from the bridge and moving toward me. The butterfly was just about eye level as it approached the bridge. I was sure that just at the last moment, the insect would veer over or under the girders. I squatted down, anyway, ready for its approach. Hardly believing it, I saw the shimmering *Morpho* weave and bob just above me, flying through the open space between the steel girders. My net did the rest. My first and only *cypris* in twenty years!

I juggled my field time between Cuesta Angel and La Tirimbina, two hours away. Blocks of two weeks at Cariblanco necessitated a change, and I would head for La Tirimbina. Challa would comment on my departures, *"Va para abajo?"* (Are you going down the road?) Yes, indeed, I would forsake the *fresquito* climate of Cuesta Angel for the warmth of La Tirimbina, eight hundred meters lower in elevation. Even so, La Tirimbina did not seem very tropical. The highest daytime temperatures reached the mid-eighties, and it dropped into the low sixties at night. It was, in short, more temperate than La Selva, which was even more *abajo* at a hundred meters above sea level. The González family knew I would return in a few weeks, and the rooms were always ready.

At La Tirimbina, I studied morphoes in a swatch of tropical rain forest bordering a cacao plantation called Finca La Tigra. Inside the forest, a thicket of low vegetation continues along a footpath as if hugging it, especially flourishing where giant canopy trees have fallen over years earlier. The sounds of insects are heard everywhere I turn. Butterflies, some with translucent, gossamerlike wings, others with bold colors, engage in endless aerial pursuits above these illuminated ribbons of brush preceding the darkened forest proper. When the clouds suddenly return, these insects disappear.

Once inside this rain forest, where I have walked many times, I see giant trees festooned with lianas and boughs of dense foliage, I hear the squawking emanating from little flocks of oropendulas and toucans, unseen from where I stand but nonetheless close by. The path now disappears into a muddy ditch lined with *Heliconia* plants, bearing upright red and yellow flowers, a species different from that in the bordering thicket. Not only are they visited by several species of hummingbirds, but I also see clusters of red and black corid bugs feeding on them. Black stingless bees flock on the flowers, collecting a resinous material. When the sky above, always partly hidden by the canopy of the forest, is clear, a smattering of sunlight reaches these heliconias, lighting up the flowers and making them incredibly beautiful against the shadows of green. To one side of this ditch, a giant *gavilán* tree *(Pentaclethera macroloba)* (Leguminosae) has fallen over many years before, creating a hole in the forest canopy. A carpet of heliconias now practically engulfs the darkened corpse of the big tree, a few of its larger branches reaching above the tallest leaves of the plants. Butterflies soar through the lighted area, into the shadows, and back out again. This strip of primeval rain forest is full of these light gaps, each one teeming with life not found in the darkened recesses of the undisturbed forest understory.

When the canopy-size trees fall down through natural means, the light gaps thus formed are quickly colonized with many species of plants. These are plants well adapted to bright sun, renegades coming in from the thicket separating this forest from the cacao only fifty meters away. The plants colonizing these openings attract specific kinds of animal life. Many species of insects found in the light gaps are similar to those in the larger thickets, but not to those of the forest understory. What continually amazes me about Sarapiquí is the way the habitats change drastically over very small distances. The light gaps keep the primeval rain forest in an ever-changing state, for it is not a static, immobile entity. Rather, it is a complex, continually changing assemblage of organisms. From the cacao grove, through the thicket of dense growth, into the openness of the rain forest, and through the light gaps within the forest, an imaginary transect I can walk in a matter of minutes, the patterns of life change dramatically, reflecting the mosaic texture of biological diversity in the tropics.

Beyond the ditch filled with *Heliconia,* the forest is open and clear. Little palms form a carpet, intermingled with woody treelets. To both sides of the very muddy path, which has reformed on this side of the *Heliconia* patch, there are several large *gavilán* trees. Their gnarled, grayish trunks are coated with dangling mosses and little plants. It is at this spot, at the edge of the heliconias, that some time ago I witnessed *Morpho amathonte* feeding at stinkhorn fungi. I had strolled along the path that afternoon, flushing out four brilliant blue butterflies from beneath the *Heliconia,* not expecting to find them there. Looking down to one side of the path, I spotted several stalks of the fungus, the delicate latticework gleba now stripped and rotted away, leaving behind the sticky column of stalk with its bulbous rotting apex. Kneeling down, I sniffed the fungi and detected a pleasant aroma, not unlike methyl cinnamate. Standing up I could not detect this fragrance, but the morphoes that eventually returned, wafting down through the rain forest several minutes later, certainly picked up the scent from even greater distances. I noticed that the butterflies were all males.

I do not know why these butterflies are attracted to the rot and decay of the rain forest, or how they benefit from that attraction. No doubt the fetid or vinegary scent of the forest's rot lures the butterflies and some nourishment is provided for them. But why mostly, although not exclusively, the more gaudily colored males? Are males after a specific substance of the rot? Males of *amathonte* and *peleides* are attracted to the stinkhorn fungus on the forest floor only after hordes of flies (Drosophilidae, Mycetophilidae, Otitidae) and stingless bees (certain species of *Trigona*) have scraped away the gleba. Only at this stage does the assaulted fungus emit that tantalizing fragrance. Is this the lure of *Morpho?* Could it be that males are collecting a scent substance they need for courtship? In their bodies, the substance might be converted into a different form and extruded from the body where it collects on the fringed inner borders of their hindwings. Once there, the molecules of courtship could be disseminated into the air to lure female butterflies. Perhaps a fanciful idea? Certainly from rearing adults from batches of eggs, I know there is an even sex ratio in species such as *peleides*. Is it just that females are much more secretive in their habits, and therefore less likely to be seen in the rain forest? Females do turn up at fermenting fruit —it is not exclusively a male behavior. But are males picking up other substances from fungal food sources in addition to food?

I suspect too that morphoes pick up fungal spores, the promise for the continuance of the decay cycle that binds together the fabric of life that defines this rain forest, when feeding at other kinds of rotting, fermenting food sources. Morphoes might play a role of dispersing the spores of fungi, which break down the forest's dying and dead organic matter. An excellent hypothesis to form the basis of future research with the marvelous morphoes, I tell myself—a footnote etched into my brain as I stand bathed in the wondrous ambience of this rain forest. I have seen *Morpho peleides* feeding at frothy white patches of fungus on fallen tree trunks, amidst the tangles of vines and general exuberance of life characteristic of light gaps within the rain forests of Sarapiquí.

A mile before the turn-off into the cacao, there now stands a lone *Coumarouna oleifera* tree (Leguminosae) on the opposite side of the road. It is an eerie sight. Its long, pale gray trunk rises high above the bottom of a gully, the trunk only slightly buttressed. It is still alive, but dead in other ways. You'll see what I mean. The little gully used to be a footpath, like the one into the rain forest behind the La Tigra cacao. But today it is a rivulet, a groove in the reddish earth where water has found a route of least resistance down the hills above the trees. All around the tree there is now pasture, an open dreary landscape where there was once, less than ten years ago, a magnificent rain forest.

During my early days at La Tirimbina, I would wander up this trail to the foot of the *Coumarouna* tree and watch the morphoes. When the big tree shed its fruit during the rainy season, the big blue butterflies showed up daily to suck moisture from the thin but fleshy skins of the hard seeds strewn about the forest floor. I couldn't even see the top of the tree through the dense understory lining that path. Walking just a few meters off the road, I felt lost in a forest. It was an incredible experience. The morphoes came in the morning, drifting down among the decaying debris to the floor of the forest, and toucans rummaged through the tree's lofty boughs in the afternoon, looking for fruit and seeds before decay had set in. The big tree gave life to other creatures, most of which I did not see. But today the tree is little more than a grave marker for the rain forest that vanished with the machete and fire. What a beautiful, mysterious place this once was before the destruction, an enchanted forest, giving us glimpses of tropical nature's special treasures, its own living jewels.

The little glade in the rain forest at La Tirimbina, together with the strip of rain forest bordering the Sarapiquí River at Cuesta Angel, became my two primary sites for assessing the population structure of *Morpho peleides*. Later, a small patch of semideciduous rain forest near the Pacific Coast would become a third site. Initially I concentrated this research effort at Cuesta Angel, deploying the field technique of capture-mark-release-resight as the primary tool for obtaining information on the population of *peleides*. Having one study site at a thousand meters above sea level and a second one at only two hundred meters, both in Sarapiquí, I reasoned, might reveal some interesting differences in population dynamics of *peleides* within the vast zone of tropical rain forest of the region.

Eager to begin capturing, marking, and releasing morphoes at Cuesta Angel in 1972, Roger Kimber, John Thomason, and I trudged along the rocky path bordering the Sarapiquí with our sacks of smelly bait. It had rained the night before and the forest was now shiny with dampness. Roger had to take a break and sit down, a risky business in the tropical rain forest. Stinging ants lurked everywhere out here, as we soon discovered. But Roger was quite sick, doubled over with chills and an acute case of diarrhea. After a few minutes he was up again and off we'd go. The several piles of bait in place on the forest floor, we waited in silence for the butterflies. For several days and then weeks, we captured every individual of *Morpho peleides* we could, gently taking each from the net, painting small code numbers on the undersides of the hindwings using hobbyists' enamel paint, and releasing the insect into the wild. Each butterfly marked had a different number.

My chief goal was to determine just how mobile individuals of *Morpho peleides* were in each of these populations. Such information is useful in understanding the population structure of the butterfly species in forest habitats experiencing differing levels of ecological

Along a footpath into the Cuesta Angel ravine (La Cinchona), where *Morpho* was baited with piles of rotting bananas.

upset and disturbance from humankind. I had always identified the morphoes as the supreme butterfly denizens of Sarapiquí's forests, but I was becoming increasingly concerned about the encroachment of humankind on them as forest was being cleared away on a mammoth scale.

It would be useful to me, and also to conservationists, to know more about the butterflies' range and mobility, as we try to predict how resilient this species will be in the face of marked human-wrought changes in its habitat. Up to this time, in spite of all of the interest in tropical butterflies, biologists did not have much data on the population structure for a single species in the American tropics. *Morpho peleides* provided a good test organism to examine such patterns in tropical nature, and Sarapiquí was the place I had chosen to do so. For one thing, in spite of walks and slow drives to and from the Cuesta Angel ravine from the inn in Cariblanco, we would see only an occasional morpho crossing the fields and other open areas, suggesting that the butterflies are confined to the forest and the dense thickets bordering the forest proper.

Jeep problems aside, the typically rainy conditions of Sarapiquí did not prevent us from pursuing the butterfly-marking study. It was not unusual for us to be soaked to the skin as we struggled to paint little numbers on the wings of butterflies netted at the banana baits. Whereas morphoes turned up at our baits in greatest numbers in sunny weather, some still came in light, persistent drizzles. They did not come in heavy downpours, times when our baits turned runny and dilute, washed clean of their alluring fragrance.

We did our census of *Morpho peleides* for several weeks, twice a year, for several years at Cuesta Angel. Each morning we poised ourselves in the foliage near the path and clearing, watching for the butterflies to appear, lured to the rancid scent of our bait. Thirsty, hungry hordes of stingless bees, flies, and rove beetles dropped out of the heavy air, the first feeders to ravish the foment of bananas.

The shimmering, electric flashes of blue drifted close to me as *peleides* settled on the bananas. There, they simply dropped out of sight. Typically we netted five or six male butterflies on a sunny morning. In the early afternoon more showed up, including an occasional female. We didn't keep any butterflies, except for a female or two held captive temporarily to furnish eggs for the butterfly nursery at the inn. From what I saw at the baits, I concluded that freshly hatched morphoes came to feed first and that much of the morning was an active period of flying, presumably for mating. By noon, when the heat of the day was starting to peak, males and females of all ages converged on the bananas, regaining the energy and moisture essential for life. Our maximal catch was twelve butterflies in a single day, not very much by most standards, but indicative of the population we were studying. We resighted marked butterflies once they alighted on the baits, using binoculars so as not to disturb them. We seldom had difficulty seeing the white or yellow code numbers on the wings.

Gradually, as our studies continued, I felt I was getting to know a little about the morphoes. It came out in minutiae of the field work itself, such as the manner in which I observed them and caught them for marking. Approaching a pile of rotting bananas, I felt light-headed with anticipation. My eyes searched the bait, looking for a shade of brown on a wing profile that gave away a butterfly. At first, I was not very good at this at all. I spooked a lot of butterflies, flushing them out from the leaf litter around the baits. Soon, I learned how to stalk the butterflies without scaring them away. I approached the bananas, one foot at a time, crouched very low and holding up the net bag with my free hand. I checked my feet to watch for dry twigs. The pounce came at the last possible moment, and sometimes I just gently lowered the net bag over the butterflies, engrossed in their feeding. But for the many times I succeeded with a catch, I had as many misses.

As gently as possible I extricated the pulsing butterfly from the folds of the net bag, angling it into position for marking. Holding the butterfly gently between the thumb and forefinger of my left hand, I painted the code numbers on its hindwings as swiftly as I could. Squatting down in the clearing, momentarily oblivious to the rivulets of perspiration rolling into my eyes and stinging my vision into blurs, I marked the butterfly, then let it go. My mud-spattered notebook paper, its once-blue lines now smudges of pastel dampness, gradually filled up this way with the entries on each butterfly marked for resighting. Date, time of capture, sex of the butterfly, and wing condition ("fresh;" "medium," or "tattered") became the fragments of information about the morphoes that would help me to understand their linkage to the rain forests.

It was a beginning. What mattered now was my ability to resight previously marked butterflies. The inner lining of the green canvas field bag I carried around became stained with yellow and white from the little bottles of enamel paint and camel's-hair brushes I toted for marking morphoes. The roll of toilet paper I carried with me at all times took on another vital role. I used the paper to clean off the brushes after dipping them into a small vial of ethyl acetate to dissolve the paint. Although I had developed a workable system, it was not trouble-free. Panic reigned whenever I knocked over an open bottle of paint on the ground. John, Roger, or another assistant quickly placed under my nose a back-up bottle. If the brush, already moistened with paint, dried before the butterfly was marked, it stiffened into a spike of matted hair. Haste was the key to prevent a brush coated with dry paint from becoming a lance through the tissue-thin wings of the butterfly when I tried to mark it.

The air was sometimes filled with the sighs of despair and boredom. Field work was not very glamorous and fast-moving for my students. I could not have been more excited and thrilled at what we were attempting to do with the morphoes. "Wouldn't it be great to find fifty morphoes on the baits today!" became a generic, stalwart comment of my helpers. Truth is, I would settle for a score of butterflies on a good day of trapping. Stalking and marking a few butterflies each day, considering the time we spent hauling bags of rotting fruit to the forest sites at Cuesta Angel and La Tirimbina, just didn't seem to be an acceptable return on our efforts, I was told more than once. It was understandable. I had a generic response, too. "I can appreciate the discouraging impact of small sample sizes, but for morphoes, this is what we are dealing with," I offered back, shrugging my shoulders and breaking out in a wide grin. "These are the data!" I exclaimed, more than once. I really felt we were getting a reasonable picture of the butterfly's population density in the rain forests. "Let me just say one more thing before we get too far down in the dumps on this. Our real excitement comes later when we have a composite picture from many samples, and when we analyze the data—just wait

Field studies on an adult population of *Morpho peleides*. Shown is a previously marked (number-coded) butterfly rediscovered, several days later, feeding at a rotting banana bait on a footpath through the rain forest.

and see!" It seemed to work.

I have to admit that most people find it strange for biologists to spend time tagging butterflies to track their movements and habits. It is not the kind of serious chitchat of cocktail parties. Painting little numbers on butterflies tends to strike people as something inherently funny. But these people have not shared in those special moments of resighting a marked butterfly. I have found myself saying, believing, "I know that butterfly; I've seen it before!" The morphoes and I fuse together at such moments, for we not only share the same patch of rain forest at this very instant, we have also shared it before! The little numbers painted on the wings and appearing in the lens of my binoculars tell me so. How else can we communicate with nature? Little marks on the wings help to bind the butterfly with the field biologist.

From the mark-resighting studies I slowly began to piece together a perception of what the adult population of *Morpho peleides* was doing in the rain forests at Cuesta Angel and La Tirimbina. Although our total sample sizes of marked butterflies were comparatively low relative to similar studies with other kinds of insects, we also obtained low frequencies of resighting of marked butterflies, indicating considerable dispersal and diffuse population structure.

There are some curious differences, though. Although we had marked fewer *Morpho peleides* at La Tirimbina than at Cuesta Angel for the same number of days of netting butterflies at baits, the composite picture of several years' data showed that a higher percentage of these butterflies had been resighted several times compared to the frequency of resightings at Cuesta Angel. Out of several hundred morphoes marked at each place, I resighted only about fifteen percent of these within a week's time at Cuesta Angel, and almost double this amount at La Tirimbina. Certain previously marked butterflies kept turning up at the baits, as if addicted to them. But there was useful information here. Their repeated returns to our baits over several weeks told me that our marking technique probably was not somehow altering the behavior of the morphoes, making them more vulnerable to attacks from lizards and birds, very likely their major predators among the vertebrates.

In sharp contrast to the general picture that was emerging for my two study sites in Sarapiquí, I would soon learn, from a third site farther away, that seeing lots of *Morpho* butterflies did not necessarily reflect the presence of an abundant, healthy population. My adventure with morphoes near the Pacific Coast began in December 1973 and quickly became one of my most memorable research projects. The morphoes ushered in the Christmas and New Year that year in all of their glory. Nature in the tropics, I discovered over the years, had its own peculiar ways of sneaking up on you, and this time was no exception.

It started with a walk through a forest one day. I was curious about this patch of rain forest that hugged the Pan-American Highway for a few hundred meters on the outskirts of Miramar. I had to pull over and see for myself. A narrow trail, wide enough for a jeep, cuts through the strip of tall grass between the Barranca Forest and the highway, barely detectable in the rainy season when it is closed over by the dense grass. The forest is held back, separated cleanly from the grass, which in some places reaches my head, by an old barbed wire fence. The little trail continues into the forest for quite a distance before fading out. When I first entered this forest, I could hardly believe what I was seeing. The open, rolling hills covered with cattle-grazed pastures that surrounded this forest, just moments away, seemed to have vanished as I gazed upon the cool, refreshing lushness inside the forest. Beyond the fence, the trail led me through low brush and heliconias before sloping downward through very tall trees and a densely shaded underlayer of palms.

The terrain is hilly, crisscrossed by several small gullies. A permanent stream flows through the central area of the forest, nestled in a deep shade that gives the spot an illusion of darkness at midday. Huge *Scheelea* palms intermingle with canopy trees such as *Samanea* and *Enterolobium*. From the very first time I walked into this forest, I was impressed with the high abundances of many species of butterflies. I surmised that this was little more than an artifact of what the Barranca Forest really is, namely, a little island refuge for wildlife in an "ocean" of pastures where the great forest once continued centuries before. What I see is a relic of what must have been a marvelous ecological theater of tropical nature, a fragment of a now-obliterated assemblage of species protected in this little patch of terrain along the Pan-American Highway.

He approached me from behind, quietly, one day, as I was netting morphoes from banana baits here. Carlos Rudín, from Miramar up on the mountain near here, had heard about some *gringo* who was spending a lot of time on his land. He came to find out for himself, as the proprietor of the Barranca Forest. At first, Don Carlos was extremely solemn, his steely eyes searching mine as I explained my mission with the *mariposas azules y grandes* in his forest. A smile cracked through his tight lips and flourished broadly moments later. He was very relieved, he sighed, that I was not coming here to cut down the trees to sell the timber. He told me that he had had lots of trouble in recent months with people coming in and cutting down trees. But he welcomed biologists. The year before, two biologists were here studying the *congo* (howler monkey) troop that dwelled in the forest, he explained. I showed Don Carlos how we painted numbers on the morphoes, his expression pensive and frozen in disbelief. He patted me on the back, jotted down his phone number on a card, and walked out of the forest into the burning sun. Any way that he could help me with my studies, he was at my service, and I could study the butterflies in his forest for as long as I wanted to. I praised him for his insight in protecting this forest, hoping that it too would not become a cattle pasture.

I decided to conduct a mark-resight population study of *peleides* in Señor Rudín's Barranca Forest to span the dry season, which was rapidly coming on by mid-December 1973. Given the small and confined nature of this patch of forest, I thought it would provide interesting data on the *peleides* population to compare with our findings in Sarapiquí, where the rain forests, while diminishing, were perhaps still not as restrictive to some insect populations as the Barranca Forest appeared to be.

As we did at Cuesta Angel and La Tirimbina, I set out several piles of rotting bananas in the Barranca Forest, replenishing our baits with fruit bought in the central market in Puntarenas, the closest Pacific port city. Because of the extreme dryness, even in the shaded forest glade some of the baits quickly glazed over with a hard crust as they dried out. I would make the rounds every hour or so, poking through the crust with the end of the butterfly net or machete to keep the air fragrant with the heaviness of fruit decay—the lure of the morphoes. How many times John and I walked the route of the baits to check for morphoes is hard to say. Each day, by four in the afternoon, we neared heat exhaustion. Near dusk we left for the day. But during the day we would escape to the Miramar Restaurant, less than a quarter of a mile away, and gorge ourselves on a succession of ice cold Fantas and *bocas* of fried *yuca* and *langostinas* (brackish-water prawns). These infrequent interludes refreshed us to head back into the heat at the study site.

Several weeks later, as our Barranca Forest study began to generate data on resighted, previously marked butterflies, I took some moments to reflect on what was most likely the situation with *Morpho peleides* here. On one particular afternoon, I stepped outside the Barranca Forest on the side opposite the highway. The sun-baked, hardened hill was steep and pock-marked with the ruts and grooves of cattle feet, sculpted in the rainy season when this land was soft like putty, but now held frozen by the blazing sun and winds of the long dry season. I reached the mount and looked down. The roof of the Barranca Forest was now a rectangle of dark green surrounded by the parched, brown pasturelands. It was easy for me from up here at such moments, when the patch of tropical rain forest below seemed silent and deathly still, to grasp what the morphoes were starting to tell me. High percentages of resightings of marked butterflies at the Barranca Forest between December 1973 and March 1974 were way out of line with what we had been getting at Cuesta Angel and La Tirimbina—much, much higher. "Of course!" I exclaimed to the wind, "the butterflies and most everything else in this island of forest are trapped, with nowhere else to move out to." Quickly resighting fifty, sixty, seventy percent of the marked morphoes on a weekly basis for several months, and seeing among these many more females than we had seen proportionately in the Cuesta Angel and La Tirimbina populations, gave further credence to my sudden flash of insight. Female butterflies had little choice but to stay within the restrictive limits of the forest to find food plants on which to place their eggs. But where rain forest is less restricted, such as in Sarapiquí, females could disperse more freely over larger areas of the habitat, thus accounting for the low numbers of these butterflies found at the baits. The population of *Morpho peleides* in the Barranca Forest was ecologically trapped.

Tentatively I suspected that the situation of the morphoes at Barranca was very different from what we were discovering at La Tirimbina. La Tirimbina, which had a lower incidence of resighted morphoes than Barranca but a higher one than we found at Cuesta Angel, would become another Barranca Forest "island" if the cutting down of the rain forest continued there on a large scale. The butterflies, through their numbers and tendency to be resighted or not, were possibly telling us how their populations were being affected by the amount of forest habitat available in each of these three localities.

At the height of the long dry season engulfing the Barranca Forest and much of the northwesterly lowlands of Costa Rica, the forest leaf litter crackles and crunches underfoot. It is a time of extreme parching with subdued shades of brown everywhere. Yet here, a fraction of the trees and treelets of the forest understory retain their leaves, giving the landscape a splotchy patchwork of vibrant green when all else seems threadbare and brown. In these patches of greenery dotting the dry terrain, I can see the hope for life's continuity, and that the forest is still teeming with life.

And so it is too with *Morpho peleides* and a small assemblage of other resident butterfly species here that all exploit rotting fruit and fermenting sap flows as sustenance. Incredibly, I have flushed from the brownery of the parched ground cover the occasional *Morpho* or two, their wings faded and tattered, as if battered against the forceful winds of the *verano* even within the depths of this forest island, from where they were feeding on the fallen fruits of the *guácimo* tree, *Guazuma ulmifolia* (Sterculiaceae). While the canopies of this reasonably abundant tree in the Barranca Forest are leafless in the dry season, these fallen fruits, little woody-textured oval objects littering the ground, often partially covered over in the leaf litter, demonstrate life's intricate perseverance in this forest. While the ripened, very hard fruits seem lifeless to the touch, the sticky film of sweet-tasting syrup adhering to the meshwork of crevices sculpting their surface is our clue for what brings the morphoes to them. *Morpho* uses its stout proboscis to soak up this sweetness exuded by the fruits of the *guácimo* tree, which leads me to believe that these insects secrete some sort of digestive substance that dilutes the sticky syrup, making it more easy to imbibe. Morphoes are incredible artisans at feeding on what appear to be very inaccessible substances in the tropical forest, a very different scenario from their feeding on the soft, pulpy mass of rotting bananas. At the Barranca Forest, several species of satyrid butterflies also feed on the sticky film of the *guácimo* fruits, alongside *Morpho*.

What I have witnessed with the morphoes in the Barranca Forest is symptomatic of a much broader malaise gripping much of Central America today. Only a fraction of the species that evolved in Central American forests can thrive in the scattered little pockets of rain forest that remain. I do not find other species of *Morpho* than the widespread maverick *peleides* in the Barranca Forest the way I do in Sarapiquí's rain forests. I believe this to be true for most other groups of species of the tropical rain forest. Islands of rain forest are just too small, and contain too few resources, to support the rich flora and fauna of the ecological "mainland" counterparts. And what I see here helps me to appreciate even more the lush verdancy that still covers much of the windward slopes of the Cordillera Central east of here, the rain forests of Sarapiquí. I can only hope too that what I see now at Barranca is not a sign of what will come to be for the Sarapiquí Valley.

I did not return to the Barranca Forest to study butterflies for several years after 1974 and 1975. But once, in 1984, Susan Borkin, Joan Jass, both of the Milwaukee Public Museum, and I stopped by en route to Liberia in Guanacaste Province northwest of here. I took them down the little trail, past the point where Don Carlos and I had chatted about his magnificent parcel of rain forest. They followed me to where the trail becomes a narrow footpath, making a sharp right through a thicket of palms and heliconias. Just before the spot where a big tree has fallen down across the path, I dumped a sack of rotting bananas. "Let's stop back here in three days to see what kinds of butterflies show up on the bait," I suggested to my companions. We did.

On the return trip to San José a few days later, we arrived at Barranca at four in the afternoon. The sky was an electric clear blue. The sights and sounds of years ago came back vividly as I poked around in the brush along the trail. The forest was still working, I thought to myself. Don Carlos had kept to his goal of protecting the forest, now a decade after our chat. Butterflies were almost everywhere I turned. Susan and I walked down to the bait while Joan hunted for jumping spiders in the brush. It was now about five-thirty and the forest was preparing itself for dusk, the way this forest and the once expansive forest covering this land had done for thousands of years before we set foot in it. The shrieks of the cicadas had reached a zenith, and the leaves and branches high above us rustled with the movements of small flocks of toucans and parrots, searching for the last meal of this day. Faintly to one side of where we stood, a howler monkey hooted in some distant tree within this forest.

Two morphoes flitted their wings nervously on the bait. Then two other exquisite creatures floated into our field of vision as we stood motionless a few feet from the rotting fruit. It was a pair of owl butterflies, *Caligo atreus*. Given the shimmer of light dancing softly off their huge wings, they were freshly eclosed from their chrysalises. Susan and I found ourselves eavesdroppers on a courtship ritual of these big butterflies. The written word cannot fully communicate the beauty of such fleeting, rare vignettes of tropical nature, especially those very occasional, elusive moments when human beings are permitted to witness nature's own choreography. Shafts of sun shot down through the fronds of the *Scheelea* palms high above us, peppering the path and bait with a dabble of dusk's light.

It seemed to me that the light was particularly golden and intense this time, perhaps because of the oblique, late-in-the-day angle of the sun to the Earth. Perhaps, too, an exquisite illusion? Here in our midst, the forest was very silent. Even though the cicadas were calling all around me, in the forest beyond this point, I could hardly hear them at this moment. My gaze was locked on these two graceful butterflies, each one the size of the outstretched hand of a man, as they darted back and forth across the path, near the bananas. Back and forth they went, their velvety wings flashing fresh, bold bands of orange and purple iridescence as they moved into the pools of sunlight. The smaller butterfly, the male, followed the larger one, the female. Aside from their sizes, the two were identical in color. But I knew something else was going on, unseen by us from where we stood, frozen with awe.

The male owl butterfly possesses small, platelike patches of aphrodisiac-scented pouches, one on each side of its abdomen. When the butterfly is flying, stiffened hairs on the inner, trailing edges of the hindwings brush up against these little pouches, picking up the

The butterfly *Caligo atreus*.

scent substance and transferring the smears to the wings, where the perfume is more readily evaporated into the heavy dusk air. We noticed that the two butterflies repeatedly moved back and forth across the same air spaces, only a meter or so above the ground. Such a movement pattern in a confined area would allow the female to pick up the scent of the male, to initiate or block continued courtship and mating. If the butterfly had already been mated, the game would have broken off much sooner, with the female rejecting the scent and moving out of the area. But this was very clearly not happening now.

Around and around the silent lovers went, oblivious to our presence, and oblivious to the fruit bait, a staple of their diet! The morphoes on the bait did not seem to notice, even when the butterflies swooped low over the pasty fruit. In the shadows between the pools of light, the big butterflies appeared as dark objects, quickly disappearing from our view. But when they came back through the dabble of sun coating this forest for the final time this day, the butterflies became creatures cloaked in beauty that rivaled that of the morphoes. I couldn't help thinking, for a brief moment, that the vivid orange band slicing through the chocolate-brown upper side of the butterflies' forewings was a sliver of the sun itself, balanced only by the shimmering dark purple sheen of the upper sides of the hindwings, as if a sign of dusk. When they shot through the sunlight, the butterflies alerted me to the aerial dances of thousands of tiny gnats everywhere, little golden specks caught in an oscillating shaft of sun above the forest floor.

I had never seen the courtship dance of the owl butterfly before this moment, and I doubt that I ever will again. Much of tropical nature is this way. I have seen hundreds of owl butterflies on my baits in Sarapiquí over the years, and I have flushed out many others from the forest understory. But I caught a glimpse of their courtship only this one time. Tropical nature gives up just little glimpses of itself to us. Even if I had set out, as a research goal, to study the courtship of *Caligo*, I am not at all certain that I would have witnessed what I was most fortunate to have, that day in the Barranca Forest.

John Wilmer has researched the possible symbolism of *Morpho* to the Arecuna Indians in the uplands of Guyana; he related to me recently that these people refer to the "blue morpho butterfly" as *avakaparu*, which translates as "wanderer of streams and trails." I suspect that the particular species alluded to is the ubiquitous *achilles*, which like *peleides* in Central American rain forests is the species most prone to considerable dispersal along waterways, borders of forest, and roadcuts. Perhaps too for the Amerindians of Costa Rica, such as the Chibcha-derived Indians of the Caribbean watershed region which includes Sarapiquí, *peleides* symbolized the "wanderer" of the rain forest? Indeed, given the huge biological diversity of these forests, one is led to believe, looking beyond *Morpho*'s astounding presence, that these peoples have many such symbols linking them to the breathtaking nature in which their own cultures evolved. Perhaps the best thing for humankind today is for each person to recognize in nature symbols of life they hold important and meaningful. For myself, based on what I have experienced in Sarapiquí's rain forests, I view my feelings for *Morpho* as personal and not necessarily those to be shared by others.

Now, after my many escapades tracking the habits of the morphoes in the Sarapiquí Valley, I reflect back on what lessons of ecology I believe these butterflies are teaching me. What I see as the relationship of the morphoes to the rest of life in the tropical rain forest, namely, their most probable role, along with many other insects, in aiding the dispersal of decay microorganisms and fungal spores, represents a whole new set of research questions. My thoughts focus on the rain forest's essential cycle of decay when I think about these butterflies.

Especially when the rains are incessant and the skies leaden throughout the days of Sarapiquí's long wet season, I see the forest as a vast reservoir of mold and decay, cuddled and nurtured by incessant moisture, as if it were some vast, living terrestrial sponge seeping with rot. Enter the morphoes and other deep forest dwellers. Dazzling blue creatures epitomize the movement of tiny spores, the purveyors of yet more rot and decay to come, lodged on their legs and wing scales, on the hairs of their coal-gray bodies, ready to seize an opportunity, to sprout new life, when they are dislodged and settled on the moisture film of a leaf, twig, or forest floor. Herein too lies the marvel of bromeliads and orchids and everything else here, for their own survival too is linked to the movement of seeds of decay through the rain forest. Many creatures surely carry the spores of rot, but certainly the morphoes, creatures that seem to belong to the sky and not the damp forest floor, exalt the irony of it all, the exquisite beauty of a citizen of the sunshine and its life-sustaining bond to the rotting fruits and fungi coating the forest floor. Could Victor Hugo have asked for a more impressive irony?

And so I can only suppose that the elusive canopy-dwelling *Morpho theseus*, which seldom comes to the forest floor to feed, possibly spreads the seeds of decay high above. For there, a tonnage of dead twigs, branches, aborted and gnawed fruits and seeds are attacked by still other kinds of saprophytic fungi and bacteria not found on the forest floor. It is often said that much of the plant matter that dies each day in the tropical rain forest never makes it to the ground, staying lodged in the dense tangles of lianas, epiphytes, and tree crowns thirty meters or more out of my sight from where I stand on the ground. So it must be in these knots of plant debris that the rain forest's rooftop morphoes, such as *theseus* and *cypris,* imbibe the liquefying fruits of nature's decay cycle. In doing so, these creatures fuel the spread of rot catalysts that do not lie in wait on the forest floor.

I do not mean to suggest that morphoes are the rain forest's most important purveyors of tropical nature's complex decay cycle, for undoubtedly many thousands of species spread mold, spores, and bacteria. Rather, for me *Morpho* is a good candidate to symbolize these legions and their concerted action. *Morpho*'s own probable role in this unifying ecological process awaits further study.

Without the morphoes, owl butterflies, and elusive satyrids, the feeders of rot, and the myriads of ants, flies, and stingless bees that come into contact with fountains of decay on the forest floor, the upper reaches of the forest would have less nutrients to offer the host of creatures that dwell here. Decay of plant matter hastens the erosion of tissues, converting them into mats of perched soil suitable as anchorage points for epiphytes. Ants, termites, and other arthropods tunneling through branches set free weakened and rotted limbs, and many of these limbs remain wedged in the forest canopy and become part of the substrate used by spores to lodge, germinate, and perpetuate their own species. Just think about it for a moment—the large, relatively unstudied assemblages of ant species that surely exist high up in the canopy of the tropical rain forest—a reservoir of insect life that endows the entire rain forest with a staggering number of species.

Converting dying or dead tissues into nutrients is what binds the creatures of the tropical rain forest into a functioning unit. Thus the giant trees, what I have come to love and admire about Sarapiquí when I stop at a ridge above the forest canopy, are supported precariously upon a thin, fragile tissue of microbes and organic matter, matter that is turned over, transformed by millipedes, sowbugs, ants, and millions of other tiny creatures. Without these hidden, largely unseen assemblages of life, the giants would be no more. But this exquisite association between big trees and the Earth's tiniest of creatures has structured and guided the development of Central America's and South America's rain forests for millions of years. With the fixation of energy from the sun through photosynthesis to make living plant tissues, and the continual absence of a cold-temperature winter season, the tropical rain forest pulses with energy, most of it tied up in the bodies of its living creatures, corpuscles of nutrients feeding into one another.

What a fascinating, elegant circle of life *Morpho* symbolizes in this regard. Plants die in the rain forest, including the woody vines *Morpho* caterpillars feed upon and are evolutionarily specialized to exploit, and saprophytic fungi and bacteria attack the dead plant material. In the process of breaking down dead plant material to feed themselves, the fungi metabolize substances that become attractive to *Morpho*. The eventual breakdown of the dead plant material provides the rain forest with the fertilizer it needs in order to survive,

A fleshy bracket fungus festooning a rotten log in the Sarapiquí tropical rain forest attracts a constellation of small insects, including the fungus flies shown in this photograph. Presumably the flies, of which many distinct species may be present, breed in the fungus, as the latter feeds on the log. Such interactions are part of the way in which limited supplies of nutrients are recycled through the rain forest ecosystem.

including the woody vines and other legumes fed upon by *Morpho* caterpillars. *Morpho* also gets nutrients from the decay organisms as well.

Morphoes symbolize a great deal about the workings of a tropical rain forest. When mushrooms break down the dying and dead tissues of a log or tree trunk, these saprophytic organisms are releasing valuable nutrients into the rain forest, to be fed upon by living plants. So too when the very large grub of a *Megasoma* or *Dynastes* scarab beetle, what the Costa Ricans call the *cornizuelo,* ingests the rotting wood of a tree stump, it also is unlocking essential nutrients to nurture the rain forest. And when birds peck holes in the trunks of trees, exposing sap that soon becomes encrusted with fermenting mold. Such mold, like that of rotting fruit in the forest's canopy or on its floor, converts nature's most ubiquitous fuel molecule, sugar, into the structural building blocks of life, proteins and other substances. *Morpho*'s own existence, together with that of legions of other insects and other arthropods that disperse bacteria and spores, ensures this rain forest will nourish *Mucuna* and other legumes that feed this butterfly's curious red and yellow caterpillars.

But this intimate biological partnership between microbes and big trees in the tropical rain forest is being broken apart by deforestation. And as I write, this situation has tragic implications for the morphoes, creatures whose own lives are also a cognitive piece of the living tapestry of Sarapiquí's forests. It takes about 150 *Mucuna* leaves to make one mature caterpillar of *Morpho peleides,* or a wet weight of about 20 grams of plant flesh to produce one butterfly. Typically a clump of *Mucuna* or *Machaerium* occupies little more than a few square meters of habitat floor space, an area not even the girth of an average canopy tree of the tropical rain forest. For one *Morpho* or several individuals growing up in the same vine patch, not much forest space is required. But even this grazing pressure on the forest is relaxed, since probably half of the caterpillars never mature, due to predation and parasitism. It must not take more than several ounces of fluids to feed an adult *Morpho* for its entire lifespan, which is most likely less than a couple of months on the average. But the food resources of morphoes, their caterpillar food plants and the juices of decay for the adults, are spread out through the rain forest. Thus the existence of a single *Morpho* is spread out through the forest as well. *Morpho* cannot survive in just one small place. Consider too that it takes about ten acres of tropical pasture to fatten a Brahma steer for slaughter.

How many more mornings when the rain forest bathes in tropical sunshine will there be for me, anyone, to witness the incredible beauty of *Morpho* dancing above the Tirimbina creek? And how much opportunity to see this will there be for much of the floodplain of Sarapiquí? Outside of the La Selva Biological Reserve and the adjoining Braulio Carillo National Park, much of what had been home for the morphoes is rapidly becoming beef cattle pastures.

Given this tragic scenario, you too might very well share my own sense of urgency in wishing that everyone could come to Sarapiquí and see firsthand this vanishing, threatened beauty about which I speak. If you came along with me, I know exactly what I would do. We would climb to the summit of a particular small, grass-covered hill at La Tirimbina to look out over the patch of tropical rain forest that is still home for the morphoes as I write. Before now, taking this perspective, going to the hill and looking toward that forest several kilometers away, never seemed a terribly important thing for me to do. For up until a few years ago, I always appreciated the predictability I enjoyed for so many years of simply knowing that this patch of rain forest was there. But now, will it still be there next year? For this reason, I sense the urgency to take you there now. While the rain forest is still there.

I can assure you that you will see morphoes when the weather conditions are correct, and that you'll experience, firsthand, the interconnections that exist among all creatures. I could assure you, too, that you'd witness the changeability of this forest, from its subdued hues and shapes when the sky was gray with mist and rain, to the sunny moments when so much life seemed to spring to life. When the brilliant blue sky of morning embraced the greenness of this place,

it would be as if the warmth of the sun momentarily jolted all creatures big and small, making them incredibly noticeable and almost
obvious to you. If you took a moment or two to duck your insect
net through the brush along the path through here, I am very sure
that you'd see all manner of insects, some shiny and bold, others
subdued and hesitant. If you could sweep up a tiny piece of the floor
of this rain forest and scrutinize whatever moved in the field of a
microscope, I am confident too that you'd see multitudes of tiny
creatures, most of which do not even have names. This patch
of rain forest is indeed alive, as it has been for thousands of years,
with the humming of life. And for me, it has been *Morpho*, with its
intricate interconnections to the rain forest, that has come to
symbolize the orchestration of species defining the magnificence of
Sarapiquí's nature.

OBSERVING BUTTERFLY ROOSTS ON A STEEP MOUNTAINSIDE

4

I really think we both saw it at the same moment. One of my field assistants, John Thomason, and I were standing together at the edge of the Sarapiquí road, looking out across the abyss where the Cuesta Angel ravine drops away into a belly of mist, rocks, and the crisp, churning waters of the mighty river itself. It was near dusk on a typical rainy-season day in June 1972. But luckily for myself, John, and my other assistant from Lawrence University, Roger Kimber, the afternoon rains had held off for a change. Roger walked over and joined us as the late afternoon rays of the sun illuminated the forest-blanketed nooks and crannies of this ancient ravine, the great channel of the Sarapiquí River. Later on, in the dark of the night over dinner, the three of us would muse how easy it would have been to have missed the butterflies.

But they hadn't escaped our attention. Even though the three of us were heartily fatigued as another field day had come to a close, and we were easily distracted by the deafening booms of the dusk chorus of cicadas now echoing through the mountain pass above us, below us those persistent flutters down the mountainside caught our eyes. It had to be one of the most fortuitous moments in my field work. We happened to be standing at a place where the side of the mountain, its thin veneer of clay-riddled topsoil, had slid away down toward the river perhaps a decade before. From where we stood, gazing down into the mist of the distant ribbon of forest far below, the place was now filled with a pale green wedge of tall grasses, a gap in the tropical rain forest of about thirty meters across. Both sides of the grass-covered scar were lined with rain forest. Because of the abruptness with which the ancient forest must have been pulled away from the mountain years before, from where we stood on the ridge the edges of the forest appeared dark and forbidding. There had not been enough time for a wall of dense secondary-growth rain forest to form a natural scab over the exposed sides. This was especially true for the left edge of the forest. It was here, about thirty meters below us, that we noticed the fluttering butterflies, their presence enhanced by the interplay of the rays of the fading sun and the sheer, stark darkness of the exposed interior of the jungle.

The light was fading fast now, making the thick swatch of tall grass in front of us appear as a pale green avenue of disruptive biological monotony violating the dark green rain forest that, from our perspective, seemed to be everywhere else. We strained to see more, stepping precariously out into the grass, hoping we wouldn't fall through as we had done many times before. Our excitement with the butterflies, originally three or four but now close to a dozen strong, seemed to cloud our sense of prior experience and good judgment. I could clearly see the medium-sized butterflies all coalescing like a knot of movement in a cluster of dead creepers that stood out boldly at the edge of the jungle's exposed darkness. From where we stood they were tiny smudges of brownish yellow, and little more for the moment. Typically I had forgotten to take along the binoculars this day, an oversight I felt I was paying for most dearly at this moment.

Their fluttering grew in intensity. With the dying sunlight, the dead creepers, suspended from the roof of the forest, were golden yellow, gently swaying strings in a place where everything else exuded the greenness of life. At first, I hadn't been sure of what I had spotted. Was it merely some dead leaves rustling about on those vines? "Say you guys, am I imagining things, or did you see that movement in that pocket of dead creepers down there?" I inquired of John and Roger. John was the first to speak up, his hand on his chin in a pensive stance. "No, Allen, those must be butterflies or moths down there," came his soft, almost muffled reply. Roger nodded in concurrence. Then it hit me, and I could feel the excitement building in my veins. "You know something, I think we've come upon a communal roost of *Heliconius* butterflies!" If so, it was my first encounter with a phenomenon I had often read about, and one I was intrigued to study.

My companions could tell that I was very happy. I am an open book that way, not prone to cover up my feelings one way or the other. The study of tropical natural history brings its share of mood swings for some people; this discovery would become a real high for me and my companions. From the literature, I knew that the communal roosting behavior itself had been well documented by several researchers, past and contemporary. Essentially what happens, as I explained briefly to Roger and John on the ridge as dusk became night, is that several or many adult butterflies, of the same or different species (within the genus), collect together on dead branches or vines to pass the night. Some reports indicated that the same vines or branches are used repeatedly over several weeks, even months. The adaptive significance of this behavior, unusual for butterflies, is largely a mystery.

"Well fellows, we are just going to have to return later tonight to check out that roost one way or another," I exclaimed, as we headed toward the jeep a few moments later. There was a weary silence in my assistants at first, followed eventually by a subdued "yes." I could tell it was time for a break, time to replace field work and shop talk with some dinner back at the inn in Cariblanco, our field headquarters. Like clockwork, John and Roger were thinking about one of Hortensia's or Fanny's famous *sopas* (soups) after a long day of catching cicadas and butterflies in the Cuesta Angel rain forest. I had to agree.

I filled part of the ten-minute ride to Cariblanco with some anecdotes of what I knew about *Heliconius* natural history. My companions perked up a bit, knowing we were taking a well-earned break, perhaps forgetting for the moment a journey back out here later in the night. It would be a challenge for us to find out if indeed what we had seen was the formation of a *Heliconius* roost, and, if so, the species of butterfly and the final tally of the insects on the roost. As I explained all of this to John and Roger, both now somewhat glassy-eyed with fatigue, my voice came out in short bursts, disrupted by the rattling of the Landrover on the bumpy road. As we pulled up to the inn, I shared my hope with John and Roger that the rain would hold off for a few more hours. I knew they surely felt the same way.

Dinner was no exception tonight: we wolfed down the delicious tripe soup, *bistec* and *ensalada* (salad). The meals always passed the *familia* González test, as I called it. Fanny and the others loved to sit nearby as we downed their great food, all eyes intently upon us, seeking some obvious reaction of approval to what they had placed before us. Each dinner was a new test for us, even though the menu hardly changed from one evening to the next. With my mouth crammed with rice, salad, beans, or *sopa*, I nodded generously with feverish exuberance to our hosts this evening as I had done on hundreds of others. There were no bad meals here at the González inn in Cariblanco; all of it was tasty and our hunger never failed.

I outlined some of what I knew about *Heliconius* roosting to Roger and John. Dinner was now over, the plastic blue-and-white check tablecloth wiped clean, and still no rain. But it was now pitch-black outside. Although the systematics was still a bit uncertain at this time, I told them that there were many species of *Heliconius* in Central America and South America, and that the caterpillars were specialist feeders on Passifloraceae. Some older research publications, such as those of the British entomologist E. C. Poulton in the last century and the study of *Heliconius charitonia*, the zebra butterfly, in Florida in the 1930s, highlighted the characteristics of communal roosting in these butterflies. The subfamily Heliconiinae, to which *Heliconius* belonged along with several other less prominent genera, belonged to the enormous butterfly family Nymphalidae, which attained a zenith of diversity in the Neotropical region. A couple of years before our discovery at Cuesta Angel, Woodruff (Woody) Benson had completed a fascinating doctoral study of communal roosting in *Heliconius erato* on the Osa Peninsula in Costa Rica. Along with other contemporary researchers studying Neotropical butterflies such as Lincoln Pierson Brower, Thomas C. Emmel, and Larry Gilbert, Woody had developed a successful technique for experimentally marking *Heliconius* butterflies in order to trace their movement patterns and roosting behavior. Their experiences would become immensely insightful in planning our own field study at Cuesta Angel and La Tirimbina in Sarapiquí.

I can tell you that part of the reason why I was so elated about possibly discovering a butterfly roost was because of my impression that it was not at all easy to find one in the wilds of tropical America. I would venture to guess that if a deliberate attempt was made to find one of these roosts for study, it would be an immensely difficult thing to do. Simply stated, we got lucky that day.

A steady drizzle soon replaced the speckling of fine mist on the windshield as we chugged out of sleepy Cariblanco, toward the forested mountain pass looming out there somewhere ahead of us. I hoped that the real heavy rain would stay away a bit longer. Roger and John already knew my plan. We would attach a rope to the front bumper of the jeep, parking it as close as possible to the edge of the ravine just opposite from where the roost was located. As we approached the spot, I tried to imagine what I would feel like going down over the edge of the mountain in the night, thrashing and groping for support and direction in the quest to see the roost.

My companions stood there frozen for a few moments in the darkness, trying to assess if I was really serious about what was about to happen. "Okay, let's go down the slope just where the grass begins, and try to stay clear of the jungle brush nearby." With our flashlights off, my voice seemed to melt away in the darkness, as if I were rehearsing a speech to no one but myself. The plan was that we would take turns going down the rope as far as we had to to end up underneath the roost. I had no idea just how far above the ground the roost was, but we were bent on finding out. We had no gloves to protect our hands against rope burns, sure to be gotten on this sixty-degree slope. Suddenly I found myself thinking back to high school gym classes and never being able to climb all the way to the top of the rope, always sliding down and burning my hands. This rope felt the same as that old gym class rope. At least by keeping clear of the jungle proper, I hoped that we would not get impaled on the thick, razor-sharp spines of the palm trees and vines that I knew grew in this habitat.

The heavens were covered with rain clouds now. Any bit of ambient light would have been greatly welcome; but there was not even a faint glimmer of those incredible displays of the equatorial heavens that I had come to appreciate in Costa Rica. The katydids and tree frogs serenaded us, as if encouraging us to plunge ahead with our little adventure that night. The drizzle had become a fierce rainstorm; a *temporal* had settled in off the Caribbean, blanketing the Sarapiquí Valley with mist, chills, and a dampness that went straight to the bones. "Let's huddle in the jeep for a few minutes, maybe the rain will die down a bit," I offered my teammates. But by the time our breaths had fully misted up the windows, I knew that the rain was here to stay for tonight. John leaped out and stood in the beams of the jeep's headlights as he heaved the coiled rope out into the darkness of the ravine. Roger leaned over to check the knots on the bumper. These two fellows, blond-haired and ruddy-faced, worked well together out here. John's glasses were fogged up and he wiped them with his red handkerchief before grasping the rope to be the first one down the mountainside.

He vanished quickly into the rain and darkness. Roger and I shone our lights on him in total silence as he slid into the tall grass. I could see throngs of tiny moths dancing around the feathery seed heads of the grasses, momentarily caught in the beams of my flashlight.

Myriads of other flying insects filled the night air along the ridge, even in the thickness of this driving rainstorm. And it seemed that, for just a moment or two, the rush of calling insects and frogs to the left and right of this spot extinguished itself as John slid down the slope. We were left with the faint howls of winds down in the ravine, and their occasional upwellings that rustled the trees up on this ridge. We were the interlopers on this wonderful nature, crashing through the night's darkness and incessant dampness, through a slice of a wild garden where frogs, insects, and the winds had been calling for eons, long before any human being stepped on this ridge or touched the slippery soil of its slope, nature's testimony to the Sarapiquí River far below where we now stood.

Roger dropped away over the side of the mountain almost as quickly as John had moments before. Then total darkness as before formed a wall of uncertainty in front of me as I gazed down the valley. Surely I'd see a flicker from their flashlights, and soon? "What have I gotten us into, anyway?" I thought to myself and the night air. There was no help out here if there was an accident. Here we were again, pushing our luck in the tropical wilds, brushing closely with danger. We really didn't even know what the terrain was actually like beyond the lip at the edge of the road. That tall grass, and the rain forest, obliterated from view the true identity of this mysterious mountain in Sarapiquí.

"Hey Allen, we're as far as the rope will go and we're just about under the roost! It is really something to see," Roger's voice bellowed through the rain. Like the katydids and tree frogs calling away, Roger was now a part of the jungle out there, an unseen voice, momentarily returned to the living nature. Then I saw the flickering beams of their flashlights aimed up at the creepers, an unnatural interlude in the inky veil that engulfed this rain forest. Gripping the flashlight in my teeth, I went over the edge and through the grass. Where my companions had gone before me, the grass was matted down, slippery as ice and oil, and I spun around on the rope, in control of the situation and out of it just as fast. What took seconds seemed to last for some agonizingly long minutes as I fell down and groped for anchorage on tufts of grass and vines. I was a blind man, one deathly afraid of clutching a deadly fer-de-lance or some other pit viper. Then it was over. I too had reached the end of the rope. I balanced myself carefully as I tried to stand up and aim my light in different directions. I am sure that all three of us had shared those same terrifying moments—a kind of primal fear that goes with poking around in the jungle at night, and with no free hands! But somehow, we managed to keep our cool. Our climb must have bordered between downright stupidity and gutsiness in the name of natural history study.

When I got to the end of my rope, my companions were not there. I sensed they were off to my right as I faced upward toward the road and the jeep. But I could see absolutely nothing up there at all—just a total blackness. They called over to me and shone their lights in my direction. Even so, their lights hardly penetrated the four-foot-tall grass and other vegetation separating us. It turned out, as I groped my way over toward them, leaving behind the rope, our lifeline out of here, that John and Roger were only five meters away! Roger grabbed me to steady me on the soft, slippery earth. John whispered over to me, "Allen, just slowly raise your light above my head to see the roost!" I could tell that we now stood at the very edge of the primeval rain forest, for at first I shone my flashlight straight to the canopy a good twenty-five meters above our heads. The undersides of the leaves shone like silvery velvet in the night.

Slowly I zeroed my light in on the sleeping butterflies. There they were! I counted twenty all clustered together in a patch of dead creepers perhaps no more than two meters on each side. I asked John and Roger to take counts to check on mine. What was amazing was that the roost was only about a meter above our heads. Even though it was raining hard, the butterflies stayed motionless on their dry perches, tucked away just inside the edge of the jungle and out of the rain. The thick leafy canopy high above the roost site would protect the butterflies from the downpours. Because there were now twenty butterflies in the roost, it was clear that what we had seen near dusk was the arrival of butterflies for the night. *Heliconius* butterflies roosted only at night, or occasionally, as we would discover later, during the daytime when the weather was exceptionally dark and overcast.

"Well, guys, we did it!" I whispered, as I gripped the arms of both assistants. In doing so, I almost caused the three of us to slip away into the oblivion of the very steep gorge that dropped for another thousand meters below where we were standing. I caught glimpses in my flashlight of their smiles of success, a parting of lips and a wiping away of raindrops from their beards. We were in this ordeal together, a team. We didn't mind the rain now, or the puddles forming in the broad brims of our *tico* field hats. I just stood there for a while, gazing up at the butterflies, shining my light on them for only a few moments at a time. I didn't want to frighten them off the roost with too much light at once. There they sat, suspended downward on their thin legs, clinging ever so delicately to the tips of dead vines. Some of them were lined up in perfect rows along a vine. A few were scattered off to the sides, away from the pack. Outcasts? As I studied them that first night, I could not help thinking that they seemed to be nature's forgotten works of art, looking almost like a bough of dried, brown leaves, ready to break off and blow away with the next gust. But I knew this was not so. These creatures clung to these vines with an inner drive to survive, to hold on, and not to be a forgotten fragment of life.

By the yellow stripes on their oblong, slender wings, set off against a background color of brownish black, I could easily tell that the butterflies on the roost belonged to the widespread, familiar species *Heliconius charitonia*. The zebra butterfly occurs throughout Central America, Mexico, parts of the Caribbean archipelago, and Florida. Like all species of *Heliconius*, it possesses elongated wings, unlike most butterflies, and the eyes are exceedingly large compared to the rest of the head structure. The ground color of the undersides of the wings varies from a chocolate brown to a pinkish tan, depending upon the angle of the light.

Long before we came here, long before Columbus and the legions that came after him, and long before the Indians of even longer ago, the butterflies settled into their nightly roosts in dead creepers. The forces of nature have given these creatures the wherewithal to stake out their roosts in the most protective of places, inaccessible and easily missed holes in the margins of the great rain forest, high above the ground and away from the danger of many kinds of night predators. John and I had gotten lucky, that's all. It was the configuration of the landscape here that gave us the chance to get close to a roost of *Heliconius*. For all practical purposes, the location of this roost, which we came to call Roost A with the subsequent discovery of other roosts along the side of the Sarapiquí Valley and at La Tirimbina, was inaccessible, given the steep slope of the hillside. To the butterflies, the roost site may have seemed high above the ground, near the canopy of the forest. Because the trees on the hillside grew straight up, the canopy was lower than usual, depending upon where you stood on the slope. The vines, including the dead creepers, came down much closer to the ground than they probably would have on flat land. It was a plus for us.

Getting back up the hill to the jeep was much more challenging for me than getting down. I groped and grasped at the tufts of tall grass whenever I could as I struggled with the rope with the other hand. On the first night out here, I slammed my hand into a nest of stinging ants (*Odontomachus*) churned up from a very rotten log almost entirely buried in the dense grass. Three or four stings, the equivalent of one good dose of the dreaded close relative of this ponerine, namely *Paraponera clavata* (a large black ant common to Sarapiquí forests, which the local folks call the *bala* [the bullet]). As I recall now, John and Roger luckily bypassed the ants. On the way back to the inn to call it a night, I told John and Roger that we would have to devise some sort of observation deck beneath the roost, so that we could study it for several months!

El patrón, Don Gonzalo, shook his head in disbelief at my inquiry the following morning. I could only imagine that he was caught off guard again by these crazy *gringos mariposeros*. How could we top, in his age-worn, squinting eyes, the blue butterflies in the bags in our rooms, and the long nights I spent the year before watching *Morpho* caterpillars in the rain and mist? But here we were again, with a new project. I explained to Don Gonzalo that I wanted to borrow a hammer and saw and buy some nails and lumber. In my fledgling Spanish, combined with a few rough sketches, I related my mission to make an observation deck down the hillside of Cuesta Angel. I even told him why, which really got him going with the other fellows who hung around the *pulpería* and *cantina*. It was a great topic for conversation on a rainy afternoon—the *gringos* are now building a deck in the jungle to watch butterflies at night!

Naturally Don Gonzalo came through for me. Out behind the little gas station next to the inn, Challa found some old lumber we could use, including part of a wooden door. It would make a perfect platform for two people to sit on. Together with the beams, we loaded the door and our tools into the jeep and hurried over to the ridge after breakfast. The sunny weather would make our task somewhat easier, but by no means simple. Much of the grass where we had slid down the hill the night before was still flattened down. Piece by piece we lowered the lumber, and ourselves, down to the dead creepers, and labored under the hot sun to build our deck. By this time, the zebra butterflies were long gone for the day. We would not be disturbing them as we scurried about the making of the observation deck. Wisely, John brought along some extra rope which we used to help secure the platform. The idea was to make the observation deck horizontal, and to position it just beneath the roost site. We used thick beams to support the deck, jamming them into the ground as much as possible. We had to cut the support beams right at the site in order to achieve the correct angle of the cut for the ends that would be nailed to the platform. At the rear of the deck we anchored the whole structure to some wooden stakes driven into the ground above the platform. We then attached the platform to these stakes with the rope. In this way, we hoped that the deck would stay in place with our weight on it. The deck itself was little more than the half-door Challa had roused up from the trash behind the gas pump. But it would do. By noon, our deck was in place, long before the butterflies would arrive for the night.

The little deck that we built measured about one meter on each side and was big enough for just one person at a time. Hidden in the tall grasses, it could not be seen from the top of the hill and the road, a desirable feature for keeping away any curiosity seekers who would surely stop to see what we were up to. Cautiously, each of us tested the deck, with success. With the incessant rains of this valley, we hoped the deck would stay in place for several weeks, perhaps months, and not be washed away down the hill with one of us on it at night. My rule was that there would always be two of us at the site each night of study. John and Roger roughed out a depressed area in the ground just behind the deck for the second person to use during observations.

Now that we had our deck in place, how would we study the roosting butterflies? What kinds of information was I after? As I usually do, I opted for some straight and uncomplicated questions about zebra butterfly natural history. Of course, I was not out here to reinvent the wheel, so I had to build on what other researchers had already reported in the literature on the phenomenon of communal roosting in this butterfly species. Could we add anything new? Clearly we could. For virtually any species studied, even those most intensely so such as *Drosophila* fungus flies, there are always new things to be discovered. We will never understand it all, for we cannot put ourselves inside the head, the brain, the psyche, of another creature. But we can try to understand as much as possible, to stretch those limits of knowledge as far as they can be pushed. I felt this

Just above the lighted area in the lower left, a student field assistant, John H. Thomason, is pointing upward to a communal roost of the butterfly *Heliconius charitonia* during the 1972 rainy season at La Cinchona, near Cuesta Angel. John is standing on a little platform built into the steep side of the ravine, concealed by the dense grass and brush. The butterfly roost is situated in a cluster of dead creepers high above John's head.

way about the very familiar zebra butterfly. I told John, and later Eleanor Williams, another student from Lawrence University who conducted a six-month field study at Cuesta Angel on the population dynamics of this species, that in spite of all that had been written about this creature and its roosting habits, there was little information available on how roost membership changed from day to day over several months.

I designed a field study to document the sex ratio, patterns of re-cruitment of new adult butterflies, and general turnover in roost membership, for this particular roost of *Heliconius charitonia*. From June 27 through August 9, 1972, a six-week period, we marked individual butterflies from the roost on twenty different days. Because of other research studies I had under way here and elsewhere in Sarapiquí and in Guanacaste Province, we were unable to spend more time than this at the roost. Yet this was enough to obtain a basic picture of how the roost membership changed over a several-week period. We arrived at the roost usually just after dawn, hoping to net as many butterflies as possible for marking as they left the roost. Using a fast-drying hobbyists' enamel paint and fine camel's-hair brushes, we painted little code numbers on the undersides of both hindwings on each butterfly netted. The code numbers, usually painted in white or yellow, were clearly visible when the butterfly perched on the roost with its wings folded tightly. Putting number codes on both wings would not alter the butterfly's aerodynamics, or so we assumed. We always avoided netting butterflies while they were still perched on the dead creepers, wanting to minimize actual disturbance of the roosting butterflies and the roost site. Aside from marking them, I wanted to disturb the butterflies as little as possible.

I noticed something striking about these butterflies. When the rays of the morning sun hit the roost directly from the east, the butterflies exploded off the roost site in a very dramatic and beautiful manner. On clear mornings, we could watch the sun come up out of the east, across the Cuesta Angel ravine. We could almost calculate when the sun's rays would wake up the roosting butterflies. All of a sudden they were up and away, settling on the surrounding vegetation to soak up the sun's warmth before flying off. Sometimes we joked about how the butterflies appeared "lazy" and hesitant to leave the roost on cool, overcast mornings when the rising sun did little to warm them. We kind of felt the same way, being out here on the deck at the crack of dawn! When the weather was cool and wet, the butterflies seldom left the roost until much later in the morning, and then it was a very gradual process.

Late in the afternoon, generally after 4:30, we would return to the observation deck to study the return of the butterflies to the roost. This was a most enjoyable exercise. It was a game of sorts— predicting which marked butterflies would show up. We ended up marking fifteen butterflies on this roost, and resighting most of these at least once within the next couple of weeks. Only a few individuals showed up repeatedly for the length of the study.

We got to recognize almost instantly certain marked individuals, the few that kept returning throughout the six-week period. I especially enjoyed watching the freshly hatched butterflies, the unmarked newcomers to the roost. In the early morning sun, when they drifted off the creepers and settled on the dew-covered vegetation beneath the roost, the upper sides of the wings of these newborn butterflies shimmered like black satin, boldly decorated with broad sweeps of brilliant yellow stripes. How vulnerable these fresh butterflies seemed to be at such moments. They perched on the damp greenness, along with the older, tattered individuals, their slender wings stretched out, as if reaching for as much warmth of the morning sun as possible. At such moments, we could almost touch the butterflies. But always, in a few minutes, they were off, springing to life in upward leaps into the air.

So you can understand why some of the most beautiful moments I had with zebra butterflies in the early morning were watching them fly off out into the vast open air space of the Sarapiquí gorge. Many flew downward once airborne, quickly disappearing over the mountainside, blending in with the breath-taking backdrop of the forest and brush-filled clearings far below the observation deck. I knew that we would see some of them again this night, the next, or a week or so later. Sometimes a marked butterfly failed to show up on several evenings, only to reappear at the roost several weeks later.

After a while, the routine of going out after dark to make a final tally of the numbers of butterflies on the roost, including marked individuals, became something to look forward to. We had informal bets about which marked butterflies would turn up on a given night. It was necessary to check the roost after dark since we did not really

A close-up view of communally roosting *Heliconius charitonia*, showing several previously marked individuals as part of a field research study at Cuesta Angel.

know just when the last butterflies arrived for the evening (the "late arrivals"). I actually think that we became attached to some of the

Butterflies warming up in the early morning sunshine on the brush beneath a communal roost at La Cinchona, Cuesta Angel, in 1972. The near butterfly has its wings fully extended to soak up heat from the sun; a marked individual is seen above.

faithful marked butterflies that always seemed to turn up. When we stopped checking this roost, we did not remove the observation deck. Even within the relatively short period of six weeks, the deck had rotted away considerably, becoming part of the organic decay that covered this damp mountainside, a place where the existence of dead wood was strictly ephemeral. We saved our rope.

In Sarapiquí in December 1972, I arranged for Eleanor Williams Thomason and Susan Parry, biology students at Lawrence, to come to Cariblanco to study the population of the zebra butterfly at Cuesta

Angel, as I was devoting more field time to the NSF-funded cicada project. John's wife had no problem settling in with the González family. In fact, she seemed to become an adopted sister of sorts to Fanny, Hortensia, Adilia, and the others. By early December, I had decided that we ought to conduct a several-month-long "mark-resight" study of *Heliconius charitonia* at Cuesta Angel, following our initial roost study in August. I was intrigued with the possibility, based on casual field observations up to this time, that discrete populations of the butterfly existed up and down the side of the mountain, and that perhaps separate roost sites were associated with each of these breeding populations. It was just an idea, an impression, based on little more than cursory information. At the same time, I pursued a study of the life cycle of this butterfly species at Cuesta Angel, aimed at disclosing the caterpillar food plants and the nectar and pollen sources of the adults, and at describing the cycle's early stages.

"Eleanora" and "Susana," as they became known in Cariblanco, learned the marking technique from us and staked out six distinct sites at various points down the side of the mountain. Their study sites ranged from the crest of the ridge above the road to Sarapiquí, through various spots along the little dirt road leading down the side of the ravine to the Sarapiquí River, and ending in the open, cleared area bordering the river, where a squatter family had set down roots the year before. From December 1972 through May 1973, Ellie, Susan, and John conducted the study, marking butterflies netted at each of the six stations with a different color paint. Over the 155-day period, they marked a total of 976 butterflies among the six sites, and spent 63 days marking and resighting butterflies. They recorded the sex and wing condition ("fresh," "middle," and "worn") of each butterfly they marked. I had turned over the Landrover to John, who needed it to visit other localities in Sarapiquí and elsewhere in the country as part of the cicada studies, his primary reason for being in Costa Rica as my field assistant. So there were many times when Ellie and Susan walked to and from the ravine each day. Ellie remained on the project after Susan returned to the States.

They breakfasted early at the inn so as to get to the ravine by 7:30, and spent the day there observing butterflies. We ended up with so much data that we sought out the expert assistance of population ecologist Laurence M. Cook of the University of Manchester in England, who helped us calculate and interpret various population parameters based upon our raw data. At the suggestion of Lincoln Brower, Dr. Cook also collaborated with me in the analysis of our population data on *Morpho peleides* from the Barranca site. He took over most ably where we, the field observers, the gatherers of natural history information on the butterflies, felt limited in deciding on the most appropriate analyses. So much of biological science is accom-

Undergraduate student researchers Eleanor Williams Thomason (left) and Susan Parry marking netted individuals of *Heliconius charitonia* with fast-drying hobbyists' enamel paint, to study the movement patterns of the butterflies at various points along the steep slope of the La Cinchona ravine.

plished this way, bringing together different talents to collaborate on an end product, such as a scientific paper, that would be of interest to other researchers.

But the analysis came much later, of course. For my students there were the many months of field study in the tropics, of becoming part of the Sarapiquí experience. During the months I had returned to Lawrence to teach, John and Ellie melted into the warmth and hospitality that defined the mood of life at the Cariblanco inn. They settled in with the family. Ellie helped cook the meals, bake bread, do the dishes, and whatever else, in the evening hours. Tirelessly, Ellie and, until she left, Susan, loaded up their backpacks each morning and headed out to the ravine, a good forty-five-minute hike from Cariblanco. They didn't mind, for they were participating in a most wonderful learning experience in the tropics, something that might not present itself again in the future. Ellie had grown up in the Door County area of northeastern Wisconsin, and felt very much at home with the out-of-doors and the butterflies.

Ah, yes, those butterflies. The more time we spent observing them, the more we learned about their habits and their relationship to the tropical rain forests of Sarapiquí. Ellie's population study, for example, showed that distinct populations of the zebra butterfly did, in fact, exist at various points down the side of the ravine, for she had discovered very little evidence of exchange of marked individuals among her six sites. She also found that there were high percentages of recaptures (resightings) of butterflies where they had been previously marked, especially in the first several days after being marked.

We scoured the landscape, as much as was possible given the rough terrain, in search of roosts. Possibly there was a relationship between Ellie's emerging picture of distinct populations and the locations of communal roosts of *Heliconius charitonia*? The first clue happened quite unexpectedly. I almost bumped into the roost! John and I were looking for cicadas in the scrubby forest at the top of the crest above the road to Sarapiquí, only about 150 meters from where we had found the first roost (Roost A) the previous year. On this particular day, February 10, 1973, I was about to stand up after crawling through the tangled, dense brush on my hands and knees, not minding the rain that was building that morning. But then I saw them, just two butterflies, jostled off their darkly shaded perch by my rumbling around on the forest floor beneath them. This was the very top of the hill, and the roost, we discovered, was only a meter off the ground! Another find! The dead creepers here formed a thick stand of gnarled, stringy meshwork in the deep shade of the forest. I had not expected the butterflies here. But then who am I to second-guess nature?

The roost was inside Ellie's first site, and eventually some butterflies she had marked turned up on this roost. In eight weeks, we ended up marking a total of ninety-six butterflies on this roost, and of these, fifty percent were resighted here at least once, and several many times. With this much bigger sample of butterflies on Roost B than we had previously with Roost A, it was feasible to check for sex ratio. We discovered a 1:1 sex ratio. Most startling, and a contrast to what we had witnessed on Roost A, was that a whopping thirty-six percent of all butterflies marked on Roost B were resighted on the roost for more than half the total number of observation days. Clearly a sizable portion of the roost's membership were highly "residential" butterflies, undoubtedly foraging for resources within the immediate vicinity of the roost, a sort of mountaintop population. Later, I recall walking along with John through this forest and out into a clearing where we watched for *Morpho theseus* coming across the ridge, climbing up from one rain forest and down into the next one. "Say, John, did you see that *charitonia* fly past me just now? . . . I could have sworn it was marked!" We stayed up on the ridge that morning longer than I had originally intended. In doing so, we discovered several of our marked butterflies, at distances ranging from 65 to 165 meters from Roost B, where they had been originally marked at dawn on nine different dates.

In this way, the pieces to our little puzzle about the zebra butterfly started to fit together into a rough, hesitant sketch of the creature's population structure. Our perseverance was paying off; a month or so later, we discovered Roost C suspended in some dead creepers high above the forest floor about two-thirds of the way down the dirt road to the Sarapiquí River. The roost dangled in a big tree, and it was about twenty meters off the ground, totally inaccessible to us and more typical of what I had expected for the roosting habits in these very wary butterflies.

The tree containing the roost was about two hundred meters down the very steep slope that fell away from the little road. There was no way we could study it. But through binoculars we could clearly see some butterflies, although we did not see any marked ones. It didn't really matter, though. What was becoming apparent to the three of us was the way in which the zebra butterfly was subdividing its breeding population down the side of this intriguing mountain.

There appeared to be several distinct "subpopulations," that is, fairly localized groupings of this butterfly species, at different places down the ravine. The chief evidence for this conclusion was the fairly low frequency of exchange of marked individual butterflies among the various observation points, from the ridge top down to the Río Sarapiquí itself. We also suspected that one or more communal roosts were associated with each of these groupings of butterflies. Thus we were witnessing some clues to how the butterfly species interprets its environment, reflected in where we found roosts relative to where Ellie and Susan had marked hundreds of butterflies over several months of hard work. It stung me sharply that we could not get close to Roost C in this respect. There was just no way we could build a deck to reach it!

Ellie and Susan did the very best they could. It became Ellie's project for an independent study at Lawrence. More than that, it taught her firsthand the challenges that go with studying specific questions in tropical natural history. Eventually we coauthored a paper in the *Journal of Animal Ecology* with Dr. Cook on the results of this project. John and I went on to publish the findings we uncovered with Roosts A and B in the *Journal of the Lepidopterists' Society*. Subsequent further studies of zebra butterfly roosts at Cuesta Angel and La Tirimbina resulted in other papers published with other undergraduate students, including Mary Ellen Carolan from Lawrence and Mark Moffett from Beloit College. Mark, who worked with me at La Tirimbina in 1977, also collaborated with me on studies of the ecology of a widespread ithomiine butterfly, *Mechanitis isthmia*, resulting in coauthored papers published in the *American Midland Naturalist* and a German entomological journal. Mary Ellen also worked with me at La Tirimbina in 1976, following our roost project at Cuesta Angel, on a study of food-gathering behavior in the giant tropical ponerine ant, *Paraponera clavata*.

What Sarapiquí taught me was that seeking answers to specific questions about just a single species, such as the beautiful zebra butterfly, always opened a Pandora's box of new questions. Through further field work, it would be necessary to examine very carefully precisely where the butterflies deposited their eggs and also where they fed. Our preliminary observations revealed at least one species of passifloraceous caterpillar food plant in the subgenus *Tetrastylis* (within the genus *Passiflora*), since we witnessed butterflies depositing eggs on individuals of this vine at different places along the ravine. We also recorded the various species of flowers visited by the butterflies, including wild cucumber vines. *Heliconius* butterflies have been found to collect and mulch pollen from the orangish flowers of wild cucumber vines, thereby obtaining nitrogenous substances (since pollen grains contain proteins) that the females utilize for the synthesis of egg tissues. But the butterflies also visited several other kinds of plants to obtain nectar for energy, since this liquid is rich in various nutrients, including sugars. These natural history observations, made alongside our marking studies, helped us to interpret the disjunct spatial pattern of the butterfly population at this locality.

To understand the existence of the zebra butterfly required knowing about every other kind of organism it interacted with out here on the Cuesta Angel mountainside. And more than this, it also meant understanding how the physical environment, the terrain, the wind,

The passionflower vine, *Passiflora vitifolia,* a caterpillar food plant for some species of *Heliconius* butterflies in Sarapiquí. The elongate petals of the large, conspicuous flower are bright red.

rain, and sunshine, came together to poise the butterfly for the evolutionary testing ground of its associations with many other species. There were moments when John, Roger, Ellie, and the others sensed my frustration with just how difficult it could be to get some simple answers. But we didn't get answers most of the time, just clues to new questions to ask about nature. Out here in this valley of rain forest, where the great river shaped the land for millions of years, ours was a world of firsthand experience, a place where book knowledge took second place to trying to unearth new facts by ourselves, as a team.

There was the period of weeks when I was doggedly determined to find the caterpillar food plant. "John and Roger, isn't it odd just how common the butterflies are here on the ridge but I haven't a clue about the food plant?" The butterflies teased us. We'd stand on the ridge looking out, in places where the rain forest broke away and low brush took over. In such places, the butterflies zipped through the morning sun, often at very high speeds, with an air of urgency about them. But I searched these open scars on the mountainside to witness those few moments when the butterfly stopped, dropping into the brush in search of something. It always seemed to us that the butterflies were just out of reach of our aerial nets. The binoculars helped, but we had to get close. Down at the bottom of the ravine, along the edge of the Sarapiquí River where the squatter had settled, our luck was much better. Where he cleared away the rain forest, the dense tangle of second-growth vegetation had taken a fast hold. He chose not to clear it all away to sow his *mulanga*, *yuca*, and bananas.

Where the forest was allowed to begin the very slow process of reestablishing itself is where the vines came in, proliferating over the terrain, now jagged with the profile of broken trees and matchstick logs. It was always hard to distinguish among the many species of intertwined vines here. I could see, however, that there were Piperaceae, Cucurbitaceae, Apocynaceae, and many other families represented. John, Roger, and I labored to penetrate this little ribbon of wild vegetation, snuggled in between the river and the point where the mountainside raised itself abruptly. We struggled over the rotting, broken logs and immense boulders, thrown off by volcanoes eons before. "You know, fellows, this is the kind of place that really makes me nervous about poisonous snakes . . . so let's be real careful out here today . . . okay?" became my standard daily opener as we parted the brush with our machetes. We slipped and fell over the moldy rocks and logs, well slicked with algae and moss where the sun could not penetrate the leafy cover. In some places, these lush plants, a tangle of incredible sizes and shapes of leaves, of spines and sticky hairs on stems and branches, towered over our heads. It was a liliputian rain forest, complete with layers of life, where the stench of mold and decay arched upward from the darkened recesses of the rotting world beneath our feet. But in these places we saw a fascinating display of butterflies when the sun was brightest.

The satiny ink-blue- and white-splotched wings of *Heliconius cydno* never failed to catch my attention as we struggled through this brush. This species shared this webwork of vines and suckers (resprouting from fallen logs) with the gloriously colored *Heliconius hecale*, its bright orange-, yellow-, and black-streaked wings fluttering just above the canopy. Tiny eddies of an unseen breeze, faint ripples of air in the very still, heavy dampness of this place, caused a *Heliconius cydno* butterfly, its oblong forewings now blurs of ink-blue iridescence and white, to miss its mark in landing on a flower. The butterfly finally takes hold, using its long slender glistening black legs to grasp the petals of the *Anguria* flower, positioning itself for a meal of pollen. Soon, the satiny *cydno* is joined here by *hecale* and by the zebra butterfly, for it is a place where the bright orange-red tuftlike flower heads of *Anguria* offer pollen and nectar to these fickle feeders. Our luckiest moments were when we watched individuals of all three species vying vigorously for a spot to alight on the flower, a sort of casual pecking order centered on who would get the goodies first. You see, the *Anguria* vine, although robust and big, did not bear many flowers at once here, so the butterflies had to converge at once on the few flowers available, especially when the clouds broke away and the valley filled with the golden radiance of the early morning tropical sun. Could it be that those butterflies on the roosts high above, like the one we studied on the deck we had built, sauntered down to the bottom of the valley to feed? Perhaps it was so.

We followed the zebra butterflies here to discover their caterpillar food plants. I let the butterflies be the plant taxonomists and evolutionary biologists all at once. For me, every vine looked the same as the next one here, or so it seemed many times. But the butterflies, guided by their keen senses of vision and smell, sorted out this marvelous riot of living diversity for me. They never seemed to fail at finding the correct vine in this morass of life. The zebra butterfly found the *Tetrastylis* for me. We struggled to follow a butterfly as it fluttered skillfully through and about the vines without breaking a wingbeat or a wing, many minutes at a time. When it found the correct plant, it hovered and fluttered intensely, as if inspecting each leaf and tendril. Just when I was certain the butterfly would place an egg on a leaf or tendril, it moved on to the next part of the vine, sometimes hidden from my view. I felt myself an intruder on a very special act of nature, a butterfly most carefully placing her babies in the jungle. It had to be exactly the correct leaf or tendril. How was it that the gravid female recognized the most tender, young leaflets of the vine on which to place an egg? What sort of marvelous evolutionary fine-tuning in food plant parts was this? The precise answers to such questions may never be known. But for now, I am humbled by this exquisiteness of the zebra butterfly, a very specialized behavior that ensures the survival of the species. One of the basic lessons of nature I learned in Sarapiquí, through studies of creatures like *Heliconius* butterflies, is that in order to begin to understand nature, we must uncover the subtle, small differences among species with similar habits, not so much the broadly sweeping grand picture.

The roosts, and their relation to other features of this butterfly's natural history, still intrigued me beyond our initial discoveries at Cuesta Angel. No one really understands why these butterflies form their sleeping aggregations. From our work, we definitely picked up the idea that the roosts were somehow connected with the spatial arrangement of breeding populations of the zebra butterfly. We were not alone. In Trinidad, Paul Ehrlich and Larry Gilbert, working with *Heliconius ethilla*, discovered that home range patterns changed when there was a drastic change in the availability of food resources within the existing home range of the butterflies. (Like us, Drs. Ehrlich and Gilbert did their study in a rugged, mountainous area.) This was a most important discovery, underscoring the adaptive, flexible nature of a butterfly species in the ways it utilizes the environment. Home range movement patterns and the locations of communal roosts were clearly related, based on our studies in Sarapiquí, key aspects of the broader picture of how tropical butterflies adapt to the availability of food resources in the environment.

Communal roosts seem to be fairly stable entities within the populations of *Heliconius*, acting as sort of brokerage houses of information about the habitat that allow butterflies to gauge the changes in their resources. Certainly one intriguing idea along these lines that has been advanced by some biologists is that newly eclosed adults recently recruited to a roost might learn to locate pollen and nectar sources by following older, more experienced adult butterflies on their daily sojourns into the surrounding habitats. Roosts might also encourage the assembly of unmated, fresh females for mating by older male butterflies resident on a roost. Newly mated females may learn to find caterpillar food plants on which to lay their eggs by following older, experienced females from the roost. Other kinds of social interactions related to butterfly survival might also be operative on such roosts, but very little is known about them. One of the classic explanations of communal roosting in butterflies has more to do with a sort of collective defense against predators. The arrival of a predatory animal in the midst of a roost might somehow alert its membership to flutter off into the forest, even though one or a few individuals might be taken as prey in the process. A related view is that some species of *Heliconius* butterflies are distasteful to insect-eating vertebrates, owing to noxious substances ingested in the caterpillar stage from the food plants, and that they are therefore capable of reinforcing this undesirability as food by a collective visual signal at the roost site. In the case of the zebra butterfly, the roost appears at night, to the human observer, as a cluster of faded, dead leaves attached to creepers. In other words, the butterflies in their typical sleeping posture appear more cryptically than warningly colored. But who knows how a butterfly predator, such as lizard or bird, interprets such a sight at night?

The butterflies often modify their foraging habits in direct response to changes in the blooming patterns of their pollen sources, while retaining the same basic population structure, home range, and roost locations. I believe that as biologists continue to study the detailed habits of other tropical insects, we will find more and more evidence of the sophisticated means by which individual species adjust their daily habits in response to changes in the availability of food resources. In the meantime, however, the habits of *Heliconius* butterflies must be viewed as elegant examples of the ways in which insects assess the environment and respond rapidly to changes in it to maximize survival on a daily basis.

We never saw lots of zebra butterflies together in the clearings at Cuesta Angel. Only on roosts did these butterflies congregate, exhibiting what the great naturalist William Beebe long ago called the "capacity of sociability." Off the roosts, the butterflies, like other species of *Heliconius*, scattered themselves across the terrain. How the butterflies could be so dispersed in going about the business of searching for resources in the habitat during the day and then so social at night remains one of tropical nature's greatest mysteries.

I am glad that I had the chance to encounter the butterfly roosts in Sarapiquí. My experiences with them were not planned events or part of a structured research program on these insects. Perhaps it was just a matter of time before I came across a roost; but finding the first roost on the steep mountainside, that special day when the rains held off at dusk, sensitized me and my student assistants to look out for other roosts later. I am readily spurred on to the study of specific events in tropical nature when confronted with a few clues. True, I had seen the largely unstructured and temporary flocking of other kinds of butterflies and some dragonflies in the temperate zone. But observing the communally roosting *Heliconius charitonia* in Sarapiquí became my avenue to seeing firsthand how this intriguing, still largely mysterious behavior is an integral part of this species's natural history.

In 1980, five years after we had completed our study of zebra butterflies in Cuesta Angel, I learned that Don Gonzalo had died. After *el patrón* had gone, Doña Virginia, his widow, had moved with her daughters back to Santo Domingo de Heredia, their original home. Not having stayed in Cariblanco for several years by this time, I was eager to learn of Challa and his family, who stayed behind to live in Sarapiquí.

Inquiring at the inn, I learned that Challa, who inherited the property from his father, had leased it to someone else, and that he and his family had moved to a new location in Sarapiquí. He now lived in the pastel blue house farther down the road from Cariblanco, closer to San Miguel but still in the mountains. Getting the directions, I was off to visit. Where the road swings down around a bend to the left when facing eastward toward the *tierra caliente*, Challa's little house sits on the right, with a coffee farm behind it. On one side of the house there is a large pile of neatly stacked *leña* (firewood), and chicken coops on the other side. Beyond the house the land drops away swiftly for a great distance and eventually meets the Sarapiquí River. Coffee bushes are everywhere on the steep slope, fusing with the crisp mist blanketing this place most of the time.

Challa came out of the house and over to the little wooden fence in a flash, as he had done many times before when I stopped, and as he would continue to do on my visits for many years. Suddenly he was there, before I turned off the jeep's engine, those silver-studded teeth flashing that smile of welcome I had missed for several years. But Challa was different now. When I stayed at the inn in earlier years, he sported a black moustache and black hair. But like me, the passage of only a few years had metamorphosed him, a shocking white replacing blackness. Challa had married late in life, about three years after I first started living at Cariblanco, and now he had two young daughters, Marta and Giselle.

Isabel offered me coffee and a *boca* of *queso blanco con tortilla*. They were at ease with me, even though several years had intervened since our last contact. But the passage of those years seemed insignificant; the warmth of a well-rounded friendship, forged at the Cariblanco inn long before this meeting, brought us back together with a spirit of camaraderie. What made the difference, too, was that we had been part of a family out here on the mountain ridge high above the Sarapiquí River. The long discussions about the *mariposas azules* and *chicharras* (cicadas), the times my students helped out in their kitchen, all of these experiences made me feel like part of the González clan.

After some *abrazos* we stepped inside to a cottage filled with warmth. Little Marta grabbed my hand to show me the two caged parrots on the back porch. Later, after *café*, Challa led me out back to see his crops. Through the dense foliage of the coffee bushes, now thick and lush and laden with shiny red berries, Challa vanished from sight. For a few moments, I could no longer see his red-checkered shirt and faded blue jeans. Then he called out, and I followed the sound, growing fainter down this wind-swept ridge. He was standing proudly next to his tomato patch. "It is the first one in Sarapiquí!" he offered. It looked like a success. Tomatoes traditionally do not make out well in the humid tropics, but Challa obviously had been weaving his magic on these healthy vines now brimming with plump fruit. Challa's sea-green eyes searched my face for a sign of approval, which I gave readily. Our mirth filled the pocket of humid air that hung over us, engulfed us, here on the ridge where the raging waters of the Sarapiquí are faint echoes for only the coffee bushes to hear. Like Challa, I too hopscotched from subject to subject as if trying to compress the passage of years into minutes. "*Qué noticias de Fanny y Hortensia?*" I inquired of my old *amigo*. "*Ah, Don Allen, ellas son en San José ahora. Pero, ellas siempre pregunta para usted!*" (But they always ask for you!) Flashes of watery eyes and teeth and more *abrazos* ushered my departure from Challa's house along the road to Sarapiquí.

What is special and appealing about Challa's place now is the simplicity of his fairly uncomplicated life, out here along the ridge of this ancient valley. He's the lucky one. He wakes up with the lush green of the rain forest on the opposite slope of the valley facing his view from the window. He can stand behind his house, perched on a flat spot before the land falls away, to see the rains coming in from the Caribbean Sea to the east. Challa's world is one of nature.

What embraces him, whether by choice or not, are the strong colors of butterflies and other insects, metallic-sheened orchid bees and beetles—the buzz and hum of life. Now when I approach his house on the curve in the road, I see brilliant colors mingling with the softness of green and other earthtones. His may not be an easy life, but it is rich in ways meaningful to human existence.

Long after I am gone, as long as there are habitats suitable for their survival, the zebra butterflies will perform their nightly ritual of flocking on roosts. We must view this behavior as one part of the broadly textured biological puzzle of how this species has come to terms with the rest of nature. I do not understand these butterflies, but I feel a bit closer to them for having shared some of their time and space. They comprised, of course, but one of the thousands of insect species that caught my eye out here on Cuesta Angel. But these were moments when I glowed with excitement and awe, and when I momentarily forgot about the rest of nature that felt our presence, close by in the jungle night, on the side of the mountain. We had stood there to be part of this ancient ritual of life, on the rugged slope where perhaps no person had ever stood before.

So too I hope that others come to stand here in years to come. Even though there is now a repaved road of glossy asphalt along the ridge, rather than the old mud and gravel with its potholes, the steepness of this ravine has preserved its rain forest, home for many marvelous insects I have sought to study over the years. Let others too soak up the rain, smell the ageless cycle of rot and decay that fuels the rain forest clinging to the gorge and giving it the sustenance for continued life. Let them see the clouds rolling in from the east, and the butterflies racing through the places where the jungle has been broken open. Then they too can appreciate that every living creature is a building block of knowledge about life, a part of the chronicle of nature of which we too are part. I hope that Sarapiquí's forests, like the one covering the steep slopes of the Cuesta Angel ravine, are still around for such introspection.

ENCOUNTERS WITH CICADAS AND OTHER FOREST INSECTS

5

Cicadas, stout-bodied, earth-colored members of the "true bug" family (in the order Homoptera), with glistening elongate transparent or translucent (hyaline) wings, have held my fascination since boyhood days in suburban New York. *Tibicen chloromera*, the common species in southern New York State, was the largest insect I had come across in my summer wanderings through marshy woodlands. I was enthralled by the loud staccato call of the males, which always seemed to crescendo during the hottest daytime hours of July and August. Walking through fields and forests, I could hear throngs of these insects everywhere, but I only actually saw a few each summer. The first time I saw the big *Tibicen* was in a marsh. Perhaps I was eleven or twelve years old. Suddenly it was there, almost in grasping reach of my hands. As I walked through waist-high joe-pye weed, goldenrods, and tall grass, there was a sudden buzz as if something had crash-landed nearby. I turned to one side just in time to see the big cicada clutching a tall thin reed, the weight of its body, powdery white below and mottled black and dark green above, bending down the plant. Apparently the creature did not see me, for very quickly it burst forth in a call so vibrant that it almost deafened me for a few moments.

Early on in my life, cicadas impressed me because they heightened my awareness of the way nature partitions the environment into daytime and nighttime components, each with its own set of active animal species. New York summers at night are filled with the sounds of crickets, katydids, and other calling insects such as the cone-headed grasshopper. Cicadas dominate the daytime in late summer, and they do not call at night under most circumstances. Singing insects of both daytime and nighttime make us acutely aware of the large segment of this planet's nature that is often unseen but surely present. Through singing insects I have come to appreciate the cycle of seasons in the north. In spring and early summer the fields and forests are filled with the sounds of birds, but not with singing insects. It is only in late summer and autumn that we realize their renewed presence in our midst, each year calling as they have done for millions of years before the advent of humankind. The reason for this pattern has to do with the annual cycle of growth in singing insects.

During the lapse of years between my teens and beginning postdoctoral research in Costa Rica, I had almost entirely forgotten about cicadas. Perhaps the greatest reason why I had not pursued my interest in them had precisely to do with their inaccessibility as a group of insects. In northern climates, setting aside the unusual and well-studied periodical (thirteen-year and seventeen-year) cicadas (*Magicicada* species), adult population densities of most of the so-called annual cicadas, such as *Tibicen* species and others, are generally very low, at least in my experience in the Northeast and Midwest. Although annual cicadas have nymphs with multiyear life cycles, usually ranging from five to nine years, the occurrence of several overlapping generations, coupled with a variable, staggered developmental period in the nymphs within a generation, ensures limited adult emergence at a particular locality each year. For this reason, cicadas are easily forgotten or ignored as objects of serious study—it is often too frustrating trying to get a good sample to work with. My experiences in the tropics changed this perception of cicadas, and led me into a fascinating period of field research on them, chiefly in Sarapiquí, which spanned several years.

Whereas in New York or the Chicago area I was aware of the presence of one species of cicada in late summer, my journeys to and from La Selva between 1968 and 1970 opened my eyes and ears to a pleasantly new and challenging situation. I had entered into a land rich with cicadas, where many species of these daytime troubadours made their presence and exuberance clear to me. Consider the trek across the mountains from the Central Valley to the *tierra caliente.* During the dry season, the coffee *fincas* above Alajuela and Heredia blossomed with the shrill calls of cicadas, easily heard from the jeep. I sensed that the calls were coming from the various species of legume shade trees, mostly *Inga, Pithecellobium,* and *Erythrina*, in the coffee plantations. When the shifting, boisterous winds of *verano* in these hills are just right, the calls are almost deafening, echoing off the jeep as we slipped by. At other times, when the wind shifted, the calls were barely perceptible.

In the early phase of the very distinctive and intense dry season characteristic of these foothills on the leeward slopes of the Cordillera Central, the air is filled with the bell-like chirp of *Fidicina amoena*, the "bell ringer."(Early on in these studies, my student assistants and myself came up with our own vernacular names for the various species of cicadas we were studying. These names were taken from the distinctive calls or songs of each species. Furthermore, since we were not sure of their actual scientific names at the time, these vernacular names helped us in keeping track of our field data.) Later in the dry season, when *amoena* is on the wane, *F. pronoe* (the "late summer pulse-whistler"), with its very different pulsating whistlelike call, occupies the same places. When I first heard these calls, I would sometimes pull over and get out to collect some voucher specimens of these species. Invariably after I crawled under the barbed wire fences bordering the coffee, or asked permission to enter the *finca* if near a house, the cicadas would stop calling as I approached them. Even though I knew they were all around me, in the legume trees, some of which were short enough for me to catch a cicada in my aerial net, I had a very difficult time spotting one of the insects. Cicadas are uncanny in detecting one's presence and becoming silent in the trees. Often these showdowns lasted several minutes, and usually I gave up first. I could hear them starting up as I drove off!

From my initial observations at Finca La Selva during my years as a postdoctoral researcher with OTS, it soon became clear to me that cicadas are a very distinctive feature of the complex tapestry of Sarapiquí's forests. During early correspondence with Tom Moore, an expert on cicadas who had studied and collected them in different parts of Latin America in the decade before I arrived at La Selva, I learned that Costa Rica had a greater number of cicada species than all of North America east of the Mississippi River. Yet in spite of this, I was surprised to learn that these creatures, by and large, are not mentioned in the various published accounts of naturalists studying the floras and faunas of New World tropical forests. And there appeared to be very little natural history or ecological information published on Central American species, save for classic treatises such as Godman and Salvin's chapter on cicadas in *Biologia Centrali-Americana* published in the last century. The study of New World tropical cicadas, including those in Central America, was clearly a wide-open field of research.

At La Selva, between 1968 and 1970, I had the firsthand opportunity to conduct some preliminary studies on cicadas occurring there. I did not go to La Selva with this intention, but it did not take me long to rekindle a long-dormant fascination with these creatures. It happened at first when I accompanied Monte Lloyd into the rain forest when he went to check his experimental boxes of leaf litter. I noticed a large chocolate-brown cast nymphal skin of a cicada clinging to the underside of an understory palm plant. I had never seen a cicada cast skin that large. Above our heads, the forest was throbbing with the call of what later I would learn to be *Zammara smaragdina* ("rainy day croaker"). But there I was, holding the cast skin, a glistening shiny object, a testimonial of nature's adulthood, in the palm of my hand. I was fascinated just to think how big the adult insect must be, judging from the cast skin, which was easily twice the size of a *Tibicen* cast skin in New York. Monte, who had been studying North American periodical cicadas, told me that tropical cicadas were largely unstudied.

During my two years at La Selva, I noticed that at certain times of the year, the calls of the cicadas were very different from at other times, and that the nymphal cast skins were also different at these times. I decided to set up study plots to measure the numbers and kinds of cicadas emerging in the rain forest understory at La Selva. And with Tom Moore's help, I was able to make a preliminary assessment that during the short, erratic *veranillo* (little dry season) characteristic of January and February here, there are peak numbers of the "summertime whistler," *Fidicina sericans*, emerging in the rain forest, while in the very long rainy season, the most abundant species appears to be the "rainy day croaker." (Tom was a big help in providing species identifications for the cicadas I eventually studied in Costa Rica.) Several other species are active in the La Selva forest and one, *Fidicina mannifera*, what Dan Janzen would later dub the "sundown cicada" in *Costa Rican Natural History* (University of Chicago Press, 1983), appears to be present in low numbers throughout most of the year.

My studies at La Selva provided a basis to apply for a grant from the National Science Foundation to pursue research on Costa Rican cicadas, especially those of Sarapiquí. While I was on the faculty of Lawrence University the grant was awarded, which provided five years of support to study cicadas. The chief objective of the project was to measure the seasonal adult emergence patterns at two rain forest localities in Sarapiquí, supplementing these with similar observations at other localities in northern Costa Rica. Several Lawrence University students, funded under my grant, assisted me in carrying out this research, which began in 1972.

Cicadas, from what preliminary data I had from my days at La Selva, exhibited a striking range of morphological, behavioral, and ecological features—all for species inhabiting the same geographical region. I thought perhaps such marked differences among different

Fidicina mannifera, the "sundown cicada," one of the largest cicadas in Sarapiquí. Its bulky chocolate brown body is difficult to spot on tree trunks within the shaded forest understory, in spite of the insect's large size. The "sundown cicada's" strong, pulsating, screamlike buzz, like clockwork, marks the arrival of dusk and to a lesser extent dawn, filling the rain forests in lowland Sarapiquí with fifteen-minute spells of intense, unmistakable cicada song.

species somehow reflected divergent adaptations to different ecological conditions within the tropical rain forest, a topic of considerable general interest to ecologists. Of the dozens of species known from Costa Rica, each one must offer a unique insight into how tropical nature functions to establish a web of life. I wanted very much to reveal some wisps of marvelous adaptation which surely formed the ecological underpinning of these intriguing insects, often heard, seldom seen, and most certainly seldom studied. Unraveling some of these stories of adaptation, and the relationships of cicadas to tropical forest, would become my chief mission in Sarapiquí and other points in northern Costa Rica for several productive years of field work.

Additionally, I set out to measure the comparative abundance of cicadas emerging in plots of forest vegetation at each locality, with an emphasis on determining if cicadas preferentially emerged closer to certain species of forest canopy trees than others. Such an objective could generate information useful in understanding the overall workings of tropical forests, from the standpoint of the interdependence among cicadas, herbivorous insects, tropical forest vegetation, and tropical seasonality. I hoped, over several years, to be able to piece together a picture of cicada seasonality in Costa Rica, especially in Sarapiquí. Another mission of the project was to determine the extent to which the same species of cicadas were widely distributed across northern Costa Rica, and the habitat associations of individual species at each locality studied. In a sense, my research design included a loose transect of distinctive vegetational and climatic zones, ranging from the rain-forested foothills of La Tirimbina near La Virgen (220 meters elevation), to Cuesta Angel's montane rain forest (900 meters), Bajo La Hondura's cloud forest (1,000 meters), forest remnants in the Central Valley (600 meters), through the seasonal mountains northwest of the Central Valley (800–1,000 meters), and into the very seasonal and dry lowlands (50–100 meters) even farther to the northwest. The design also allowed censusing cicada populations not only in natural forest, but also in agricultural habitats, including some coffee *fincas* more than a century old.

At each locality, my basic methodology was to set out blocks of usually contiguous quadrates, usually measuring five by six meters (varying with the nature of the terrain and habitat), a size I chose because it was big enough to encompass at least one tree of very large girth (2–8 meters in diameter) and yet small enough to enable us to really survey and collect the cast skins within its boundaries. The object was then to make exhaustive collections of cicada cast skins in each quadrate on different dates scattered throughout each year, for several years. By this time I was fairly confident that I could distinguish species on the basis of the cast skins, since they exhibited distinctive morphological features such as color, size, degree of waxy coating on the underside of the thorax and abdomen, and other attributes. I could also distinguish sexes of cast skins, because the ovipositor sheath casing is prominent on cast skins of females.

Although the number of quadrates and the size of habitats examined varied between localities, I focused much attention on study plots at La Tirimbina and Cuesta Angel. At both locations, several plots were set up along the margins of the Río Sarapiquí and various creeks, places where I seemed to hear many species of cicadas. At La Tirimbina, my principal study site was a hillside of regenerating rain forest where the tree *Goethalsia meiantha* (Tiliaceae) was dominant. Interspersed with these trees were several large *gavilán* trees and scores of seedlings and saplings belonging to these species.

What is unusual about the *gavilán* tree is its high local density, something not generally found in most tree species in tropical forests. Gary S. Hartshorn, whom I met at La Selva in 1970, did his doctoral thesis on the population dynamics of the *gavilán* tree in Costa Rica, uncovering some fascinating aspects of this tree's ecology that contribute to its widespread abundance in the lower-elevation rain forests of Sarapiquí. After many years based in Costa Rica at the Tropical Science Center, Hartshorn went on to join the World Wildlife Fund in Washington, D.C., as a coordinator of tropical biological diversity programs.

The seeds of *gavilán* are extremely toxic to many herbivorous in-

Looking skyward into the canopy of the tropical rain forest in Sarapiquí. The big tree in the middle of the photograph with feathery leaves is the *gavilán (Pentaclethra macroloba)*.

sects and other animals, and they are dispersed mechanically, being literally shot out of the tough, woody pods under pressure. As a result, seeds are scattered typically beneath the parent trees, which annually have one large peak of flowering and subsequent pod-set, rather than being widely dispersed into the forest by vertebrate animals such as monkeys, *pacas*, and birds. Thus small groves of *gavilán*, containing both adult trees and younger ones, tend to sprout up in the Sarapiquí lowland and premontane rain forests such as the one at La Tirimbina. La Tirimbina, about two hundred meters above sea level, is most likely close to the upper elevational limit for *gavilán* in Sarapiquí. It is not at all common in the rain forest at Cuesta

Angel at a higher elevation, but other legume trees are found there, scattered mostly as isolated individuals in the forest. At the time of the year when the *gavilán* seed pods are mature, the rain forest at La Tirimbina, as in much of lowland Sarapiquí, is riddled with the "snap!" sounds of its pods splitting in half, twisting apart, and shooting forth the squarish, flattened, soft-shelled brown seeds. The *gavilán* illustrates that the tropical rain forest is not dependent on animals to disperse its seeds, something very different from the norm for most north-temperate tree species.

This particular patch of rain forest on the La Tirimbina hillside, the Padre Núñez Forest, became my principal study site for the project. I had ready access to it, and to other sites in the area, by living at the farm headquarters at La Tirimbina. It was the cicada project that prompted me, with Bob Hunter's encouragement, to use the La Tirimbina farm and its adjacent *fincas* and forests as my principal field research site in Sarapiquí. La Tirimbina has remained a major focus of my field work in Costa Rica; and over the many years in which I have lived here a part of each year, I have come to appreciate the friendship and hospitality of Bob and Nancy Hunter, and later that of their son Charlie, who eventually took over the management of the farm from his father in the mid-1980s.

In the old days, when Challa González Serrano and his family still operated the inn at Cariblanco, I used to stop there for diesel or gas on my way into La Tirimbina from San José. La Tirimbina is farther down the Sarapiquí Valley from Cariblanco, the terrain becoming rolling hills rather than high mountain ridge. At times when I did not stay at Cariblanco but just stopped there for fuel, Challa would ask me, "*Va para abajo?*" (Are you going below?), his way of inquiring if I was headed toward La Virgen and La Tirimbina.

At La Tirimbina, I lived initially in a wood-frame building called a *galerón*. When this farm building burned down in 1976, I stayed in a one-story office building constructed on the site of the old *galerón*. Here I had a little room outfitted with a screened window, bed, work table, and shelves. Although small and inhabited by the usual array of house-living vagrants, such as bats, scorpions, coral snakes, opossums, ants, and giant cockroaches, this spot proved very adequate for my living needs during much of my research career in Sarapiquí. Although I originally used an old outhouse with its own stable of creatures lurking in its depths and on the inside of its mold-encrusted walls, the later building had a toilet. Both buildings I lived in at the *galerón* had a shower, its dimly lit stall home for many creatures such as tailless whip scorpions, bats, and bona fide scorpions. Several years later, when this wooden building was destroyed by ants and termites, I moved into a well-built cement house on the hill overlooking the *galerón* work area. And in the past two years I have stayed in the Hunter cabin located in a little clearing along the Tirimbina Creek. When I first started living at La Tirimbina in 1971, a diesel-driven generator, which did not work all of the time, provided lighting at night. But many times when the noisy generator did not work, I used candles, enjoying the night sounds of katydids and tree frogs from the nearby rain forest that ran along the Tirimbina Creek. Years later, Bob Hunter built a small hydroelectric dam on a different creek, providing a more reliable source of electricity for the farm's workers who lived in little houses along the public access road and near the *galerón* area.

While living at La Tirimbina, unlike at Cariblanco, I had to bring my own food from San José, usually packing an ice chest with perishables and stocking up on plenty of cans of tuna fish and jars of peanut butter and jelly. Part of the ritual in leaving San José for La Tirimbina was to purchase a large block of ice from the *fábrica de hielo* near Parque Morazán, and transport this in the styrofoam ice chest to the farm. The ice usually lasted about a week, and sometimes I was able to supplement its loss with smaller chunks of ice I negotiated from Dagoberto at his store in La Virgen. Ice was a scarce, relished commodity in these parts. I was also able to purchase Cokes, other soft drinks, and food from the farm's *pulpería*, and venture into La Virgen, the nearest town, for an occasional evening meal. Many times, too, the Hunters invited me over to their cabin for dinner.

Staying at La Tirimbina also fanned my interests in the rain forest habitat adjoining the nearby La Tigra cacao, a place unusually rich with many kinds of butterflies and other insects. It would be at this place, over the years, that I would come to learn more about the intriguing habits of tropical insects, especially butterflies and orchid bees.

To reach La Tirimbina from the main road through Sarapiquí, you take the first dirt road to the right just before arriving at La Virgen de Socorro when coming from points south and west. From the main road, you can see a steel suspension bridge dangling above the frothy waters of the Sarapiquí River. Crossing this particular suspension

The *galerón* building erected in 1976–77, following a devastating fire that destroyed the original *galerón,* at Finca La Tirimbina near La Virgen in Sarapiquí, as seen in 1979. The author's room for several years was at the second window from the right in the wooden building.

bridge while riding in a jeep or pickup truck, or bouncing around on the back of a tractor, has been a startling, if not deathly frightening, experience for many guests I have brought to La Tirimbina. You see, the steel beam underpinnings of the bridge have been broken in several places for quite a while. The bridge swiftly swings up and down, to and fro, high above the Sarapiquí's furious, boulder-strewn waters, under the weight of a vehicle inching its way across, the driver doing his or her best to keep the tires square on the loose, wooden planks. Through the spaces between the scattered planks, the river is easily seen below. A new guest receives the "La Tirimbina christening" by sticking it out, in the vehicle, as the knowing driver straddles the planks and hopes for the best as the bridge oscillates, with loud creaking, from one end to the other across its hundred-meter span. Once across this bridge, you have to bear to the left for about four miles before reaching the hill where the roadcut finally snakes its way down to the *finca*'s headquarters. Before this point, however, the road passes through rolling farmland dotted with patches of chiefly secondary rain forests and pastures with scattered huge trees of the primary rain forest that once graced this landscape. The road crosses several little *quebradas* such as the San Ramón, before swinging through the El Uno farm and arriving at La Tirimbina proper. Over the years more and more little homesteads have started up along the road, and the swatches of rain forest have diminished. This is a private property on a public-access road, one where visitors are welcome with permission from its owners.

La Tirimbina, a conglomerate of three separate, contiguous *fincas*, La Tirimbina proper, El Uno, and La Tigra, sits on the back side of La Selva, near the El Peje river. Not long after I began living at La Tirimbina proper, the *finca* that included the headquarters for the agricultural operations of the conglomerate, I learned that each *finca* was devoted to one or a few kinds of perennial cash crops. Thus, El Uno was planted chiefly in cacao and rubber, La Tirimbina proper in black pepper, spices, and later vanilla, and La Tigra in cacao. These farms represented separate companies managed by Bob

The infamous suspension bridge across the Río Sarapiquí at La Virgen,
which one must cross to reach Finca La Tirimbina.

Hunter, such as Granjas Tropicales, Compañía Agrícola Myrisica,
S.A. (CAMSA), and Huntrosa. The three *fincas*, constituting an area
of about 450 hectares (1,100 acres) of rolling hills blanketed with
a patchwork of rain forest and cultivated lands, were the mission
of Bob Hunter, a U.S.-trained agronomist, born of American mis-
sionary parents in China, who came to Costa Rica in 1951. To acquire
land near La Virgen, Bob formed an alliance with Alfredo Echandi,
brother of Mario Echandi, Costa Rica's president in the late 1960s.
Alfredo Echandi owned the land encompassing the El Uno and La
Tirimbina farms, and in 1958 Bob was able to raise the capital necessary to initiate a program for diverse cash crop agriculture on it.

Bob's dream was to introduce nontraditional crop diversification into the tropical rain forest region, the Sarapiquí Valley. When I first met Don Roberto, as he is known to everyone up and down the valley, he owned Finca Las Vegas, a cacao and pejeballe palm farm on a wedge of rolling terrain at the confluence of Sarapiquí's two great rivers, the Río Sarapiquí and the Río Puerto Viejo. Bob purchased the Las Vegas *finca*, consisting of 75 hectares (180 acres) in 1955 for about four U.S. dollars an acre. Farther upriver from Las Vegas is Finca La Selva, purchased by the Organization for Tropical Studies, Inc., in the 1960s from Leslie Holdridge, a forestry specialist who, together with Bob Hunter and Joseph Tosi, founded the Tropical Science Center in San José. Les Holdridge had bought the *finca* he would name La Selva in the 1950s from Alberto ("Chino") Torres, a soil scientist employed by the Organization of American States. At the time of this transaction, Holdridge asked Hunter if he would buy the piece of land immediately north of the La Selva property, located at the confluence of the *ríos* Sarapiquí and Puerto Viejo. Bob bought this land, naming it Finca Las Vegas (the "River Bank Farm"). In the 1980s, the Las Vegas farm, with the involvement of Bob Hunter's company and the Hershey Foods Corporation, was donated to OTS to become part of the greatly expanded La Selva Biological Reserve. Much of the land on the eastern flank of the Río Puerto Viejo was owned at the time by a Costa Rican named Ludwig ("Vico") Starke, whose father had worked for the United Fruit Company at the time when it was dismantling much of its banana plantations and selling off the land at a very cheap price. Much of the land to the right of the road on the other side of the new bridge across the Río Puerto Viejo (when traveling from Puerto Viejo to Las Horquetas) is the Finca Starke. Although consisting of about 500 hectares at the time it was originally purchased by OTS, the La Selva reserve today comprises more than 1,500 hectares of primary and secondary rain forest habitats and pasture land.

Bob's vision of agronomic development in Sarapiquí was tempered with an appreciation for the need to conserve its rain forests, as he strove to implement farming methods that entailed protecting sizable stands of forest habitat. When I first started staying at La Tirimbina in 1971, I did not think about such issues as the importance of rain forests. What I found chiefly attractive there was the availability of a broad range of ecological habitats, from pristine, untouched rain forest to many stages of successional secondary (marginal) and agricultural habitats nestled within the rain forest. La Tirimbina offered a wealth of research site potential for a young tropical biologist.

When I first met Bob and for several more years, he was the director of the Associated Colleges of the Midwest program in Costa Rica. For some years before joining ACM in 1963, Bob had been on the faculty of the IICA (Instituto Inter-Americano de Ciencias Agrícola) in Turrialba, Costa Rica, where he had done research on cacao, coffee, rubber, and the pejeballe palm. After finishing his Ph.D. in farm crops at Michigan State University, under a fellowship from the Farmers & Manufacturers Sugar Beet Association, Bob eventually headed for Costa Rica in 1951 to work for various U.S. agricultural aid programs, including STICA (Servicio Técnico Inter-Americano de Cooperación Agrícola). STICA's mission was to develop research, training, and extension programs in tropical agriculture, and Bob would be this program's last director in Costa Rica. STICA was a vehicle for providing U.S. aid to developing agricultural programs in various Latin American countries, including Peru and Costa Rica. In Costa Rica, the program was headquartered in San José. Later, while at the Tropical Science Center, Bob helped to create the Association of Tropical Biology and became editor of its newsletter, which evolved into the ATB's scholarly research journal in tropical biology, *Biotropica*. He was also involved in the founding of OTS in 1963.

Over many years of staying at La Tirimbina, I developed a great admiration for the way in which the Hunters lived there. A muddy road ran by the side of the *galerón* area opposite the creek, continuing along the creek through a shaded swatch of rain forest and into a flat clearing. This is where the Hunters lived. When I first arrived, home for Bob and Nancy and their youngest boy, Charlie (who was very young at the time, but who today manages the farm), was an A-frame house completely open at the front. Bob and Nancy called it the "hippie hut." The A-frame had a large wooden deck in front of it, a place where the Hunters and guests could sit in the shade. The edge of the deck was adorned with "pre-Columbian" Indian artifacts, including *metates* with various species of orchid plants growing on them. Between the house and the river, the ground was covered with grasses that Bob kept mowed neatly. Many college students stayed there during the early days of ACM. Later, when roosting bats and an occasional *terciopelo* beneath the loose flooring got to be too close for everyone's comfort, the A-frame house was replaced on the same site with a wooden-frame cabin having a large screened-in living room, kitchen, two bedrooms, and bathroom. Both the open side of the original A-frame house and the screened-in living room of the cabin faced the Tirimbina Creek and the sharply rising wall of rain forest on its opposite side. Just before the creek there was a large rotten tree stump completely engulfed now by an immense *Philodendron* plant. The plant's rotting fruits attracted *Morpho* butterflies, which skillfully weaved their way through the tangle of stems and leaves, going every which way to seek the succulent rot, and its nourishment, dangling in the dark shadows of the huge plant.

Behind the cabin Bob planted citrus trees, just a few. Beyond these trees, ravaged by leaf-cutting bees, the hill rises swiftly, covered with a dense bramble of secondary rain forest teeming with all kinds of insect life. Attached to the back side of the little cabin is a rain-collecting tank used as a source for drinking water, shower, and washing dishes. This tank was pressure-fed from a much larger one located high up on the hill behind the cabin, and connected to it by a long, thin pipe.

Grassy lawn, oddly incongruous with the luxuriance of the surrounding rain forest, bordered the cabin for a little way. In one corner of the clearing, which measured about two hundred meters square, where the creek bends and crosses close to the front of the cabin, Bob erected a little palm-frond-thatched roof on wooden poles. He stored the lawnmower here. The palm thatching was home for snakes, nesting ants, and other creatures. Beneath the roof, where the dirt was dry and protected from rain, there were hundreds of depression pits made by ant lion larvae. Since this modest structure sat close to the remnant trees of the rain forest still hugging the creek, at certain times of the year its wobbly poles and thatched roof were festooned with cicada cast skins, especially those of the "summertime whistler."

In this forest strip, less than ten meters wide, between the creek and the border of the grassy area, and farther upsteam where it followed the entrance road to the cabin area, there were scattered young *gavilán* trees, although no mature ones. Presumably these trees got here from seeds either shot out from pods borne on older trees across the creek or washed downstream from the older *gavilán* trees located where the creek swings by the Padre Núñez rain forest. Where this rain forest, as small as it is, meets the open, grassy area, there were little tangles of vines such as *Aristolochia*, which thrived in a transitional zone of shadows and stippled sun. A couple of old cacao trees flourished in this shade, often adorned with lots of developing pods, a sure sign of good pollination, induced, I am sure, by the proliferation of pollinating insects that dwell in the moist, shaded forest near the creek.

What I also enjoyed about staying at La Tirimbina was the opportunity to immerse myself in the vignettes of tropical nature that surrounded the little *galerón* area. I was easily able to walk up the nearby hills and absorb the vistas of Sarapiquí's landscape and its wildlife. Sometimes just before dusk, when I was through with my work, I would take a short walk up the roadcut above the *galerón* area. Here and there, down the hillside and above me, the land came alive with the rustling of toucans, parrots, and oropendulas. Silhouetted against the fading sun were the boughs of *Cecropia* trees, their spindly trunks, rosette-shaped leaves, and dangling fruit giving them away immediately and distinguishing them from the other trees dotting the hillside where most of the rain forest had been cleared away long ago. It was because the rain forest was gone that I could gaze down, from near the apex of this hill, upon the *galerón* area in the flattened ribbon of land between the hill and the Tirimbina Creek. Keel-billed toucans, groups of three or four, seldom more than this, would often silently slide onto a branch of a *Cecropia* here, hopping alongside dangling fruit to feast before day became night.

Off in the distance on a different hill, in a stately *Tabebuia* tree, its crown of leaves now obscured by a full complement of yellow blossoms evident even in the quickly fading sunlight, one day when the rains refused to come, another toucan called out across the glen, its straining voice reaching a frantic pitch against the darkening steel-blue sky. The citizens of the rain forest, our brethren in life, were going through their ancient rituals, playing out a script written by the hands of evolution over millions of years, readying themselves for the night. In the fading light, the bluish-gray roof of the *galerón* looked like some geometrically sharp-edged pond or small lake, as it glimmered into dusk perhaps ten meters below where I stood on the roadcut. The earthtones of the buildings blended with the hues of nature filling the glen, an illusion, in the waning daylight, of marriage between that which is wrought by humankind and that which has been shaped by the forces of nature in this ancient valley of the Sarapiquí River. What gave away the illusion were the intrusions, thin wisps of blue smoke rising up from the *galerón* as firewood burned to dry the harvest of peppercorns, the glow of embers peeking through the slats of the building, and the unwanted blasting sounds from radios in little houses along the creek. The fires burned in cement boxes underneath the roof of the *galerón*, sometimes well into the night.

Surprisingly, it is often while standing out here, in a landscape that is not richly blanketed in rain forest but pock-marked with occasional rain forest trees in a carpeting of pastures and shrub, that I begin to understand how the rain forest struggles to reclaim the terrain. The answers are here, amidst this vast area of human disturbance that reaches down the side of the hill from the roadcut, between here and the *galerón* below. As I gaze out upon the *Cecropia* and the *Bombacopsis*, I sense that the rain forest is fighting valiantly to come back. Mind you, all of this is a very slow and orderly process. You cannot witness quickly the return of the rain forest, but from where I stand, you can sense the presence of some strategic players in the complex process. In a sense, I imagine this slope a large light gap, a place where the rain forest fell down, certainly not of its own accord in this case. Light gaps within the forest, holes in the tree cover created when a giant tree topples over, help the forest ecosystem to change, evolve, and remain resilient. The rain forest is not a static assemblage of life, rather a continually changing one. There are creatures in it, on its boundaries, that are evolutionarily programmed to participate in the forest's cycle of birth, growth, and death. The players, by necessity, include plants, animals, and microorganisms.

What I especially enjoyed about my stays at the La Tirimbina farm complex were the soothing theatrics of tropical rainstorms heading in off the stormy Caribbean east of this place, especially at night and at dusk. In the temperate zone, rain seldom affected me the way it did here. In my little room in the *galerón* area, sleep came quickly with the soothing of rain. In my room in the new building next to the new *galerón* I found great comfort in the rain hitting the metal roof, and each time, my bed felt enticingly dry and warm. Luxury did not matter, for I had the basics, and keeping dry when sleeping was one of them. Even through the torrential rains beating against the corrugated metal roof of my dry, snug room, the enchantments of the Sarapiquí rain forest could be heard and felt. Giant *Bufo* toads knocked against the wooden walls of my room as they jumped up high to snare insects bumping into the lighted window screens. Farther off in the distance, in the strip of rain forest along the Tirimbina Creek, a mixed chorus of tree frogs, katydids, and squeaking bats filled the damp air, their sounds slicing through the staccato of rain on the roof. And on some of these nights, before the rains intensified to their sometimes deafening crescendos, the air near my room hummed with the soft melodies of a local balladeer or two, a *finca* worker strumming a guitar and singing a beautiful country song. At such a moment, the softness, gentleness of this music blended magnificently with the echoes of nature also close at hand, reaffirming humanity's continuity with this broader tapestry of life.

From 1984 on, when I lived in the new guest house on the hill, my appreciation of rain at La Tirimbina took on a new complexion. During the rainy season I would stand on the veranda of the house, or on top of the knoll behind it, and look toward the east. I did this late in the afternoon when the ashen hues of the clouds told me that rain must not be far away. Looking across the undulating hills, some covered with pepper vines, others in rain forest, I listened closely. At first it was just the faint humming of the winds coming in from the Caribbean. Then a new sound was added, a slight roar echoing off the hills far off in the distance. The roaring grew steadily in its intensity. This land, and the sky, were speaking to me and to the rest of nature. Sarapiquí was being kissed with the treasure of rain, and the rain was heading my way. At such moments the colors were subdued, broad sweeps of green and brown on the land, and above it thick bands of bluish gray, the storm. Soon I could see the leading edge of the rain, perhaps a quarter of a mile distant, as a thin veil of silvery white, its presence almost unnoticed but ascertained by the advancing roar. Now the skies were devoid of toucans and parrots, and the choruses of cicadas muffled. The land responded to the rain. At first I heard its metallic sound on the broadleaf rain forest. Then I became mesmerized, failing to notice how rapidly the rain was advancing to the spot where I stood. Rain has a way of doing this to me. All my life I had looked upward to the skies to see the rain. But here in Sarapiquí, in these ancient foothills, I learned to look out toward the horizon and see the march of rain as it swept across the land.

This scene seldom fails to transfix me. There is something dramatically special about looking broadside at a wall of rain. Now I understand better the magic of rainbows that sometimes appear and disappear across the distantmost hills of La Tirimbina as I stand on the knoll, munching a *crema* (cookie) or just gazing. The world's most precious finite resource, water, is speaking to me. In its tiny ricochets off the rain forest, I can sense its message of life. In no other place on Earth do I feel as close to water and its role as life's cradle as I do out here in the rolling hills of Sarapiquí. Not even when swimming in it. There is nothing comparable, for out here the rain hugs the forest the way the rain forest clings to the land. And then, suddenly, the rain is hitting me as the storm moves across the *finca*, rumbling on toward the *cordillera*. In the subdued pall over the landscape before me, I sense the rapture of life, even though I cannot see the butterflies, orchid bees, cicadas, and other creatures thriving in the rain forest. But because the warm tropical rains sweep across these hills this way, I know there is the potential for life to continue and manifest itself in the diverse ways it has for millions of years.

It was within this setting of the La Tirimbina farm that I did much of my study of cicadas and their relationship to tropical rain forests. Each time a census of cast skins was taken, we would crawl through the habitat on our hands and knees, with plastic bags tucked into our belts, and collect every cast skin we found. The cast skins were later examined to determine species of cicada and the sex ratio of the emerging adult population at each census. Most importantly, voucher specimens of adult cicadas were also taken, whenever possible, at the time cast skins were being censused. In this way, over several years, I was able to build an inventory of the cicada populations occurring here and at other study localities. The many bags of cicada cast skins were saved as specimen vouchers of this project. In 1973 and again in 1976, Tom Moore, through funding from my NSF grant, was able to join me in the field to make tape recordings of the cicada species being studied. These recordings were used to help verify species names assigned to our collections, since these designations were not always clear-cut.

My little room in the farm's headquarters doubled as a makeshift laboratory and insect nursery. It was here that I carefully prepared my insect specimens and updated field notes, often by candlelight at night. Bags of cicada cast skins quickly filled up the room on many of my stays here.

Voucher specimens of insects from my research were preserved in the field using a number of standard methods. Adult butterflies, moths, and dragonflies were slid into glassine envelopes and stored in redwood or Schmitt insect boxes. Bulky insects such as beetles and cicadas were either pinned or layered between tissue paper in these boxes, along with collecting data. Collecting data were written directly on glassine storage envelopes for butterflies and moths. These boxes of insects were sprinkled with paradichlorobenzene (PDB) crystals to prevent mold and repel vermin. This was often not good enough in the field, where I lost many useful research specimens to unwanted corpse-eating ants that seemed to be everywhere. So I ended up doing to the boxes what I had done to loaves of bread ravaged by ants and roaches in my room: I stored them inside tightly closed plastic bags. This was the only way to protect the specimens. Soft-bodied insects were preserved in 70 percent ethanol in vials.

In my cicada studies I often found it necessary to collect vouchers of plant species as well. This was particularly true when regularly discovering aggregations of cast skins beneath certain kinds of trees, adult cicadas clustering in trees, and female cicadas ovipositing on treelets and saplings in the forest understory and edge habitats. Tropical biology dictates this collaborative approach, in which insect ecologists such as myself come to depend heavily upon plant taxonomists to provide accurate determinations of plant material. While plants do not move around the way animals do, with the exception of their seeds and fruit being dispersed in the forest, it is nonetheless a major challenge to secure specimens of various taxa. As I usually did not have access all of the time to a standard plant press, I prepared dried plant specimens by pressing plants on newsprint between sheets of rigid cardboard cut from cartons given to me by the clerk in the *pulpería*. I taped a small index card with the collecting data onto the newsprint with the specimen. I stacked books from Bob Hunter's office on top of the plant specimens in the makeshift press for several days, and then dried them on the seed dryer in the *galerón*. When leaving La Tirimbina, I bundled the pressed specimens between sheets of cardboard, tying them with string and eventually putting the parcel into a suitcase or field box going back to the U.S. with me. Whenever possible, I tried to obtain identifications of plant specimens at the herbarium in the National Museum of Costa Rica in San José, between trips into Sarapiquí.

Many times, while returning to our lodgings at the *galerón* area,

Moncho Morales and his daughter on the trail at Finca La Tirimbina in 1983.

our hands full of bags of cicada cast skins, people would stop us and ask why we were collecting *cáscaras de chicharras*. Gradually, as a result of such spontaneous dialogues along a muddy road or path, some folks brought us not only cicadas and cast skins but other kinds of *bichos* as well. One particular fellow named Moncho even wanted to share with me a special talent of his with stinging wasps. One day, in the presence of myself and Mary Ellen Carolan, Moncho did his thing. He led us to a spot where a healthy, grapefruit-sized paper nest of a *Polybia* wasp was attached to the underside of a leaf on a banana plant. Moncho made a fist with his right hand, rubbed it in his left armpit, and then slowly picked off the wasp nest from the leaf. The hundreds of churning wasps appeared dazed and drugged as they coated Moncho's hand, in which he had crumbled the nest. He did this without getting stung, and we were both amazed. Neither one of us opted to repeat his feat for the sake of science.

At La Tirimbina I also got to know Jorge Mejías, a man who would be very helpful to me over many years. Jorge, who was from La Virgen, began working here in 1976, eventually becoming fore-man of the farm, or *mandador*, in 1983. From the very beginning, he was sensitive and interested in my studies of insects, often volun-teering to show me places at the farm I had not seen before. A superb woodsman, Jorge led me through the rain forests, sometimes clearing a small trail with his well-sharpened machete. Although he came on the scene near the end of my cicada project, even after this research ended he took me to forest habitats where I was able to discover at least one species of cicada I had not found before. Jorge, deep inside a patch of rain forest, once showed me the *bejuco de agua*, the water vine, and how to slice through its woodiness with a machete and sip the drops of sweet water to quench a thirst in the field. Not far from this place, he showed me how he used the seeds of a certain species of tree to trap *tepisquintle*, a large rodent prized in the *campo* for its delicious meat—a treat Jorge tried to give his family at Christ-mas. Through Jorge my eyes were opened to features of rain forest wildlife that I would otherwise surely have missed. It was against this backdrop of helpful friendly people and the style of living here that I was able to conduct my multiyear studies of cicadas and other insects.

Although we spent much time looking down at the ground for cast skins, I did look up to discover other attributes of rain forest cicada biology, such as oviposition sites. You must bear in mind that we are talking here about some very basic natural history information, since very little, up to this time, was known about the habits of Central American cicadas. We were starting from scratch and attempting to build a data base of sorts. All in all, the study revealed that Costa Rica had at least twenty-three species of cicadas, representing nine genera. By far the most predominant species, especially in my field experiences in Sarapiquí, included several of *Fidicina*, two

Some Sarapiquí cicadas. From left to right: *Quesada gigas*, *Zammara smaragdina* (male and female, respectively), *Fidicina pronoe*, *Fidicina sericans*, and *Fidicina amoena*.

Cast skins, final–instar nymphal skins (cuticles) of the cicada *Quesada gigas*.

of *Zammara*, and the ubiquitous *Quesada gigas*, the largest species of all and the one that Costa Ricans call *la chicharra de Semana Santa* (the Holy Week cicada), owing to its penchant for eclosing in prodigious numbers during the week of Easter each year, at the end of the dry season. Among the vegetation zones covered by the census, I discovered that the highest number of species, twenty-three, occurs in the lowland tropical rain forest region, that is, in Sarapiquí. Although the cicada faunas of the Caribbean slopes of the great *cordillera* tend to be distinct from those of the Pacific dry zone, some overlap occurs in species such as the "sundown cicada" (*Fidicina mannifera*) and the genus *Zammara*.

It was really the patterns of cast skins that began to tell me some interesting features of cicada natural history in the tropics. At Cuesta Angel, for instance, the abundance of cicada cast skins was much lower than in the La Tirimbina plots. While cast skins at Cuesta Angel were found scattered beneath various genera of canopy-tree legumes, cast skins in the La Tirimbina rain forest were dramatically clustered around *gavilán* trees, compelling me to believe that somehow legume tree species, especially abundant ones, figure prominently in the ecology of Costa Rican cicadas. The "summertime whistler" (*Fidicina sericans*) was the abundant dry season cicada up and down the Sarapiquí Valley, replaced in the rainy season by *Zammara smaragdina*, the "rainy day croaker," especially at La Tirimbina.

The data from Cuesta Angel sketched a portrait of cicada natural history fairly unique to this region of Sarapiquí. While several species thrive here, including a very skittish and elusive species of *Fidicina* near the top of the ridge above the roadcut where its adults aggregate in tall trees, their emergence population densities are very low, as if the hatches are spread out thinly over large areas of this rugged rain forest. This is also true for a beautiful green *Carineta* whose adults perch head-downward like cone-headed grasshoppers (an unusual behavior in most cicadas I have seen), near the bases of trunks of *Cecropia* (Moraceae) trees growing on the side of the ravine below the roadcut just beyond reach of the aerial net. At dusk, a particular stretch of the roadcut, not far from where we observed roosting butterflies, sprang to life with the ear-cutting "chug-chug-chug" call of this medium-sized cicada (body length about eighteen millimeters). At such moments I am reminded of my boyhood days, not so much of cicadas in the marshy woodland as of the cone-headed grasshoppers themselves. But unlike the cone-headed grasshoppers, which sing nocturnally, *Carineta* is a dusk insect, bridging the world of the daytime cicadas with the night world of the rain forest's orthopterans.

As insects go, most of the familiar species of cicadas I came to study in Sarapiquí's forests are good-sized creatures, with body lengths ranging generally between twenty-five and forty millimeters, excluding the wings which extend well beyond the body when at rest. Of course, some cicadas, like the smaller species of *Carineta*, are considerably smaller, but typically the species of *Fidicina* and *Zammara* are large-sized insects. But this did not always facilitate observing the habits of these insects in the wild. Consider, if you will, our experiences with the "rainy day creaky gate" (*Zammara tympanum*) in the Cuesta Angel ravine. Throughout the year, but especially during the long rainy season here, the ravine echoes with the shrill, almost ethereal cry of this large cicada. The adult males seem to be calling everywhere one turns, but in reality, as my studies reveal, there is usually one male on a tree and considerable distance between trees having the insects. Thus the densities of chorusing males appear to be very low, something corroborated at least partially by the observed low densities of this species's cast skins in the rain forest.

In fact, it took me a couple of years to collect my first specimen of this species. I was walking along the footpath that runs parallel to the river at the bottom of the ravine, not far from where the squatter had cleared the forest to plant *yuca* and bananas. Ahead of me, as I entered the forest, streams of sunlight highlighted the outlines of the tall trees and filtered through the delicate pale green lacework of thick mosses and epiphytic ferns clinging to these trees. Then I heard the insect, quite unexpectedly, for the rest of nature in the ravine had been silent. But there it was, a single male cicada whose piercing call had started up from a source less than fifteen meters in front of me, slicing through the silence and echoing off the trees. I judged that the calling insect was perhaps ten or twelve meters up in the tree, which had a diameter of about a meter. Would I be able to spot it against the mottled earthtones of the tree, especially if the creature suddenly became silent again, as I continued my stalk? Now at the base of the tree, which stood in a tiny clearing where the squatter had started to clear away more forest for his fledgling *finca* or *parcela*, the cicada has ceased calling. Then, as a light drizzle sprinkled on my face as I stared up the tree, my body rigid and frozen to the spot, the creature started up again. Up close, it sounded like a screechy, rusted gate swishing back and forth in the gusts of air. When the cicada started calling again, I thought I would be able to locate it without difficulty. But I had no idea what I was looking for in terms of body size and color patterns, for at this time I did not even know that it was a *Zammara*. From what I had learned from Tom Moore and from examining insect collections in museums, I knew that *Zammara* cicadas are large insects with somewhat dorso-ventrally flattened bodies and conspicuous lateral flanges on the pro-thoracic shield. These features, in addition to their mottled brown and green colors (which are sexually dimorphic in that females tend to be more olive-green and the males bright green) and the presence of brown markings on the wings, make them readily distinguishable from most other Central American cicadas.

Finally, I stood right up next to the tree and looked almost straight up the moss-covered trunk. For a while I saw nothing, except for an extremely cryptically colored tiny mantis postured in sticklike fashion amongst the mosses. It barely moved; rather, its little body swayed to and fro, as if mimicking a twig being jostled in the breeze! Was this part of the mantis's act of deception, allowing it to go unnoticed by wandering prey? The mosses, from my vantage point next to the tree, looked as if they were covered with a patina of tiny prisms, for flecks of colorful sunlight danced off the tiny droplets of rain clinging to them. But suddenly I noticed a prism surface much bigger than this speckling of brilliance against the carpet of green above my head. As shadows from foliage high above moved around, this flattened prism appeared and disappeared, as if some ephemeral phenomenon in a state of flux. I struggled to stand on my tiptoes and looked closely at this object, which was about a meter or so above my head and nestled in the thick moss. Then I saw the creature. The glistening prism was a wing of a mottled green and brown cicada, perched as if it was squashed down into the mosses and lichens which, from here, seemed to enclose the creature's large body. Had it not been for the sun dancing off that wing, I would not have seen the insect at all.

What beautiful crypsis this was! A perfect match. This elegant camouflage, in which an animal object fused with the color hues, shadows, and contours of matted epiphytic plant life, was more extreme, a sort of "inverse conspicuousness," than I had noticed for *Zammara* cicadas elsewhere. It is a matter of match. At La Tirimbina, these cicadas perch on slate-hued trunks of many tree species, where they stand out when one scans a trunk in search of a calling male. Even up close, cicada in the hand, males of *smaragdina* are more brightly colored than their counterparts in *tympanum*. The same is true for the third Costa Rican species, *smaragdula*, on the lower leeward slopes of the *cordilleras* and farther west. Crypsis is a matter of perspective, as *Zammara* teaches us. Still, individuals of all three species, males and females, with their boldly mottled body splotchwork, are striking objects of tropical nature, rebelling against the solid, continuous greens and browns and blacks of most other cicadas here. Intuitively, I can imagine that Amerindians must have been inspired in their own decorative painting of pottery and other objects by the innovative sweeps of nature's own paintbrush on the backs of *Zammara*.

Luck was on my side as I swung my net hard against the tree where the cicada sat, hoping that the insect would leap back and fall into the net bag. As I swung the net, I could hardly see what I was doing since I did my best to keep my balance on my toes. But the net, cicada in it, and I came crashing down together as I lost my balance. I fell down on a thorny bramble covering jagged volcanic rocks, but I had my prize in tow! My first specimen of the elusive "rainy day creaky gate" cicada, one of two specimens I would find in my several years out there.

For just a few seconds before my catch, as I stood there transfixed by a cicada I had yet to see, my thoughts flashed back to a couple of weeks earlier. Not far from this tree, farther into this rain forest along the footpath, I had been treated to an elegant nighttime concert, with the glen filled with the raucous love songs of katydids and tree frogs, coming mostly from the forest canopy high above my head. There I was, standing alone at nine in the evening at this desolate spot in the Sarapiquí River gorge, lured by a star-studded sky, an unusual occurrence in this land of perpetual mist and rain. Yet I was surely not alone, for a refreshed feeling of oneness with nature overcame me, as if I was lulled into a trance for a few all too brief moments. In the chill of this night I sweated with the radiance of awakening to the melodies ringing through the forest embracing me, a sole wanderer out here. The rain forest was indeed alive, the flickering starlight off the slicked leaves and rocks along the tiny footpath telling me of a much deeper story of life, beckoning me to look high above my head—not to see the forest, reduced to a dancing assemblage of foliage silhouettes against the stars, but to feel its unseen presence in the ethereal calls of its katydids and tree frogs sitting up there. I felt so happy and so humbled by this presence of nature's beauty in the darkness! It helped me to understand, through its very contrasts, the dramatic transformation of this same rain forest in the day, when the rain, mist, and sun bathe its foliage and branches with the vibrancy that brings to life the cicadas and birds. It brings to life too the swiftly passing buzz of giant orchid bees streaking along this path, going by so quickly I hardly see them. Oddly enough, it is the nighttime immersion into this forest that heightened my awareness of the cicadas as symbolizing, along with the katydids and other singing Orthoptera here, the vast majority of life forms comprising this wellspring of evolution's ancient and fragile testing ground, the most often unseen plants and animals.

Even the low brush along a footpath through the rain forest, as where I stood this evening, is filled with the throbbing of an incredible assemblage of life. In a mere two-hundred-meter stretch along such a path, one can find representative species belonging to as many as forty families of amphibians and reptiles. These are curious groupings clinging to the slick leaves, a fine-tuned balance among herbivores, carnivores, and scavengers. Take just the Orthoptera alone. At night, one can discover that an impressive sixty percent of all creatures seen on leaves belong to this group. These are interesting insects, skillful at jumping and flitting from leaf to leaf, plant to plant, at a moment's disturbance. Roaches, crickets, the rain forest's chief insectan scavengers, and a smattering of herbivorous grasshoppers, long-horned and short, comprise a major share of this nighttime diversity of life in Sarapiquí.

Not far from here, along the road between Cuesta Angel and Cariblanco, a dilapidated wooden church stood across from the Echandi *finca*. Walking by this church one morning, I paused to check the single light bulb dangling from the front porch for insects that might have been attracted to the light the night before, a practice I have come to appreciate since my great successes at Vara Blanca. On this occasion I found two huge grasshopperlike creatures, apparently both the same species, clinging to the rotting ceiling beams near the threadbare wire attached to the light bulb. Mottled in cryptic hues of brown, these insects were radically different from Orthoptera species I knew that inhabited the expansive scrubby pastures of this *finca*. I have never again, since this moment of discovery, seen an insect of this type anywhere in Costa Rica, reinforcing my belief that these primeval forests are rife with legions of unknown species, behaviors, and entire assemblages of life, all awaiting both study and appreciation.

And so it came to pass one day, soon after my night stroll in the rain forest along the Sarapiquí River, close to the spot where I caught *Zammara tympanum*, that I spotted a large, leaf-green katydid perched rigidly on the upper side of a rain-slicked leaf of an *Anthurium* plant along the footpath. I had almost missed this creature of near-perfect camouflage, for not only its color but also the reflection of light from its glistening wing covers matched incredibly the light reflections off the leaf on which it sat motionless. It is still a puzzle today how I even noticed the animal. It bore a striking resemblance to our North American "true katydid," *Pterophylla camelifolia*, and perhaps it is a closely related species. (Its occurrence on the upper highland slopes of the *cordillera* once again suggest the temperate-zone biological affinities that course through the uplands of Central America.) In any case, discovering this katydid startled me, as if I was suddenly brought face to face with a player in the night's unseen symphony of this rain forest. There it was, a resident of the forest but thrust out of its proper niche, perhaps fallen down from the canopy, perhaps jostled from its foliage-rich lair by a bird or other animal rummaging around for a fine morsel of food, and now starkly out of place within inches of the forest floor. Still, the creature blended in so beautifully, and I hoped, after photographing it, that it would eventually find its way back into the canopy. Now I suspected, at least, that I had met face to face the creature whose arboreal populations blessed this land with raspy "czit-czit-czit" calls in the night!

Even when I jostled the mammoth, flattened leaf on which it sat, the katydid did not move at all. Up close, I could see tiny droplets of crystalline dew adhering, beadlike, to both its long antennae; splashes of the tiny crystals dotted its legs and body. Perhaps, too, it had been knocked down from the canopy by a torrential rainstorm, a common occurrence up here on this valley between great ridges, and now it sat, its body chemistry and rhythm too cool to permit it to fly or crawl away. I would not collect this magnificent katydid; I would leave it alone, hoping that its mortal foes on the forest floor, insectivorous lizards and such, would miss it. But if it behaved like our "true katydid" does, gliding from branch to branch and largely incapable of sustained flight, it might well be doomed in its predicament near the forest floor, unable to reach its natural abode high above my head. But this was not for me to worry about. The splendid katydid of this glen, a creature I have not seen since, would be left alone. And so it was. For me, it is captured in my mind, many years later, as if I had just seen it the day before, and it is there, too, in my picture.

In the rain forests of Sarapiquí and elsewhere in the tropics, one must be largely content just to discover these vignettes of the broader tapestry. Surely the living diversity is there, but it is not readily seen or experienced otherwise. This is always the big disappointment of naturalists and natural history buffs who rush to the tropics to see firsthand the land's floras and faunas. As I have learned in Sarapiquí, even over decades of field work, of enthusiastic immersion into the rain forest day and night, one is treated to just small glimpses of what is actually living there. Perhaps no creatures more than the cicadas and other singing insects have inured me to this maddeningly frustrating truism of the tropical forest. Yet this is all the more reason why these habitats should be studied and appreciated broadly.

It is perhaps for this reason that my capture of the "rainy day creaky gate" cicada (*Zammara tympanum*), a seemingly small incident in its own right, had such a large significance for me. It became another small piece of knowledge about the elusive, crafty creatures I had set out to study scientifically. In this line of work, voucher specimens of species being studied are essential. Ecologists collect vouchers with a sensitivity to taking just enough material for adequate species identification purposes. Sometimes the specimens then become useful to systematists studying particular groups of organisms, especially from the tropics where many species in most groups wait description and naming, not to mention interpretation of their evolutionary affinities.

My quest of the "rainy day creaky gate" cicada was strikingly similar to searching for another montane rain forest cicada, *Procollina biolleyi* at Bajo La Hondura. *Procollina* is also a large-bodied (thick as a man's thumb) mottled green and brown cicada with brown splotches on its otherwise transparent papery wings; it is not as dorsoventrally flattened as *Zammara* and its call is very distinctive. But like *Zammara* and unlike many other tropical cicadas, it often perches on tree trunks rather than in the branches of the forest canopy. Only after several months at Bajo La Hondura was I able to collect several adults of this species, which prior to my studies was known from only a handful of specimens collected a long time ago and kept chiefly in a few European museums. Like *Zammara tympanum*, *Procollina* sits on the moss-covered tree trunks inside the rain forest, where its loud song fills the rugged landscape even through the rain and when the clouds come down to meet the crown of the forest here. This cicada shares this rain forest with only one other species, to the best of my knowledge, *Carineta postica* the "whispering chug-chug," a small-bodied cicada with a very low, barely audible call. The censuses of cast skins at Bajo La Hondura revealed that *Carineta* is far less abundant than the boisterous *Procollina*. The study plots here also revealed a characteristic that I would come to appreciate virtually everywhere we studied cicada hatches, namely, that more than half the quadrates yield few or no cast skins, while other individual quadrates were usually the high producers.

We know very little about the nature of survival in cicada nymphs beneath the rain forest floor. Soil ecology is a fledgling realm of tropical biology, one in dire need of amplification and attention. Undoubtedly the soil harbors suites of pathogenic microorganisms that kill cicada nymphs for food. Consider again *Procollina* at Bajo La Hondura. Clearly the rain forest here is filled with these cicadas, for their coarse, grating call, even through the frequent rain and mist and above the roar of the river at the bottom of the ravine, gives them away instantly. As if guided by some great unseen clock, the males start up, first a few and then a boastful chorus, saturating the forest with the delightful noise of nature. But through my research I have found that many *Procollina* are killed by a certain kind of fungus, even before they have a chance to fly off to an existence above the ground. By placing out in the forest floor several "emergence cages" built in San José and transported here on the top of my jeep, I was able to trap large series of emerging cicadas. These cages, each a meter in length and with a rectangular base (open at the bottom), consisted of a sturdy wood frame with heavy mesh screening tacked to its two sloping sides (forming a peak about a half-meter in height) and ends. The cages were placed flush on the ground so that emerging cicadas would be trapped inside. What prompted me to trap cicadas in this manner? Before this, I had encountered many dead, mummified *Procollina* clinging to understory plants, and further examination suggested the culprit to be an entomophagous fungus, *Entomophthora echinospora* (the result of a collaboration in 1973 with David Tyrrell and Donald McLeod of the Insect Pathology Research Institute, Canadian Forest Service, in Sault Ste. Marie, Ontario). Infected cicada specimens were sent to Canada for laboratory diagnosis and isolation of the suspected pathogen. Using the cages, I discovered that five percent of the emerging *Procollina* were killed by this fungus during the peak adult emergence in the rainy season. The cages also told us that the *Procollina* is infected with the killing fungus either before the final molt or immediately following it; infection does not occur after the insect is fully sclerotized and ready to fly up into the forest.

Curiously, the only other cicada hatching in the same plots, the less abundant "whispering chug-chug," escaped from attack by the fungus. Here is another fascinating attribute of tropical nature: two different species, belonging to the same group of insects and both undergoing their life cycles in the same patches of rain forest, exhibit different response patterns to the presence of a pathogenic organism adapted to digesting cicadas. Such patterns of unexpected ecological partitioning among species, within quite small parcels of rain forest, contribute to the richness of biological diversity in the tropics. Such things tell me that there is much to know about the structure and dynamism of nature in small pieces of the habitat, and that to achieve a semblance of understanding the whole rain forest, we must examine these spatially, and often temporally, compacted phenomena.

It is the widespread emergence of *Procollina* to which the killing fungus has adapted as its prey, not the rarer and more spatially patchy *Carineta*. We should not be surprised by this manifestation of an age-old concept in population ecology, that of density-dependent predation. Rather we should be cognizant of what it takes to uncover such events in nature. Without the census of the cast skins in representative areas of the rugged landscape here, and without attempting to measure the incidence of the disease, we could not begin to piece together this story about cicada biology at Bajo La Hondura. And by no means do we have much of the picture clarified. But what we have done has given us some helpful clues, allowing us or other researchers to look further.

From the viewpoint of the cicada, the tropical rain forest contains microorganisms and other creatures both beneficial and detrimental to its survival. Once, at La Tirimbina, I unearthed a mature nymph of *Zammara,* dead and hardened, sprouting an antlerlike fungal growth from its head. Who knows what else ravages cicada nymphs in these rain forests? Do burrowing mammals such as the *taltusa* (a pocket gopher, *Macrogeomys*) graze on nymphs in their search for succulent tree roots? I have been intrigued too that cicada nymphs undergo their final molt in Sarapiquí after dark. Is this because air humidity and temperature regimes at night are more conducive to a successful molt, whereas daytime hatches, with perhaps drier conditions, are more prone to cause death? In the temperate zone, it is not uncommon for many aquatic insects to eclose at dusk, night, or dawn, rather than strictly in the daytime. Could it be that predatory animals, such as ground-cover lizards and forest understory birds, are less active at night in the rain forest? I do not have the answers to such questions. But I have crawled through the La Selva and La Tirimbina forests well after dark to search for molting cicadas clinging to understory plants.

On rainy or starlit nights, my flashlight would reveal a tiny patch of something pale-colored against the backdrop of shadows everywhere. Looking closer, sometimes what the light captured was an understory katydid or walking stick, and sometimes, when I got lucky, an adult cicada half in and half out of its cuticle. When I came upon such a sight, I would pause just to watch the arduous process, the birth of an adult cicada, transfixed at the silence of the event against the noisy backdrop of nature's hidden nightlife. Perhaps less than an hour before, this succulent creature was burrowing beneath the mulch and soil of this rain forest, preparing to leave one world and enter, even if so briefly, another. In doing so, it would perhaps add its own genetic heritage to the biological melting pot of thousands, perhaps millions of others, producing before death another generation that would return the species to its mysterious subterranean existence. By dawn, the big "sundown cicada" struggling to extricate itself from its glistening chocolate skin, pushing itself out with jerking motions, would no longer be the soft, pale creature it is at this moment. By that time it would become the majestic, earthtone, plump insect whose vibrant call awakens the rain forest to the sun, clouds, and sky.

Our field measurements at La Tirimbina reinforced my idea that some patches of rain forest are more productive in hatching cicadas than others, as we had also discovered at Cuesta Angel. During a five-week period in 1975, we gathered up 903 cast skins of *Zammara* (9.3 skins per square meter) from the river-edge plot near the Quebrada San Ramón, while for a total of *three years*, 1,800 cast skins of this species were collected from the *gavilán* tree plots (about 5.4 cicadas hatching per square meter of forest floor). Furthermore, the river-edge plot collections represent almost a tenfold greater abundance than that in the *Goethalsia*-dominant Padre Núñez forest study plot. There can be as much as a hundredfold difference between the total numbers of cast skins of this species collected annually in each study quadrate in the Padre Núñez forest. Of close to 2,500 cast skins collected from the plots in the Padre Núñez forest for a three-year period, a staggering fifteen percent came from just one quadrate! On the basis of cast skin data for this species from all study plots at La Tirimbina, I estimated that the rain forest here produces an average of one *Zammara* per square meter each year.

This was also the general pattern for other habitats I studied across northern Costa Rica. Cast skins of *Zammara* and some species of *Fidicina* are most abundant within close range of large legume trees. Thus, in spite of the tropical forest's strict floristic heterogeneity, many species of cicadas, based on our observations of the distribution of cast skins, appear to be associated chiefly with one component of these habitats, although not exclusively so. I have no clue as to why this pattern should exist. At La Tirimbina, as in the Barranca site near Puntarenas and Miramar, I found the greatest densities of *Zammara* and *Fidicina* cicadas on flattened, sandy-soil stretches near streams well dominated by legume tree saplings. Even in the central highlands, cicadas are clearly associated with the periodically flooded stream banks where old, stately individuals of a legume tree (*Zygia*) still flourish.

Looking at our data more closely, we found that the tree plots alone (plots including the trunk of a substantial tree), representing less than ten percent of the total area of our study plots at La Tirimbina, accounted for nearly eighty percent of all cast skins collected here. From such data we concluded that the absolute size of the forest area had little to do with cicada abundance. Sampling bigger and bigger segments of rain forest did not, at Cuesta Angel, provide a larger sample size of cicada cast skins; clearly, hatching cicada populations here were highly disjunct in their spatial distributions through the rain forest. This is not meant to imply, however, that large areas of rain forest are not needed to maintain breeding populations of cicada species. In spite of the very low densities of cast skins here, our data pointed to the tremendous spatial heterogeneity of the rain forest environment, as experienced by cicadas. Although the total river-edge area was about twelve times greater than that of the tree plots, cicada abundances here were not much greater than in the tree plots. Curiously, the river-edge plot contained a greater diversity of tree species, whereas the tree plots were quadrates deliberately established around the bases of large legume tree species on the steep slopes.

A cicada density estimate, based on counts of cast skins in the rain forest, of six-hundredths of a cicada hatching in a square meter of Cuesta Angel rain forest means that about seventeen square meters of forest are needed to produce one cicada in this time. But at La Tirimbina, a lower-elevation rain forest, an average of one cicada of this species is produced within a single square meter of rain forest in the same time span, a sizable difference from Cuesta Angel. Taken at face value, these data suggest that populations of the "rainy day croaker" in the rugged forest at Cuesta Angel are sparsely distributed over large areas compared to those at La Tirimbina. Such information, the result of field research, is helpful in appreciating why large tracts of tropical forests must be·protected in the long term. This information also suggests that, at least for cicada populations, different types of tropical rain forests must be viewed differently in decisions on setting aside protected areas. Naturally, in all situations, the larger the area protected, the better for all of nature.

Perhaps the single greatest lesson about tropical forest ecology the cicadas help us to understand has to do with tropical seasonality. In the temperate zone we are accustomed to expecting to hear cicadas in late summer and autumn, as I did in the Northeast and Midwest of the U.S. Under such conditions there is little ecological opportunity for seasonal displacement in adult activity among different species, although certainly this does occur to some degree when North American periodical cicadas emerge in a given year, which usually occurs in May and June. But by and large, cicada seasonality, for annual species, is confined to a single hatch in late summer for regional species. In Sarapiquí I found the situation to be very different. Clearly we identify what I term "rainy season cicadas" and "dry season cicadas," even though most Costa Ricans I speak with identify cicadas as insects of *verano* (summer, dry season).

Seasonality in the tropics assumes a different complexion from the standpoint of cicada ecology. In Sarapiquí, and confirmed by more incidental field censuses of cicada cast skins elsewhere in Costa Rica, including the Meseta Central and the lowlands of the Guanacaste dry forest, certain species of cicadas predominate during the dry season while others distinctly do the same in the rainy season. Thus, unlike the majority of temperate-zone cicadas (though I am certain there are some notable exceptions), by and large tropical cicadas exhibit a dramatic seasonal displacement of species. Such allochronic hatching patterns, while not well understood in terms of the underlying causative factors, may help explain why there are so many more species of cicadas, per unit area of habitat, in the Costa Rican tropics than throughout much of North America. If indeed cicada species in some

An aggregation of chorusing males of the cicada *Fidicina pronoe* in a
Gliricidia sepium tree, at the height of the dry season in late March 1979,
at Finca La Tirimbina.

tropical habitats exhibit a form of ecological convergence for exploiting the same tree species as egg-laying sites and nymph development
sites, then allochrony in adult activity patterns may function to reduce
some degree of interspecific competition for a limited resource essential to their survival. While this is little more than conjecture at this
point, such ideas can serve as a basis for further studies, especially
in the American tropics where many species of cicadas occur and
virtually all are largely unstudied.

The comparisons of cicada field hatches at several localities across
northern Costa Rica also revealed distinct patterns of both habitat
and geographic displacement of species and their abundance. I found
that agricultural habitats such as coffee *fincas* planted with legume
shade cover trees such as *Inga* generally supported only one to three

species of cicadas, similar to what I discovered in nearby remnants of forest vegetation bordering creeks, and far less than what was typical for large stands of primary and secondary tropical forests. Cicada faunas were very different between the Caribbean and Pacific slopes and adjoining lowlands of the Cordillera Central, even though a few species, such as the big "sundown cicada," *Fidicina mannifera,* were widely distributed on the lower slopes on both sides of these mountains. By far the greatest number of cicada species was in Sarapiquí, where extensive areas of rain forest still remain. Most of the other localities studied had little or no intact forest cover. Cicada populations in such areas may have been obliterated long ago when much of the forests were cleared to make room for large-scale agriculture.

From our data, there can be little doubt that both geographic and habitat heterogeneity have played major roles in shaping the overall high number of cicada species occurring today in northern Costa Rica. My studies of Costa Rican cicadas thus heightened my awareness of an ecological and evolutionary process deemed pivotal in molding the great diversity of floras and faunas in the tropics, namely, that both temporal and spatial heterogeneity in the environment over relatively small distances contribute greatly to the elaboration of many distinct species possessing ecological specializations.

What are the ecological factors regulating seasonal hatches in Costa Rican cicadas? I do not have an answer to this question, but some indirect observations may provide some clues. At La Tirimbina during the dry season, when the rain forest throbs with the steady buzz of the "summertime whistler," a succession of four or five days of unexpected rainy weather, which is not uncommon here and which locals call a *pinta*, brings forth a small hatch of the "rainy day croaker." Clearly there are overlapping generations of cicadas in these species waiting in the ground for the appropriate time to hatch, since adults emerge every year and presumably the nymphs have multiyear life cycles, not unlike our North American annual cicadas. Bouts of dry weather within the long rainy season bring forth little, localized hatches of *chicharras de verano* such as the "summertime whistler." Could it be that the mature nymphs of rainy season and dry season cicadas possess different tolerance levels to soil moisture or dryness, or to some indirect factor affecting the consistency and nutrient content of phloem and xylem fluids in roots of their food plants?

Experiencing this ebb and flow of cicada hatches in Sarapiquí leads me to believe that such a biological trigger fits well with the often whimsical nature of seasonality in this land of rain forests. A naturalist can say that of the eleven species of cicadas thriving in La Tirimbina's forests, seven are active in the rainy season, but is this strictly the case? One must be attuned to the senses to understand the fluid nature of cicada activity in Sarapiquí's rain forests. What I feel out here, when strolling through the rain forests in either season, is the presence of cicadas, through their calls of courtship and their sudden screeches, or "disturbance squawks," emitted when being chased by a bird or some other enemy. One must learn the calls of cicadas to interpret the resilience of the rain forest's animal life. Through the cicadas, and their opportunistic responses to changes in the environment, as when rainy season species hatch in the dry season, one comes to a new awareness of the rain forest as a changeable, shifting web of nature's players, in which it is not always feasible, nor desirable, to pigeonhole the activities of individual species into fixed time slots.

In my studies of cicadas, I have also come to appreciate the natural history of other insects and of the floras of Sarapiquí. Take the phenomenon of convergent evolution. Plants belonging to different taxa often have strikingly similar vegetative parts, only their flowers and fruit giving the essential clues about their identities. Consider the rain forest understory at La Tirimbina or Cuesta Angel. Here one finds many understory treelets with leaves bearing "drip tips." A drip tip is the elongated, pointed apex of a leaf that allows rain water to roll off the leaf more effectively. Drip tips are a distinctive morphological adaptation of many tropical forest plant species, all confronted, through evolutionary time, with the problem of their leaf surfaces being ideal colonization grounds for microfloras, those legions of fungi, lichens, and epiphytic mosses that require a surface coated with a sustained film of water. Heavy loads of epiphytic organisms on leaves cut down on the amount of photosynthetic surface available and may weigh down leaves to the point where they break off, further weakening the plant. Widely divergent taxa of plants in Sarapiquí's rain forest display the drip tip leaf design, providing an outstanding example of convergence.

I believe that drip tips provide an additional advantage to the overall design of the tropical rain forest. Channeling rain water off vegetation and directly to the soil, for the large quantity of rain that actually makes its way down through the dense tangle of foliage, branches, epiphytes, and lodged rotting debris in the forest canopy, nurses the decay cycle on the forest floor, breaking down dead plant and animal matter through the concerted action of both litter organisms and water. In this way, nutrients are released and shuffled through the soil, providing a food matrix for plant roots and the symbiotic microfloras attached to them. Such a system of nutrient cycling enriches the food supply in roots for the subterraneous cicada nymphs tapping into these plants for their own nourishment.

Walking through Sarapiquí's rain forests, there is no escaping the feeling that the ground cover, that dampened, moldy leaf mulch, fortified with fallen branches, twigs, and rotting seeds and fruit, is a vast, immensely complex nutrient bed for life. One must view the floor of the tropical rain forest as a dynamic receptacle for nature's dying and dead organisms, the carcasses of life that rapidly become broken down and reabsorbed into the forest ecosystem. And chiefly because of my fascination with cicadas, I have spent much time with my face practically pushed down into this world of decay, searching for one thing, cast skins, but always discovering much more. It was on a morning in August of 1972 in the Padre Núñez rain forest that John Thomason, crawling along beside me in the litter, came face to face with a large, dead katydid, obviously recently fallen into the leaf litter, of a kind I had never seen before. Almost intuitively, one has the mysterious sensation of encountering something new when doing field work in the tropics. This was the case with this large insect, adorned with incredible leaf-mimicking forewings garnished with brown spots and holes, counterfeit insect-feeding damage.

Imagine just how intense the selection pressures on insects must be in the tropical rain forest for a katydid, a creature of foliage, to evolve wings bearing a remarkable resemblance to herbivore-perforated, fungal-spotted leaves! Judging from its appearance, I guessed this katydid to have died and fallen to this spot in the rain forest perhaps only minutes or an hour or so before John's discovering it in the spongy leaf mulch. Seeing such a creature in this circumstance of death, it is challenging to think about the millions of dead and dying insects and other animal life surely showering down from the forest canopy every day. A few days later, fly maggots exited from the katydid carcass, signals that nature's cycle of rot and decay had already set in. But the katydid was still in good enough condition to be sent to the Museum of Zoology at the University of Michigan, where it was identified by Irving J. Cantrall as *Celidophylla albimacula*. Retained for Michigan's insect collections, our specimen was the second of its species ever found, and the first female specimen. Furthermore, the first specimen, a male, had been collected in 1898 at Chontales, Nicaragua, more than seventy years before John's discovery.

Yet when you think about it, such rare finds should not be terribly surprising, given the immense diversity of insects inhabiting Sarapiquí's rain forests. There is a feel of this diversity reflected in the audacious color patterns, sizes, and shapes of foliage-inhabiting and floral-inhabiting insects here. In just one group, such as the leaf hoppers, one does not have to look too far to sense the riotous pulse of evolution's diversifying processes.

Nonetheless, I still tingle at those fleeting encounters with the rain forest's dramatic insect citizens. Part of my challenge in seeing the more elusive of these is learning not to be distracted by little annoyances. Take, for example, my prowess with leaky Rapidograph pens.

Rapidograph pens are mainstay field tools of the tropical biologist, the black ink being ideal for writing field notes, specimen labels, and diaries almost guaranteed to withstand the humidity and rain. Now, many years later, I cannot recall just how many cotton field shirts I had, each with a large black stain directly beneath the left breast pocket. It seems I had a special talent with pens leaking out on my shirts, often unnoticed until much later. When this sort of thing first happened, I was always annoyed, distracted, in a meaningless, fruitless way. But soon, it was "What the heck!" for my already barbed-wire-torn work shirts.

An irrational preoccupation with ink stains on my shirt one night had rewarded me years earlier with a painful, piercing slice through my finger by a most unusual creature I encountered in the La Selva rain forest. My flashlight beam picked up a large grasshopper struggling to crawl from the underside of a palm frond to the upper side. This large, pale green katydid had an enormous head that was flattened frontally, looking as if the insect had crashed head-on into a wall. Looking closer at the ambling creature, I could see that the edges of this flattened surface were adorned with tiny yellow spikes, and the creature possessed glistening large black mandibles. Wanting to slip it into a plastic bag, I maneuvered the katydid onto the palm of my hand. The rain trickling down my forehead now cascaded down my nose, causing me to look down at my shirt. Then I saw the spreading splotch of blackness beneath the pocket of my brand new J. C. Penney's blue cotton shirt ($2.95 in those days—definitely not Banana Republic chic!). Rain and sweat, the stuff of nature that christens work shirts of field biologists in the tropics, work an interesting magic on Rapidograph ink, encouraging the dark stain to move along, expand, even to run. And that's what I was contemplating at the precise moment the "flattened-face" katydid swung its powerful mandibles, those beautiful, shiny structures presumably designed to process tough plant tissues, into the soft, pink flesh of my little finger on my right hand! Angered and in pain, I grabbed the insect, after it had dropped to the ground, or after I had thrown it there, I am not sure which, and threw it into the plastic bag. From that point on, I tried to ignore the inevitable leaky pen, rain, and sweat that are standard features of field work.

I learned later that the "flattened-face" katydid was a copiphorine grasshopper, *Lirometopum coronatum,* thanks to David C. Rentz, an internationally recognized authority on tropical Orthoptera. I guessed that the species name had something to do with that conspicuous ring of yellow spikes adorning the lateral edges of the insect's huge head. Dave told me that this species was related to species of *Copiphora,* such as *C. rhinoceros* at Le Selva, which are seed-eating grasshoppers. *Copiphora rhinoceros* is a slender, brilliantly green insect, with a slanted-downward/inward head bearing, at its apex, a conical reddish "horn." Its body is studded with cuticular rivets of yellow, making this rain forest grasshopper a striking, unusual creature, much like its stouter close relative *Lirometopum.* At both La Selva and La Tirimbina, I have come across *C. rhinoceros* ovipositing in palm frond axils in the forest understory. The females have very long ovipositors engineered to pierce through tough palmaceous tissues and deposit flattened, ovular eggs deeply in the fronds' axils. The powerful mandibles of copiphorine grasshoppers are designed to pierce tough seed coats, although the precise feeding behavior and seed preferences for most species are virtually unstudied. Perhaps the elusive *Lirometopum coronatum* is also a seed eater?

While searching the ground cover and rain forest understory for cicada cast skins, it was not unusual for us to encounter the sharply crackling sounds of army ants, *Eciton,* millions of them, on the move along the forest floor. These marauders of the rain forest must find booty for their nurseries while rummaging across the gound cover. Sometimes different lines of the ants, from a single colony, intersect at deep angles, as if crisscrossing, while on other occasions a single dense raiding column dominates the scene around my feet. There is a terribly frantic aura about army ants; they rush along in such huge abundance that their urgency, instilled in their genes over millions of years, causes me to jump quickly aside every time I encounter them. Most times I hear them before I see them. That curious sound, as if tiny rain drops were pelting dry leaves, implores me to look down, swiftly, at my feet. Suddenly I discover them, almost too late to step aside, as many of the workers have already crossed my field boots, even begun exploring up the legs of my pants. I jump hard, instinctively, every time, even after many years of encountering army ants. They are tropical nature's incessant raiders, always on the move, attacking many kinds of arthropods, dismembering the larger ones, and feeding them to their larvae. Army ants are nomads, without a permanent nesting site.

Along openings in the rain forest, such as footpaths, light gaps, and the lighted edges of streams, army ant raiding parties on the move kick up a lot of dust—not so much dirt and debris, but other creatures. In their prodigious movements in the rain forest, the ants flush up many kinds of insects, especially the larger, nocturnally active ones, such as katydids, roaches, and moths. Ant birds follow the ant raids, plucking out of the air these other insects and leaving the army ants alone. The crowning glory of this interaction between *Eciton,* flushed-up insects, and ant birds is that certain kinds of ithomiine butterflies follow the birds along the ant raiding party routes on the forest floor. Tiger-striped *Mechanitis* and various blue-and-translucent-winged species partake in this army ant follow-along. Ant birds splash low-lying foliage with their feces, and it is the feces that attract the butterflies. The delicate-winged ithomiines gracefully alighting on the fresh, soft bird feces are all females in search of amino acids and nitrogenous waste substances they need from the environment in order to produce eggs. The butterflies carefully insert their proboscises into the soft, watery feces to imbibe the nitrogen required for the synthesis of egg proteins. When the feces dry out, they are no longer suitable for the butterflies. Female ithomiines alight on the leaf and sometimes form little clusters of different species around the feces. I have seen this behavior to be most evident in the lighted places along the army ant raiding columns, minutes to hours after the ants have left the area. I do not believe, however, that ithomiines depend solely on ant birds as a source of feces, for I have seen the butterflies exhibiting the same behavior on bird feces and other rotting animal substances away from the army ant columns. Ithomiines appear to be excellent opportunists in this regard, with an adaptive flexibility that enables them to seize prized resources that may appear and disappear quickly.

Once, in the rain forest behind the La Tigra cacao, I came face to face with a freshly gouged out chrysalis of an *Eurytides* swallowtail butterfly, attached to the branch of an understory tree. As I examined the gaping hole in the shell, presumably made by some kind of bird, a butterfly, the ithomiine *Hypothyris euclea*, fluttered around the chrysalis. I drew back slowly from the spot, only to see the butterfly alight on the plump shell of the chrysalis and insert its proboscis inside the large wound. Slowly approaching, I noticed that the proboscis tip settled on some matted strings of glistening muscle tissue still adhering to the inner wall of the insect shell. The butterfly remained at the spot for almost an hour before flying off.

Being face to face, or perhaps more appropriately, leg to leg, with army ants can be a very startling experience. Mary Ellen Carolan, one of my student field assistants, learned this lesson very well at La Tirimbina many years ago. We were walking through an open, grassy area toward a rubber plantation when I heard Mary Ellen, who had paused to take a picture, scream. There she was, perhaps a hundred feet from me, dancing wildly on the path. Frantically slapping her pant legs, she soon wriggled part-way out of her pants— an admirable attempt to shake loose the hundreds of ants crawling up her legs. It is truly a dramatic thing to have equally frantic ants swarming up your pants and legs, especially when you had not noticed just how far they had gotten in their quest.

In searching the rain forest for cicada cast skins, the *bala* ant, *Paraponera clavata*, and its close cousins, species of *Odontomachus,* became one of our greatest fears. Both kinds of ants are powerful stingers, and both are common in Sarapiquí rain forests, especially

Butterfly, *Hypothyris euclea*, adult stage, with its proboscis inserted into an *Eurytides* butterfly chrysalis gouged out by another animal.

at La Tirimbina. But painful encounters with these ants were few and far between, for which we were always very thankful.

Here at La Tirimbina, about two hundred meters above sea level, massive seasonal hatches of mosquitoes were much less of a problem than other biting or stinging insects. The most annoying threat from mosquitoes here, however, stemmed not from biting but from their role as intermediary egg carriers for the botfly, *Dermatobia hominis,* a rather large fly whose maggots burrow into and feed on human flesh, in addition to that of other mammals (such as monkeys) and birds. Gravid females of this particular species of botfly skillfully capture the females of certain mosquitoes, belonging chiefly to the genus *Psorophora*, and place their eggs on the mosquito's body, which they then release. Since *Dermatobia* is a daytime flier, these captures, converting female mosquitoes into botfly egg carriers, occur during the day, although the mosquitoes are active at night. When a mosquito bites a person or other warm-blooded animal, the botfly's eggs drop off and hatch immediately; the tiny maggots or larvae burrow into the flesh and begin feeding on it. A great mystery in the American tropics is how such an exquisite, highly specialized and complex association between the botfly and mosquito evolved in the first place. Other species of botflies, those parasitizing small mammals including rodents, glue their eggs to vegetation where they are picked up inadvertently when an animal brushes its fur against the eggs. In botflies, heat from the mammalian body triggers the hatching of their eggs once they are lodged on the host. Agile primates are capable of swatting away flies. Anyone who has encountered a Costa Rican deerfly along a jungle trail can attest to the need to be very persistent at doing this. But deerflies come at you to feed, not to lay eggs like the botfly. Clever mosquitoes soaring through the night air in search of a hearty blood meal are much less detectable to the host than the big botflies, making them ideal "egg droppers" for the botfly species attacking humans and other primates.

The botfly larva or maggot is rather unpleasant looking, being somewhat pear-shaped, especially later in life, with stout, hooked black bristles allowing the creature to fasten itself stoically to its feeding burrow, living flesh. As it grows, which takes about ninety days, the maggot hangs upside down in its burrow, breathing by means of a tube at the rear of its yellowish white body that slips in and out of a hole broken through the host's skin. This breathing hole is a helpful diagnostic sign in detecting the presence of this creature, called the *tórsalo* by the Costa Ricans. The *tórsalo* larva secretes an antibiotic substance that prevents its subcutaneous feeding site from becoming infected by microorganisms, ensuring a supply of fresh meat on which to dine.

What starts out appearing as an itchy mosquito bite develops gradually into a large swollen reddish nodule with a tiny hole in the middle. The jerky movement of the maggot's rigid bristles, often eliciting a sharp pain, provides another telltale sign of this most unwanted guest. The growing maggot feeds on minute quantities of living flesh. More harm can be done to one's body if an attempt at extricating the tenacious maggot ends in failure. An injured larva left to die in its burrow can cause serious infection. Some biologists have been curious and heroic enough to allow the creature to complete its development, especially if it is nested in a leg or arm. The fully grown larva exits its burrow on its own accord and drops to the ground where it pupates in a damp place. The unusual pupa is stubby, black, and sandpapery to the touch.

Costa Ricans sometimes dislodge the *tórsalo* by strapping a small chunk of raw pork or bacon over the larva's breathing hole. The larva, in an attempt to wriggle out of its niche to avoid suffocation, hooks itself into the meat with its strong anal hooks and can be pulled away intact. I have not tried this method, but have resorted to others with varying success. Let me also state that I have always opted not to bear the pain of a twitching *tórsalo* larva in my flesh until it pupates. Depending upon its location, either myself or someone else would gently but firmly knead the flesh around the wound, sometimes slowly nudging part-way the maggot from its burrow, exposing enough to permit careful removal of the parasite with forceps. In my twenty years of living intermittently at La Tirimbina, I have been host to the botfly on several occasions. Feeding some *tórsalos* involuntarily with your own flesh goes with the territory, even if your stay is just a short one. Once, I had three *tórsalos* at one spot in an armpit, and it was fairly easy to knead the flesh here to extricate the maggots, one by one. In other places, such as the wrist, it was not so easy. Thoughts of the *tórsalo* often prompted me to search my room at La Tirimbina for mosquitoes and swat them quickly. Often, just after the candle or electric light was out, I would hear a mosquito buzzing close to my ears. Reaching for the flashlight, I usually spotted the culprit-to-be perched on the wall next to my bed; dispatching it quickly was about a fifty-fifty proposition.

There is certainly much to gain in appreciating tropical nature by having strange, close-up encounters with marvelous creatures one would not see without crawling through the forest floor and poking around. And yet, at the same time, there is much to be gained by stepping back and gazing at the rain forest as a collective unit of life. When I stand high on a grassy hill at La Tirimbina, in a spot where the rain forest was cleared away long ago, I can see the still-standing smudges of rain forest, veiled ever so gently with feathers of white mist in the mornings, off in the distance. From a mile or two away, the rain forest appears as little more than a uniform ribbon of green. But the flocks of parrots, toucans, and oropendulas appearing and disappearing in the dense canopy foliage, their positions given away by their noise, tell us, even from this distance, that any uniformity is but an illusion. The birds know which trees are bearing fruit, or succulent new shoots, and which are not. These organisms and all else that dwells in the forest interpret this assemblage of life as a heterogeneous mix of resources. Over short distances, the diversity of trees, vines, and herbs is tremendous; only a few notable exceptions such as the *gavilán*, marginal patches of *Cecropia, Pourouma,* and *Cordia* trees, and massive stands of palms and lady's lips in the understory give some impression of uniformity.

Cicadas, too, interpret this environment as a mixed bag. Over the years, I found that cast skins of forest species are clearly clumped around certain species of canopy-size trees, particularly *gavilán* and other woody legumes. I suspect that cicada nymphs in rain forest habitats may preferentially associate themselves with the root systems of legume trees as their primary host plants, though I have no direct data to support this. Other factors might also produce such a clumped pattern. Do mature cicada nymphs, emerging from their subterraneous rookeries, gravitate toward large trees based on configurations of shadows? Is there a differential survival of nymphs in different kinds of tropical soil formations? Perhaps nymphs do best in sandy floodplain soils rather than claylike upland soils. One intriguing idea is that rain forest cicadas thrive in greatest abundance along the margins of forest, such as along streams, rivers, and boundaries with various kinds of natural disturbances to the landscape.

I have tried to dig up cicada nymphs, hoping to determine specific associations with roots of certain species of trees, all to no avail. You must remember that the ground beneath the rain forest is a mass of tightly interlocking networks of root systems of hundreds of species of plants. Even attempting to penetrate the ground, as I have at Bajo La Hondura and La Tirimbina, has been almost impossible, the trowel or shovel being blocked by exposed roots and roots just beneath the leaf litter layer. Once, at Bajo La Hondura, I managed to dig up less than a dozen nymphs of what appeared to be *Procollina biolleyi*, unearthing several distinct size classes of the insects. But is there a relationship between body size and nymphal instar in these cicadas? Do these size classes represent distinct generations of cicadas inhabiting the soil? What has been presumed to be the case in temperate-zone annual cicadas like *Tibicen*, that is, the occurrence of several overlapping generations of nymphs in the ground during any one year, and high variability in the growth rates of nymphs within any generation, may be operative in tropical cicadas as well. What this pattern of development yields in *Tibicen* is an annual emergence cycle, in which some adults emerge every year. All tropical cicadas I have studied thus far in Costa Rica likewise have annual emergence patterns.

Far more enigmatic about these "annual" cicadas is the length of the nymph stage in the ground. Do annual cicadas have life cycles shorter than the 13- and 17-year North American periodical cicadas, say within the 5- to 9-year range, or are they much longer, within the 20- to 30-year range? An animal species with an extremely long juvenile stage, such as cicadas, might be able to stagger the hatching year of the adult stage over a wide range of years, causing considerable overlapping of generations at a locality. If this is the case, adults of a species appearing above ground in a given year might well be the offspring of parents from different years. A very lengthy life cycle of this kind might indicate extremely specialized adaptations to a biotically diverse but climatically stable environment such as the tropical forests.

A life history involving a longevous larval or nymphal period coupled with an annual adult emergence pattern exposes the phenotypic (and therefore, genetic) constitution of the animal population to natural selection on a frequent and regular basis. This allows for changing arrays of genotypes to enter into the population frequently, stockpiling the species with a heritage of genetic variability that allows the population to adapt to subtle, changing conditions to which cicada nymphs are exposed in the soil. Tropical soils are likely to be rich spheres of selection pressures arising from their substantial biotas of microorganisms, fungi, and invertebrate and vertebrate animal life, some forms of which might impact on the survival of cicada nymphs. Longevity beneath the ground, as suspected to be the case in tropical cicada nymphs, might be an evolutionary consequence of cicadas evolving to exploit a subterraneous niche in the first place, perhaps freeing them from competitive interactions with other plant-sucking bugs above ground.

Herbivorous insect associations with floras beneath the ground, on the root systems, are most likely much less diverse than those above ground. Cicadas therefore might have been locked in to slow development by feeding on nutrient-poor xylem fluids in roots. Yet because of the large amount of time in the nymphal stage, it is this stage that might be subjected to an intense, subtly changing array of selection pressures—perhaps much more so than the briefer existence of the adult stage. Annual cicadas both within the tropics and in the temperate zone are far less numerous in the adult stage than the massive hatchings of periodical cicadas, whose prodigious populations of both nymphs in the soil and adults might well satiate their predators and pathogens—something annual cicadas cannot do. Therefore selection pressures affecting annual cicadas might be more acute than those operating on periodical cicadas. If so, then a pattern of annual adult emergence yielding cohorts of mixed generations might be an effective means of ensuring the genetic variability needed to counter selection pressures, especially those affecting nymphs. But no one knows for sure the length of the life cycle of annual cicadas within and outside of the tropics—a crucial piece of information needed to understand better the adaptive significance of annual hatches versus periodicity in cicadas.

As a tentative working hypothesis to help explain the observed spatial patchiness of cicada hatches, I favor the idea that rain forest cicadas in Central America and South America, and perhaps elsewhere in the equatorial regions of the world, coevolved with canopy size legume tree species in primary-growth (climax) tropical rain forests. While different kinds of tropical rain forest habitats clearly have both different species of canopy tree legumes and associated different populational distribution (such as the preponderance of *Pentaclethra macroloba* [the *gavilán*] in the lowlands of Sarapiquí and its conspicuous scarcity or absence in the foothills), what is crucially unifying is the occurrence of legumes as floristic components of climax forests in the tropics. This is also the case in tropical dry forest. Legume trees are absent from climax forest formations in North America, even though a handful of species, such as black locust and honey locust, occur in marginal habitats, often forming large monoculture strips or stands. These north-temperate legume trees are host plants to assemblages of Homoptera, including leaf hoppers and tree hoppers but not cicadas, which are not typically associated with tree species in climax forests.

All around me as I climb up the hill in the Padre Núñez Forest at La Tirimbina, I see the feathery leaves of the *gavilán*, crisscrossing blotches of vibrant green shot through with pinpoints of sunlight, a marvel made possible by the symbiosis going on in the soil beneath my feet. I can only surmise that the *bala* ant, *Paraponera clavata*, has brushed through the forest floor's webwork of fungi and roots, and that the cicada nymph too knows these big ants very well. *Pentaclethra* belongs to the legume subfamily Mimosaceae, one of the two ancient groups of legume trees (Caesalpinaceae is the other) that evolved millions of years ago in conditions similar to that of the extant lowland tropical rain forest. A third subfamily of legumes, the Papilionaceae, is found chiefly in the temperate zone, represented in North America by honey locust and black locust, and reflects a more recent evolution of the Leguminosae.

I am left with the intriguing idea that especially mimosaceous and caesalpinaceous legumes figured prominently in the early evolution and development of Central American and South American rain forests, undoubtedly associated early on with nitrogen-fixing bacteria as symbiotic partners on their roots. Today these groups of legumes dominate the floristic makeup of canopy-size trees in rain forests, as I have seen firsthand at Cuesta Angel, La Tirimbina, and La Selva in Sarapiquí. Could it be that rain forest cicadas such as the "sundown cicada," the "summertime whistler," and the "rainy day croaker" coevolved with these legumes as the principal host trees for their nymphs in the soil? Nitrogen is an elemental building block of amino acids, the subunits of life's structural integrity, the proteins. Various laboratory studies using different species of insects (though not cicadas) generally indicate that immature insects grow up quicker when fed on plants containing greater levels of nitrogen. Nitrogen deficiencies have been shown to reduce the fecundity of insects and to retard the developmental time of eggs in some species. The early evolutionary acquisition of nitrogen fixation, through symbiosis, by these legume trees undoubtedly contributed to their sweeping ecological success as dominants in climax rain forests, and may also have provided an ideal host tree complex for herbivores such as cicada nymphs (given their higher nutritional content). A similar scenario can be hypothesized for herbivore associations with other rain forest tree species having mycorrhizal-derived symbiosis.

I am prompted in this line of reasoning by the monumental, classic paper "Butterflies and Plants: A Study in Coevolution," by Paul R. Ehrlich and Peter H. Raven, published in a 1965 issue of *Evolution*, in which it was pointed out that general patterns of herbivorous insect diversity could be explained in large measure by the joint evolution of individual groups with different groups of plants, especially in the tropics. Extending this reasoning from foliage-feeding insects to subterraneous herbivorous insects associated with roots, I envision the tropical forest as a highly complex network of herbivore-feeding substrates provided by the root systems of individual tree species.

I can stand on a hill and imagine that the rain forest I see has been flipped upside down, exposing a vast meshwork of interlocking, crossing-over root systems, a massive, whitish "root crown" in place of the green foliage. What constellations of herbivores and symbionts are intertwined with these root systems, hidden away as they are? Surely phloem- and xylem-sucking cicada nymphs, tunneling away through the soil, must figure high on this list. Imagine the webwork of root systems of the rain forest being somewhat analogous ecologically to the canopy or foliage of the forest. It is a substrate, rich in nutrients, on which unique themes of evolutionary adaptation, shaping root characteristics and the creatures exploiting them, can be played out through time.

Imagine being able to examine closely the meticulously complex, even frustrating tangle of roots in an acre of a Sarapiquí rain forest. That interconnecting meshwork would not go very far in the dimension of depth, compared to the root systems of trees in temperate forests. To understand the sprawling, elegant buttresses gracing many rain forest trees, which signal our presence in a very different kind of nature, one must consider the shallow roots of tropical plants: winglike buttresses of canopy trees; dangling aerial roots from lianas high above the rain forest floor; the spinose stilt roots of certain species of palm trees. But this shallowness assumes another complexion as we probe through the patina of life, leaf mulch, and soil defining the floor of the rain forest.

Looking closer at the roots, we would also see crusts of microorganisms associated with the finest, thread-thick rootlets. These living clots of symbiotic bacteria, coupled with another constellation of rain forest life, mycorrhizal fungi, mediate life's biggest challenge, the mobilization and transfer of energy among creatures, allowing the rain forest to sustain itself. The rain forest floor is alive with the concerted movements and actions of billions of microorganisms, different orchestrations, some breaking down the rain forest's carcasses, its fallen branches, twigs, dead leaves, rotting fruit and seeds, and the bodies of animals. In this symphonic assemblage, death of plant and animal tissues brings forth the sustenance to feed the life of the rain forest in a continuous cycle of energy exchange, releasing, by nature's fine-tuned mechanisms of micro-food-processing, a product of millions of years of evolutionary experimentation.

Surely as you walk through the rain forest, such matters of biology can only seem remote, though these interconnections spell the fate of life here and go on, in perpetuity, perhaps within twenty centimeters or so of our feet. We must stretch, bend, and listen to the calls of the cicadas to become even faintly acquainted with this pathway of interdependence structuring life beneath the floor of the rain forest. For me this is, perhaps, the most fascinating lesson embodied in the cicadas of Sarapiquí: as creatures spending the bulk of their life hidden away in the floor of the rain forest, a period of perhaps several years, they represent, symbolically, a large slice of tropical nature that is seldom seen or studied. Only as creatures of the air, tree trunks, and treetops do the cicadas remind us of this hidden wealth of biological intricacy and diversity. In some ways, this lesson is taught by other creatures of the rain forest too, such as the *bala* and leaf-cutter (*Atta*) ants, who also spend a great deal of time actively engaged in the games of survival beneath the rain forest floor.

The rain forest's elegant proclivity to yield new life, variants of life past or more of the same, rests on the foundation of energy shuffling through food chains. The fine threads of tiny roots, a latticework of pale lines embedded in the tawny clays and deep browns of the gritty soil spawned on the banks of the Sarapiquí River, a rich nursery for cicadas growing up beneath the ground, reflects a brand of ecological intimacy that unites trees, soil life, and food. Billions of bacteria scour the thin soils of the rain forest every minute of their tenuous existence, picking up and processing whatever sliver of submicroscopic organic matter there is, releasing nutrients that would otherwise not be available to the trees, lianas, and all else forming the living spandrels of this unexcelled cathedral of life. But here and there, where the stands of gnarled *gavilán* dominate the land as they have for thousands of years, and where *Pterocarpus, Pithecollobium, Inga,* and legions of other giant legume trees reach toward the sky, now graying with the threat of the afternoon rain, this hidden webwork of life in the soil takes on a different complexion. What is happening here can only be presumed, in large measure, from what little has been studied in the more accessible crop legumes of the tropics.

We must imagine these microorganisms invading, as they have for millions of years, the root hair tissues of the tropical forest legumes, causing localized proliferations of tissue cells, creating nodules encasing the now-trapped bacteria, and ensuring the continuance of a great, fine-tuned biological partnership. These bulbous structures attached to the little roots, the nodules, are furnaces of energy change and transfer, enhancing the life of both bacteria and the tree. It is within these nodules and fungal brushes, mycorrhizal fungi, attached or embedded as vesicles and arbuscules in roots of legumes and other trees, that the survival of the rain forest is prescribed, as it surely has been for eons. Furthermore, filamentous tentacular hyphae in some forms of mycorrhizal fungi proliferate through the upper layers of soil, the staging area in the rain forest where nature's decay becomes refreshened soil, producing a vast and energetically efficient harvesting machine. Together with diverse legions of other soil microflora, the mycorrhizal fungi gather up minerals and other nutrients from the otherwise food-deficient tropical soil. For the webs of the rain forest's more obvious life, its "charismatic" flora and fauna, the legions of orchids, epiphytes, lianas, vines, trees, butterflies, beetles, bats, birds, frogs, snakes, and so much more, exist ultimately because of this thin veneer of microscopic life nudged within the silty clay soil, leaf mulch, and roots of trees.

It is a system free of wastage. Elemental or gaseous nitrogen is taken up by these bacteria attached to the roots of legume trees, which draw at the same time upon the energy reserves of the tree, locked up as photosynthate. In the roots of trees and all that associate with them, as with the leaves, flowers, stems, and fruit, we see the soul of life, the sun. This nitrogen now takes on a life of its own by becoming fixed through the bacterium's intricate metabolism. The nitrogen-containing substances are shuttled back to the root tissues where they are modified again by the tree's own evolutionary game plan, becoming, in short, the nutritive materials that build new structures and, along the way, become food for herbivores such as hungry cicada nymphs digging through the soil, seeking out the rain forest's meshwork of fine roots.

What little we know about this amazing process suggests that different species of legume trees match up with either different species of nitrogen-fixing bacteria or different "strains" within species. Equally dramatic in their two-way games of life are the mycorrhizal fungi embedded in the roots of various rain forest trees, offering another example of the way in which trees take up what little nutrient matter there is in the forest floor. In the upper layer of soil, certain kinds of fungi, already living saprophytically in the soil, invade fine roots ever so selectively, not damaging or killing their hosts in the process. In these mazes of living tissues, it is often difficult to ascertain where one life form ends and another begins.

It is the movement of life again within the forest floor, the rumblings that ensure the cycle of life uniting all creatures of the rain forest. Even though the invasions of roots by mycorrhizal fungi go on out of sight, we know these fusions of life with other life are happening. You can smell the life of the rain forest when your nose is next to the damp earth. I have done this many times along the Quebrada San Ramón, where the land is flat just for a short distance, and where the sandy clay soil mixture is a nursery for the "rainy day croaker" (*Zammara smaragdina*) and the "summertime whistler" (*Fidicina sericans*). You can almost trace the steps of ancient life's upheavals and challenges in this little corner of Sarapiquí. Where the bigger rivers and the little *quebradas* reach down from the mountains to these escarping foothills and gently rolling floodplains, the sculpting of the land by water has left behind the cicada's medium for life, the clays, sand, and gravels that are thrown aside. It is in such places, down low, deep in the rain forest or near its margins, rather than at the crests of hills where the soil is much more richly compacted with many stripes of clay, that the *gavilán* trees thrive. And here too is where the rain forest cicadas thrive in greatest numbers, insofar as their nymphal cast skins are an indication. What music there is at such places in Sarapiquí! The rushes of crystalline waters across the soot-dark boulders and smaller rocks, signposts of the old volcanoes far from here, Poás, Barba, and others, the gulping sounds of fish jumping up, splashing back ever so quickly, to snatch from the water's surface an insect or feather-weight seed, fuse with the unrelenting calls of cicadas, rainy season or *verano*.

What cannot be felt out here in Sarapiquí's shrinking stands of pristine rain forest, against the backdrop of incredible colors, shapes, and sounds, all wound into one intricate living tapestry, is the way bacteria and fungi in the soil mop up valuable resources for trees, prerequisites for survival that would otherwise be inaccessible to the giants of the forest, and to most other plants as well. The soil here holds only a scant sprinkling of minerals, such as potassium and calcium in addition to nitrogen. Wondrously, areas of soil where these elements are in lowest supply are places where the mycorrhizal fungi are presumably most prolific and dense. What series of sophisticated chemical and physiological properties monitor such a response system between the fungus, tree roots, and prevailing soil conditions? How does the fungus proliferate in response to changes in the availability of minerals and nitrogen in the soil, and how do the fine roots of host trees accommodate greater quantities of the fungus? Specialized cell surface interactions with soil constituents and between fungal tissue and root tissue must be mediated by chemical signals still unknown to science. How do the mycorrhizal fungi affect the soil's stores of minerals and other substances potentially available as nutritive complements to the photosynthetic food-processing cycles of the rain forest's trees and lianas?

Time is running out, even here in Sarapiquí, to explore the answers to such questions. The rain forests are coming down. Not too long ago, I struggled over a hill with two others to witness the death of a giant tree, the act itself a symbol of the broader picture, of the obliteration of what these tropical rain forests once were like.

I believe Jay Reed, the outdoors writer for the *Milwaukee Journal*, a Hemingwayesque man who generally writes about hunting and fishing, felt the misery of nature's staggering losses as he trudged along with me up a deforested hill near La Tirimbina in 1983. On an unusual day for Sarapiquí when the sky was bright blue, Jay and the newspaper's photographer Sherman Gessert, a veteran himself of previous times with me in Sarapiquí's rain forests, had come with me to witness an execution, one I could not stop, for I had no legal right to. A mammoth *roble* tree (*Tabebuia guayacan*), a doomed holdout of a stop-and-start biological holocaust, a good eight meters in width from buttress to buttress, was coming down, a victim of humankind. The destructivenss of human beings, like many times throughout the tropics, would be announced by the dreadful sputter and whine of the chainsaw. Soon, we stood well inside a pocket of hills where extensive clear-cutting had been under way now for several months. This balding, parched brown landscape, strewn for at least a mile or two in various directions with a litter of felled tree trunks and twisted ropelike vines, was but a small microcosm of the greater malaise engulfing much of the humid or wet tropics in recent decades. Unlike the small, scattered plantings of cacao, spices, Para rubber, and other perennial crops, nestled within corridors or *finca* plots surrounded by rain forest, these hills were being clear-cut on a greater scale, to make room for cattle pastures in particular.

We struggled across a sea of fallen tree trunks and branches. One hill gave way to another and another, as we sweated and strained across this wasteland that was once a beautiful rain forest. Jorge Mejías led the way through this labyrinth of stumps, logs, and branches, here and there wielding his machete to ease our passage. In spite of this helpful gesture, we stumbled and fell many times. Not terribly far from here, over the next sun-scorched crest, is a spot where several years earlier (February 4, 1977), when the rain forest still blanketed these hills, I had a chance encounter with a pair of adult lantern flies, strangely sculpted and elusive relatives of the cicadas (Cicadidae) but in a different homopteran family, Fulgoridae. Charles L. Hogue, a colleague at the Los Angeles County Museum of Natural History, has studied the host tree associations of these creatures in Central America. The two large insects, each about ten centimeters long from bulbous, peanut-shaped head projection to the tips of its folded wings, were sitting side by side, ever so still in the daylight, on the trunk of a *Zanthoxylum* tree at the edge of the forest. Locals call the lantern fly *machaca*, and a charming bit of *tico* folklore is that if a girl is "stung" by this insect (the lantern fly does not sting), she must go to bed with her boyfriend within a day's time or else she will die! Even though lantern flies or peanut bugs are supposedly quite common in Costa Rica, I have not noticed many at all at La Tirimbina over twenty years. But today, that dome of rain forest is gone, replaced with cattle pasture.

The land seemed parched, washed in the dying hues of a rain forest, broad strokes of grays and browns, the profiles of mammoth tree trunks. Jorge and I were taking Jay and Sherm through a biological graveyard, through what I had seen from the jetliner more and more frequently in recent years—hills denuded of their veneer of nature, the rain forest now looking like piles of match sticks. How I never wanted to be a part of this, to walk through such a cauldron of wholesale death in a land I had come to love and cherish. The air was so still that afternoon as we labored on. I wished for a sign of life besides our heavy breathing and drenching sweat. Jay paused for rest and sat on a tree stump. Then I saw it, a very modest sign, a sliver of optimism amid this tragedy. It was a line of leaf-cutter ants along a log, disappearing into the thick mishmash of twigs, rotting leaves, and shadows at either end of the log, a few meters from where Jay sat. Where were these forlorn wanderers headed, out here in this land of death? These ants were our collegial sisters. Seeing them, moving very slowly and without leaf fragments, I could not help thinking about the death going on in the soil beneath us. For surely the life that once stirred in the soil, that nourished the rain forest that was no more, was dying. I traced the ants for a while, noting their perseverance, akin to ours, to forage along, but who knows to where?

Yet I admired the ants in a different way at this moment. They had purpose and direction, even here. Their instincts would try to lead them away from this death and toward a patch of healthy rain forest, perhaps the nearest one to this spot, a hefty half kilometer away as the toucan flies. But consider too this distance to travel for a column of ants! Eventually they might move their colony away from here, mesh themselves with the equilibrium of the undisturbed rain forest to which they rightfully belonged.

We would have greatly welcomed a breeze and a rain shower as we resumed our journey. Stopping at the crest of a hill and looking northward, we could see the crests of two more small hills on this folded landscape. Through the haze of heat, I could barely make out a thin wafer of dark green just peeking over the top of one of the distant crests. Jorge paused. "Jay and Sherm, look . . . that must be the big *roble* over there." Thirty minutes later and dog-tired, we arrived at the crest of that distant hill. There it was, a magnificent, stately being, still bursting with a promise of life, and reaching high out of the valley and into the sky. A mammoth tree, perhaps five or six centuries old. It just stood there, by itself, with only an occasional small palm tree beneath its huge expansive canopy. Thick rope lianas dangled down from its tallest limbs, which were festooned with epiphytes, including some tank bromeliads two meters across in size! We plunged down the hill, barely noticing the field hand, Julio, in his dark blue T-shirt, earnestly priming the chainsaw for the dreadful task given to him by the owner of this land, a business-man who lived in San José. Drawing closer, almost under the shadow of the tree's canopy, a domed roof of greenery, I could now see other, smaller trees growing out from the trunk of the tree, some very high up. The *roble* itself must have been fifty meters in height.

Aside from the dried branches crackling beneath our feet as we stumbled toward the spot, and Julio's priming of his instrument of doom, the valley was eerily silent. No toucans, parrots, or cicadas. No buzz of orchid bees. Farther down the valley, perhaps two hundred meters from where we now were, the rain forest still stood. It was a ribbon of green that now seemed strangely incongruous. Every time I visited these hills, the rain forest had been pushed back more and more. Soon there would be no more forest, save perhaps for narrow strips bordering steep *quebradas*.

Jay sat down again, breathing heavily, beet-red in the face. He was silent, head down, occasionally looking up to see when this final curtain call of wasteful tragedy would begin. Sitting there, he reminded me of that gnarled, pensive fisherman in *The Old Man and the Sea*. But out here, today, neither Jay nor the others came to conquer nature. We came to pay a last respect. Others had already sealed the fate of these foothills in Sarapiquí long before we set foot here. Ironically, Jay cooled himself in the only remaining shade, in the long shadows cast by the *roble*'s canopy. Even now, in its final moments, the *roble* replenished the spirit and body. I could not help admiring it, its full body exposed by the death that preceded it. The mammoth tree no longer stood proud in the rain forest. It was a sentinel to what once was, a terrible reminder of the majesty of Sarapiquí's nature, already lost forever. None of us could be upset with poor Julio working feverishly to start the chainsaw, for he was just doing his job. Nor could we stop, not even Jorge, what was about to happen.

The majestic and stately profile of this lone tree, rising as it did high above the twisted, rotting bramble everywhere, made me think about all the life this tree had supported during its multicentury lifespan. Later, it was Jay Reed, in an article for the *Milwaukee Journal*'s Sunday Magazine (May 15, 1983), who thought of the time depth of what was happening here this day—that this tree had started flourishing with the advent of Columbus. When Columbus first set foot on this isthmus, calling the land the "Rich Coast" (Costa Rica), this tree was already a vigorous sapling, perhaps a meter or two tall, straining upward through the pristine rain forest that once blanketed these hills with all manner of life. By the time a group of businessmen and lawyers met in Philadelphia in 1776 to forge a document that would chart the governing destiny of a new nation, the *roble* had already nursed millions of bacteria, thousands of caterpillars and leaf hoppers, and perhaps an occasional cicada nymph. When humankind first set foot on the moon two centuries later, the tree had long been home and food for thousands of birds, bats, monkeys, and snakes. Its festoon of bromeliads and orchids harbored whole microcosms, worlds within worlds of creatures, magnifying the biologically rich fabric of life that is Sarapiquí's rain forests. Yet even today, in spite of many years of research in the tropics, we still do not fully understand the complex interrelationships among organisms taking place within a single-meter stretch of canopy branch on a *roble* or other species of rain forest trees. Its massive *Philodendron* plants, with their dangling, pulpy fruits, had nourished legions of morphoes, which I am sure had paused in its shaded recesses to sip fermenting juices seeping from the fruit. How many ant colonies had also dwelled here? How many nests of stingless bees, the rain forest's most catholic of pollinators? What manner of life, microscopic and macroscopic, had existed beneath the tree's loosened sheaths of bark? How much life did the tree return to the Earth through the cycle of water exchange with the atmosphere?

The sputtering of the bright yellow chainsaw, being steadied in Julio's hand, quickly brought my thoughts back to the ground, where Jay and Sherm now sprang to attention. Soon the air around the base of the tree, where Julio shifted from one buttress to the next, the jumping chainsaw sinking deep into the *roble's* flesh, was filled with a powdery mist of yellowish sawdust. This was nothing compared to fifteen minutes later, when the tree came crashing down, sending up thousands of wood splinters, a cloud of dust, billions of tiny pieces of plant flesh blown apart by the impact. Below the bramble and ground cover in the merciless sun, this swift decapitation sent signals of trauma to the *roble*'s roots, shutting down forever that marvelous microorganism and fungus life support system that embraced the tree's roots with food as it had done for hundreds of years.

A magnificent life, a grand old goddess of the rain forest, a spot where cicadas called and morphoes soared, had died a most unnatural

A mammoth tropical rain forest canopy tree comes crashing down, seconds after the final cut with a chainsaw, near Finca La Tirimbina, during the dry season, 1983.

and unforgiving death. In the loud, crashing noise as it came to earth, it seemed to the three of us that the tree had screamed, sending a shivering death wail that echoed over these denuded hills and became muffled on the wall of rain forest in the distance. And none of us said a word for several very long seconds. We just stood there, frozen to the shaken earth, staring into a void of blueness where the *roble* had stood just moments before. Now the last tree was gone, the hills were clean, ready for the burn-off. When the silence was complete again, we turned and walked away from the carnage, whiffs of saw-dust now settling as a fine rose-hued patina on the rubble of twigs and branches beneath our feet. As we passed the crest of the first hill, I looked back one last time. The landscape had been truly trans-formed by the execution. That misty crescent of green that we had spotted earlier this morning, the slain giant tree's majestic dome peek-ing over the ridge, was gone. Everything now was in shades of brown, with no smudge of green to disrupt this harmony of non-life. Death of the life that once blanketed these rolling hills was now com-plete, a triumph of humankind's destruction of nature.

And now, much of that hilly terrain where the big tree once stood, itself one of hundreds interlaced by expansive canopies of lush foliage, no longer exudes that special fragrance of the intact tropical rain for-est, the dampened perfumery of its spongy leaf mulch on the ground. Now this ground is hardened and cracked by the baking rays of the tropical sun. Life has been snuffed out, even those legions of hidden players in the soil cover that once wrapped these hills with the prom-ise of life yet to be. But while there is still time, one must venture into the surviving patches of rain forest to sense the cycle of leaf mulch decay that helps fuel this habitat with the energy that seeds new life.

In such a place, when I am down on my knees next to the damp earth and leaf mulch with the cicadas screaming high overhead, crea-tures so seemingly disconnected from the movement of life stirring within the forest floor, I cannot help appreciating the biological rich-ness of the rain forest as an array of packages of life, some submicroscopic and beyond our imagination, others small yet noticeable, and some, of course, the charismatic obvious flora and fauna. One must seek to sense these interconnections if one is to fully appreciate the glory of life that exists in these pockets of remaining rain forest. Sarapiquí's earthy fragrances, the clinging dampness of life every-where, is as unmistakable as the hint of tropical fragrance that hits you stepping off the plane in the Meseta Central. Vesicles, some very tiny and others larger, cells and tissues, establish the movement of life hidden in the floor of Sarapiquí's rain forests. There can be no meaningful separations between the top of the rain forest, its sunlit dome, and its darkest depths. These forests thrive on life's smallest components, its legions of microorganisms and fungi. No wonder, then, that the dazzling *Morpho*, a creature of sunshine, spirals to the depths of the rain forest to feed on this decay, bridging two phases of the same world, and that even more intimately the calling cicada in the upper reaches of the rain forest is born in its deepest depths.

6

ALONG THE EDGES OF THE RAIN FOREST: PHARMACOLOGICAL BUTTERFLIES AND ORCHID BEES

La Tigra, one of the *fincas* formerly managed by Bob Hunter, includes a winding band of cacao trees between the road to Magsaysay and the tropical rain forest east of La Tirimbina. Where the cacao plantation meets old growth rain forest, there are dense thickets of vines and shrubs. Often you must cut through this profuse vegetation to enter the rain forest. Once you have done this, walking through the forest is almost as easy as exploring the cacao: in both places there is heavy shade, precluding the exuberant growth of vines and shrubs. But this is not so with the boundary zone between these two habitats. Here, there is relatively little shade, allowing for lots of photosynthetic activity close to the ground, producing an ecological zone of considerable intrigue for the field biologist. I came to spend many hours at this particular place on each of my stays at La Tirimbina over many years. In doing so I came to observe and explore the habits of some of the many kinds of insects inhabiting this ecological boundary between the cacao and the rain forest. Here, more than elsewhere in Sarapiquí, I learned about the unique ecological ties between certain insects and the chemistry of plants. Although I did not pursue these insects quite as fervently as I did the morphoes and cicadas, I came to appreciate through them some important aspects of tropical biology.

Not until you have journeyed on foot, horseback, or in a rattling jeep on the winding dirt and gravel road between La Tirimbina and the nearby Finca La Tigra do you get a gripping sense of what the gently rolling terrain of Sarapiquí is really about. On foot, this journey is a solid hour of thirsty, sweaty work, a good way to get in shape for a marathon. Virtually no destination in Sarapiquí is a straight or level shot, at least not in these foothills, a transitional zone between the *cordillera* west of here and the flattened floodplain to the east. Walking and driving through these hills gives you a sense of Sarapiquí's rich topographic heterogeneity.

The road connects La Virgen and the main road through Sarapiquí with the tiny settlement of Magsaysay near the Río Peje. Not until the 1950s, when Philippines President Ramón Magsaysay visited Costa Rica, did this former penal colony acquire a name. The other side of the broken, rotten bridge across *el Peje* is Braulio Carillo National Park land, including the La Selva Biological Reserve. From the air, this winding public-access road appears as a reddish, flat ribbon, a bold streak against the greenery, easy to negotiate on foot or by jeep. Twenty years of intermittent living out here tell me a different story. In a jeep, even with four-wheel drive, this road can be downright terrifying, even though it is only a twenty-minute trip between La Tirimbina and one of my favorite study sites where the La Tigra cacao meets the rain forest.

Especially during the long rainy season, the challenge of this road comes up quickly as I leave the La Tirimbina headquarters area. The road first climbs and cuts around a very steep hill, lined with black pepper vines to the right and a steep drop-off followed by secondary rain forest to the left. After many years of heavily laden logging tractors, hauling immense trunks of ancient rain forest trees from the interior, the entire road is now deeply gutted with multiple ruts. The first hill sets the pace for the rest of the journey. Even with four-wheel drive, the jeep often fishtails from one side of the road to the other, wheels spinning madly, golf-ball-sized lumps of red, oozing mud pelting the windshield and ricocheting off the doors and fenders with bullet fury. Coming down this hill on the return journey is sometimes even more hellish. There is little you can do to control the direction of movement of the heavy vehicle, its destiny more or less prescribed by the deep ruts which become little rivers in the heavy rains. Occasionally I have come down this hill part of the way with the jeep almost at a right angle to the road!

At the crest of the first hill, the terrain levels out for just a half kilometer or so before dipping steeply down around another hill. This pattern of following the contours of the hills continues for the rest of the way to La Tigra and beyond. One learns quickly not to brake too hard coming down a grade out here, for the jeep may

The first hill leading from the La Tirimbina farm to Finca La Tigra, along the road to Magsaysay. Going up or down this hill, even with a four-wheel-drive vehicle, can be quite a challenge in the rainy season.

lurch off the road completely or swing sideways. These are not easy situations to rectify once you are into them. Until recently, the jeeps I used did not have seat belts, so it was not uncommon to be tossed to and fro, from one side to the other, at rough points on such a road. Sometimes a terrifying lurch forward came when least expected, such as while going through what appeared to be a shallow muddy puddle where the road passed through a swale between hills. I would be charging ahead, thinking nothing of the puddle, only to find myself suddenly flung forward, hitting the windshield on rare occasion, and with a knot in my stomach—all of this a response to the unanticipated depth of the puddle as the jeep sank down deeply into it. More than once I have stalled the engine by such foolishness.

It did not take much more than a sudden lurch to one side of the soft road to create the big problem of being stuck in the deep, oozing mud here. *Finca* workers, passing by on foot, often stopped to help me push the heavy vehicle out of the mud. Once, many years ago, my jeep was stuck on a particularly difficult hill at La Tirimbina at night, an evening of incessant rain. A kind man whom I had known over the years of staying at the farm, Javier Angulo, became my salvation that night. After encountering me in the inky darkness, he walked a few miles to fetch a pair of oxen to pull the jeep out of the mud. It was this sort of very helpful assistance along these back roads that allowed me to continue with my research. People living in the *campo* of Sarapiquí were always willing to help me out, and I learned much about this wonderful aspect of these people on the long, winding public-access road between La Tirimbina and La Tigra.

Because of the challenge presented by the road, it was not for several years that I learned at which points along it I could risk peeking out to check for wildlife and scenery. And there were some delightful places along the road, especially where the rain forest almost closed over it, creating a deep shade, a cool respite from the blazing morning sun. In the early 1970s, when I started staying at La Tirimbina, both sides of this road were lined with dense stands of rain forest, evi-

Part of doing field research at Finca La Tirimbina and adjacent areas is getting stuck in the thick mud of the back roads.

denced in the old photographs I took here. But such scenes have long since been snuffed out here. Now many of these hills are little more than pale green scalps, cattle pastures, with little plots of bananas and *yuca* (manihot) and occasional giant trees in the swales, the latter stark reminders of what I once enjoyed here.

Years ago, it was only the occasional absentee *finca* owner from the Meseta Central who dared to journey out here on weekends with his family, for an overnight stay on the property being taken care of by local *campesinos*. Nowadays the roar of weekend motorcades is much greater as general commerce along the road has blossomed. The death of the rain forest has tracked the mushrooming of traffic and commerce along this little road. But even today I still meet country folk on horseback, making the journey to and from La Virgen for supplies and weekend recreation. While some of these people work the land for absentee *finca* owners, others are squatters or *parasitos* on someone else's *finca*, and more and more are start-up homesteaders. The Costa Rican government in recent years has set aside a large tract of land near this road to be available to those who wished to establish their own *fincas* or *parcelas*.

This road symbolizes now a land of marginal habitats, places where ecological anachronisms, organisms that once thrived in the rain forest, hold on ever so tenuously under new environmental challenges. Naturally what is seen here today is but a small fraction of the species once found within a short distance of the road. There is little evidence to suggest that there was once a majestic cathedral of life, the rain forest, thriving here. There are no arching spandrels, no gateways for the movements of sloths from one tree to the next, no intertwining networks of lianas, mats of epiphytic canopy debris, and interlocking crowns of giant trees. Today, in the rainy season, there is too much exposed grayness in the afternoon sky, or in the dry season too much sun-baking blueness, where there were once only hints of sky, fleeting smudges of lightness against a dark canopy of foliage. The struggle of nature here is now largely stunted, with hints of tenacity expressed by tender vines, with succulent, richly veined heart-shaped leaves, clinging here and there to the barbed-wire fences. Ashen-gray fenceposts of *manú* (*Minquartia quianensis*) are the new roadside sentinels. They stand bent over, like jagged stakes poking through the sea of grasses around them, where the big trees of the rain forest, its skyward-shooting pillars, once stood.

Can you begin to sense how dramatically this land has changed in a mere decade or two? The demise of life out here is written on these sun-scorched hills, in the baked red clay of this endlessly winding, rugged road. This was once a sacred place where I walked under a succulent canopy of life, a place where sun and shade, wetness and dryness, nature's universal gifts to life, were seemingly in harmony, in balance. Toucans and oropendulas clattered about in the

Pockets of old secondary rain forest, surrounded by expansive pastures strewn with the obvious reminders of when the forest stood tall: signs of the changing landscape of Sarapiquí within the last two decades. Shown here is a little homestead along the road to Magsaysay, beyond Finca La Tirimbina.

Along the road between La Tirimbina and Magsaysay, with Finca La Tigra on the right side of the road. This photograph was taken in 1976, at a time when the rain forest was being cleared away on the left side of the road. Today (1990), all of the area to the left of the road is cattle pasture.

trees above my head. Rare species of butterflies flitted across the sun-streaked road where dampness once reigned supreme. It seemed as if every few meters along this road were starkly different from those that came before and after. This road was once the binding of an elegant story book about nature, where different places, different turns, held the promise of new knowledge and discovery, each of these a chapter in the book. What I see out here today speaks of a sad ending. The epilogue is the sound of the tractor hauling huge tree trunks, of cattle crushing down invader species of exotic grasses that now swamp these hills. There are no more sultry nights out here where I once sat, on the fender of my parked jeep under a soft rain, to watch Sarapiquí's most spectacular light shows. These were nights, many years ago, when huge click beetles danced high above the road, their presence given away by the flashing of twin bioluminescent spots on their bodies—smudges of eerie brightness appearing and disappearing in the forest canopy that nearly closed over the road. Against the soft spatter of drizzle, the haunting cries of toads, and the metallic calls of tree frogs and katydids, the rain forest once stood here lit up in the inky darkness with these stunning silent flashes of soft glow.

And this was not a treat to be had every night—only at certain times of the year when the click beetles added their glowing presence to the blush of life that thrived in, defined this tropical rain forest. For these are seasonal insects whose natural history has barely been studied. What a magnificent story of life is inscribed in their wondrous, alluring bioluminescence. Now there is little chance here to explore it. Sometimes I netted one of these beetles, a brownish slender creature about four centimeters long, to capture the essence of its beauty close at hand. One of these beetles in a small jar created a pulsing lantern, almost enough to read by in my little room at the *galerón*. At other times of the year, the rain forest was speckled at night with the tiny lights of "fireflies," a different kind of beetle closely akin to the fireflies or "lightning bugs" of North American summer nights. But it is the giant bioluminescent click beetle, the one the Costa Ricans called *carbunclo*, that makes a lasting impression. Given what is known about click beetles in the temperate zone, most likely the larvae of the *carbunclo* dwell in rotting tree stumps and among decaying roots of old trees. Its existence is tied closely to the rain forest.

At a certain spot, where conditions were just right, a patch of lady's lips peeked through the brush at the margin of the forest. At a different place, the richly red blooms of a passionflower vine, *Passiflora vitifolia*, lay strewn on the low herbs along a trailbreak into the rain forest. And at each of these places, as at others, the butterflies and other creatures were different. The passionflower patch supported the caterpillars of *Heliconius cydno* and *H. hecale*, while the lady's lips, some distance away, fed these creatures as adult butterflies. The rain forest is this way, its different organisms scattered about providing multiple resources for other creatures, with survival hinging on the availability of the necessary resources for each kind of creature.

There is no doubt that I miss the melodies that once filled my days and nights along this road—the drumming of life itself. Today the winds carry no sound of calling insects, frogs, and birds, no soaring butterflies and hawks. The nights are now truly dark, all year long, for the *carbunclos* and their magical lights are long gone. Monotony and homogeneity have replaced the heterogeneity of life that once hugged this road. Yet today I forge ahead, convinced with a guarded optimism of sorts that there is still much to see and study

The lady's lips (*Cephaelis tomentosa*) understory shrub in the Sarapiquí rain forest. The two-part floral bract seen to the right is bright red, with the light central area (yellow) being the flower. The small tubular flowers are absent in this photograph. To the left, a second, expanded floral bract bears four fruits, which are blue.

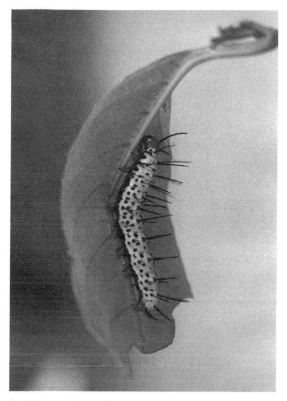

A *Heliconius* butterfly caterpillar on the underside
of a leaf of its *Passiflora* (passionflower) food plant
in the La Tigra rain forest.

—not in the cattle pastures and scalped hills, but where the "cacao
forest" at La Tigra meets the rain forest that still stands next to it.

To enter this band of cacao and make your way toward the rain
forest that stands beyond it, you must locate an old access road now
fenced off with barbed wire, near the eastern flank of Finca La Tigra.
Seldom did I drive my jeep beyond this point even in the dry season,
because the ground here is still so soft that the jeep would get stuck
very easily. I found this out soon after starting to do research here;

once it took six men to push my jeep out of the mud. Here, the road rises up a small grade as it curves to the left. Don Sisto, hired by Bob Hunter to oversee the La Tigra cacao, had a little wooden house (now rotted away) that sat up on the left side, at the apex of the bend in the road. Just before his house, the embankment had been shaved away years before, forming an entrance into the cacao grove. To reach it, I drive the jeep onto a grass-covered dirt road, passing on the right a *guava* tree that has been there for many years. I know this particular tree very well because every time I come by this point, I stop and check the tree for wasp nests.

This entire cacao plantation is more or less rectangular. At the point where I park the jeep and walk through the cacao, following another little road, this one little more than a grass-covered trail, the grove is about a half kilometer in width. One branch of the trail turns right and courses through the long axis of the cacao, while the other branch heads straight back to the rain forest. Don Sisto walked with me on this trail several times when I first started coming here. Near the site of his house, the cacao grove gives way to scrubby pasture-lands. Along another border, the hilly terrain is planted in black pepper. From where I park the jeep I can see the canopy of the rain forest looming up in the distance behind the cacao. I must bend down very low to crawl under the lowest string of the very taut barbed wire to resume my journey into the cacao, or to the rain forest beyond it. Before crawling under the wire, I throw over the fence my field pack, collecting gear, insect nets, and other equipment. Sometimes I even toss over this gate heavy sacks of rotting bananas used to bait butterflies in the rain forest. I believe that barbed wire is one of humankind's nastiest inventions. I cannot tell you how many scratches and ripped field shirts I have amassed over the years at this particular spot. Maneuvering through barbed wire is not a skill I have mastered very well. And it is not a quick task; usually it is done on all fours, face squashed down into the dirt, with face and hands in direct contact with swarming, irritating ants on more than one occasion. And take my word for it—there is little you can do to swat away hordes of stinging ants when you are halfway through barbed wire!

Just inside the barbed wire gate, in front of the embankment, there is a second *guava* tree. This tree grows off to the side of the trail leading back into the cacao. On this tree I have not found wasp nests as on the one outside the gate, but when this tree is shedding its pulpy yellowish fruit, its trunk becomes a stake-out point for "cracker" butterflies, *Hamadryas februa*. Usually I find one or two of these medium-sized butterflies perched, with their marbled gray and white wings stretched out perfectly flat against the smooth bark in the hottest hours of the day. They position themselves in the direct sunlight on the tree trunk, swiftly darting out at me as I walk by. Sometimes their aerial onslaught is accompanied by a loud clacking noise produced by the wings. At other times, it is a silent swipe within inches of my brow. These are pugnacious butterflies, for sure. This sort of assertive jitteriness is believed to be related to the courtship tactics of this species, and of the several others of this genus found in Costa Rica. Male "crackers" stake out an air space to be used for courting mates, and they defend these trysting spots against perceived intruders, even wandering field biologists and cacao field hands. The caterpillar of *Hamadryas* exudes a different kind of pugnaciousness, one seasoned by the manner in which it successfully feeds on the poisonous-latex-rich euphorbiaceous food plants that grow as pockets of weeds near this trail through the cacao.

Beneath the tree, the fallen *guava* fruits are crushed open, the work of passing livestock, horses, and people. The dark pink inner flesh of the smashed fruit, scattered in the grass, permeates the still air with a strangely sweet aroma with a touch of tanginess—a potent lure for hungry *Hamadryas*. The butterflies come to feed, sitting on the fruit with their wings held out flat against the ground, an unusual feeding posture for most butterflies. Many butterflies hold their wings in such a position only in the sunny early morning hours, a behavior that allows them to soak up the sun's heat—an essential act if the butterfly is to be thermodynamically warm enough to fly after a cool tropical night. Out here in the hot sun of the late morning and early afternoon, when the "crackers" are most active, there is little point to thermoregulating. Under this tree, in the openness of the cacao and bananas, the "crackers" have few to share the tangy crushed fruit with. The majority of butterflies that feed on rotting fruit, like the morphoes, satyrids, and brassolids, avoid the direct heat and dryness in favor of the damp coolness of the rain forest. When the fruits are gone, the "crackers" disappear from the tree; I know they will be back shortly after the next crop of *guava* blossoms forth next year. But this has not been the case at the other *guava* tree close by. Although this tree produces lots of fruits too, the "crackers" are absent from its trunk and fallen fruit.

There are several giant tree stumps of the old canopy trees closer to the rear of the cacao, within fifty meters or so of where the rain forest begins. They are blackened memorials of a time past, their outer surfaces festooned richly in creeping vines with great heart-shaped leaves. In the center of one of these stumps a little tree is growing, undoubtedly the result of a seed blown in or dropped here by a passing animal. These old stumps are still giving this place a sheen of life, even though they died perhaps two decades ago when the land was cleared for the cacao. In one of the stumps, I discovered a nest of stingless bees, *Trigona*, an amber-colored species with glossy green compound eyes. The nest's presence was given away by the cloud of silent bees hovering about the tree trunk; on closer inspection, I discovered a small waxen tube jutting out from a split in the trunk, the entrance-exit portal built by the bees to their honey-filled nest deep inside the trunk. This tube, less than ten centimeters long and as thick as a man's thumb, is sealed each night by the bees, presumably to keep out marauding army ants and other predators. On a different trunk, hidden from the trail in the thickness of the cacao branches and foliage, there is a huge termite carton nest, its dark rough exterior looking like a giant tumor on its long dead substrate. Yet this is a tumor of life, a colony of millions of termites, breaking down even further what little is left in the skeleton of the once mighty tree, and sending out debris-covered trails to discover other sources of decaying wood on which to feed. These tree trunks inspire me to believe that in existence there is really no death, no end point, for they are testimonials to this very fact of nature.

As I cut across this band of cacao, the sun is merciless. Even in the steely grayness of the afternoon skies, a preamble to the rain surely coming this way, the trail is bright compared to the darkness that looms beneath the cacao trees to either side of me as I walk along, always awkwardly carrying my field stuff. At some points, the monotonous grassy layer along the trail gives way to pockets of tall, woody plants with dark green, sandpapery leaves. This is *Solanum*

The resinous-tube entrance to a nest of a *Trigona* bee species in the La Tigra rain forest. Bees can be seen at the opening of the tube, which they fashioned from resinous material and secretions. The nest itself is hidden in a cavity inside the tree to which this tube is attached.

rugosum (Solanaceae). On these plants I am always certain to find some beautiful, metallic green, blue, and yellow grasshoppers. Could it be that these insects, in chewing on the leaves of this plant species, sequester noxious alkaloids contained in the plant's tissues? Of this I cannot be certain, but the bright colors of these insects, and their penchant to coalesce into little groups on the leaves, tells of a deeper story. I cannot resist the thought, as I watch these exquisite creatures, their metallic cuticle glistening in the sunlight, that they are distasteful to predators with good visual acuities. Every time I pass this spot, I look for the *Solanum* and check for the grasshoppers, which are usually there. They exhibit the curious habit of slowly rotating their positions to the opposite side of the leaf or stem as I approach, as if hiding from me.

There is one kind of ant that stands out on *Solanum* along the trail before the rain forest. It is a large purplish brown ant, *Ectatomma ruidim*. The workers, the ants seen roaming on *S. jamaicense* and other plants long this trail, are about the size of leaf-cutter ant workers, about a centimeter in body length. Thus they are easy to spot and make ideal subjects for studying the feeding habits of ants. *Ectatomma* is not a random wanderer on the brush. Tight knots of greenish leaf hoppers appear as little bumps on the thorny stems of *S. jamaicense*. As adults, the hoppers themselves resemble the green thorns. Typically I see clusters of ten or so hoppers, mostly the nymphs lacking the thornlike body profile of the adults. In some species, the nymphs are coated in a fluffy white flocculence, concealing their blackish or green bodies. These are small creatures, about five millimeters long. In clusters they become a bit more conspicuous. The leaf hoppers do not live alone on these plants, for in their midst I often find two or three *Ectatomma* ants, behaving as if shepherds tending their sheep. The ants carry between their strong mandibles a droplet of clear liquid, garnered, I believe, by stroking the abdominal plates of the feeding nymphs. The nymphs suck up plant sap, using a powerful stylet, and produce a sugar-rich exudate collected by the ants. Given that many kinds of insects and spiders occupy *S.*

A metallic-sheen grasshopper commonly found on *Solanum* plants in Sarapiquí.

jamaicense, including species that may graze on leaf hopper nymphs, which are wingless and incapable of rapid escape (except for running, jumping, or falling down), one can imagine there is strong selection pressure for leaf hoppers to capitalize on other kinds of protection.

Ectatomma is a noticeably pugnacious ant, rearing itself up instantly on its hindlegs and assuming a menacingly defensive posture aimed at the source of a perceived threat. It is one of the most commonly encountered ants associated with the extrafloral nectaries of many kinds of rain forest plants in Sarapiquí. *Ectatomma* is keen at chasing away many kinds of insects, ones that potentially could defoliate a plant, while protecting its own herd of nectar cattle. This is a marvelous story of compensatory evolution. What *S. jamaicense* lacks in extrafloral nectaries, it has in the form of leaf hopper herds, which, from the plant's standpoint, function as extrafloral nectaries. In both scenarios, the ants are enticed to stick around for an energy-rich reward, in exchange for keeping at least the stems of *S. jamaicense* relatively herbivore-free. Within the cacao, where natural vegetation joins the trees, there is much to appreciate about tropical nature in Sarapiquí. There are many more questions here than answers, many more avenues of intense research than one biologist has time for in the field. Every plant holds a special story, of the insects feeding on it, of others defending it within the context of a mutualistic gain for both, and of other creatures that come to the plant to feed on the insects there. And no two species of plants hold the same story, for the players are often different as is the natural history of each one.

At certain times of the year, the coarse leaves of *S. rugosum* are skeletonized by the gregarious caterpillars of an ithomiine butterfly, *Hypothyris euclea*—a slender-winged butterfly with tiger-striped wings of orange, yellow, and black. Scattered throughout the La Tigra cacao are openings in the grove where *S. rugosum* grows in clumps, reaching a height of one and a half meters or so. *Hypothyris* females do not lay their rafts of tiny eggs on tender meristem leaves; rather, the eggs are carefully placed in neat rows to form tight clusters, on the undersides of the older, tough-textured leaves. The youngest caterpillars feed by scraping away the mesophyllic layers of the leaf tissue, and only when they are bigger do they chew all the way through the leaves. The caterpillars are striking objects in their own right when full-grown, being slender of form and streaked crosswise with bold stripes of alternating yellow, light blue, white, and black. Although the *Solanum* food plant is often stripped clean of leaves, the adult butterflies are seldom very numerous, perhaps a result of intervening ecological factors that thin out the populations, or well-expressed dispersal tendencies. The metallic grasshoppers on this plant species do not seem to defoliate the many scattered clumps that riddle the cacao plantation every year when I visit this site.

As I approach the band of brush forming a thin boundary between the cacao and the rain forest, I begin to see other kinds of insects;

even here, at the edges of the rain forest, biological diversity is humming away. Brownish crickets weave and dart across my field boots in places where the trail is clear and I can see my feet. Boldly spotted black and white jumping spiders spring from one leaf to another with lightning speed. Others, metallic green and black or orange and black, catch my eye as I gently part tangles of unknown plants that come up to my waist. Before me, I can see where the little trail starts to disappear into the forest, and the land now rises steeply to my left and more gently to the right. The rain forest, from a few meters' distance, appears from this perspective as a straight-cut wall rising fifteen to thirty meters above the ground. Farm workers, armed with stone-sharpened machetes, have kept the rain forest from spewing out its citizenry into the cacao. The breakway into the forest in front of me is barely perceptible, for vegetation presses closely along the sliver openings and the muted shade beyond—the rain forest understory. It has been about three months since this margin of dense brush was last chopped, I guess to myself, and the place is teeming with insects.

Just from where I stand, I can see the nymphs of at least three species of grasshoppers scurrying across the vegetation near my feet. A pale green katydid, *Orophus tesculata*, not unlike its North American counterparts, struggles to hide under a leaf as I poke the brush with the handle end of my insect net. This species occurs here in several distinct color morphs, including brown, tan, and pink. I am told by David A. Nickle, a leading expert on Neotropical katydids at the Smithsonian Institution, that this species exhibits a genetic polymorphism. I have seen the pink morph only once. Is each color morph adapted to a different ecological niche in the rain forest? No one knows for sure. And in spite of its color, the pink morph is surprisingly cryptic, as are the other nymphs.

It is during the long rainy season in Sarapiquí that I find the adults of *Orophus* most numerous along the trail leading into the rain forest. Even with their leaflike appearance, the hopping or flying katydids become very noticeable as I part the brush. *Orophus* is a katydid of the lower reaches of the rain forest. Only on rare occasion here have I spotted a canopy katydid, *Aegimia elongata*, with its incredible flattened green wing covers sporting tiny brown spots resembling rust spots or insect bites. The upwardly curved hornlike projection at the front of the head resembles a leaf petiole, and when the insect is frightened, it may drop on its side and lie motionless, as if a freshly fallen leaf. When I see *Aegimia* I think to myself how very much I wish this rain forest would share with me more fascinating glimpses of itself. There is not enough time to see it all, to come even close to what actually lives here. If I were to spend any time here, at the edge of the rain forest, looking closely at just a small patch of the brush, I would surely get a sense of the immense biological diversity inherent in Sarapiquí and rain forests in the Americas in general. Beneath my feet, the plant life supports a miniature world of leaf hoppers, leaf beetles, aphids, ants, and other creatures—each group represented here by many species of varying sizes, colors, and habits. One can get a sense of the species richness out here, even in places where the forest canopy is inaccessible.

I can sense too the change in the complexion of this land as I leave behind the cacao and approach the forest. To the right of the break into the forest, there stands a small cluster of *Heliconia* plants, *H. latispatha* I believe, with their large pendent red inflorescences, rotted and studded, at certain times of the year, with small shiny black seeds. Now the land is cool and subdued, and the footpath soaked with a perpetual dampness that never seems to go away. In order to enter the forest, I must bend down beneath low-slung branches festooned with herbaceous vines belonging to at least three species. Just beyond this portal, the vegetation is now up to my shoulder, forming a narrow passage that continues for about twenty meters before thinning out into the understory of older secondary rain forest. Every time I pass through this break into the forest, I am over-whelmed by the maddening number of plant species, all entangled together and filled with many kinds of insects. At first, what I see seems to defy order and pattern. Seldom is there a lot of one kind of insect within a small stretch of vegetation-enclosed path to give a quantitative understanding of how this particular species relates to the rest of the forest. But with time, patience, and good observation skills, one can begin to see the ordered structure of tropical nature, taken one species, one ecological association, at a time. Where the rain forest looms high overhead, and where deep shade cascades down over a large bed of *Heliconia*—a species different from the one on the boundary of the forest and cacao—is the place where I have baited morphoes and conducted studies on cicadas.

On one particular morning, as I eased my way slowly through the dense brush and thorny vines along this path, the sunlight, a speckling of brightness struggling down to the lower strata of the forest, took on a peculiar personality. Sunlight swept across my area of vision, becoming a dancing staccato of gold against the dark roof of foliage as I looked skyward. I could feel a light rain sprinkling down from high above, an ever so gentle tickling of silvery and golden powder on my face and hands. Yet, still, this was a sunny morning. Velvety *Parides* butterflies, just one or two, glided in and out of focus just above my head, the iridescent greenish splotches on their hindwings capturing the dazzling light mixed with rain and throwing it into my face. Farther inward, I reached a point where translucent-winged ithomiine butterflies suddenly swirled around in the open air space along the path, obviously agitated by my encroachment on their turf. The presence of these small, slender-winged insects was disclosed to me by little more than slivers of silver glistening from their wings, like shimmering fragments of cellophane snared on a puddle of oil and water—dancing pieces of shiny foil reflecting transient hues of color. This vignette of staggering beauty, creatures gliding through the stagnant air among corridors of lush foliage and the patter of an almost invisible rain, was fashioned from the sun and foliage, and the pocket of many butterflies took me quite by surprise.

I noticed that one of the ithomiines resettled quickly on a plant near the ground, just ahead of me where the path widened out. Making a very slow approach to the perched butterfly, I noticed that it had landed on a lighted spot on a leaf, and that its proboscis was extended and inserted into a crystalline droplet, what I presumed to be a drop of rainwater. I was intrigued that the butterfly retained this posture for several minutes, compelling me to believe the creature was actually drinking or feeding. But water? Then it occurred to me. That sprinkle of water on my face signified rain being washed down from the canopy of the rain forest. Do droplets of presumed rainwater splashed on leaves near the forest floor carry a treasure of chemical, perhaps even nutritive, exudates gleaned by the rain high above the forest floor? And do deep-forest-dwelling butterflies, such as many species of ithomiines, tap this resource, perhaps drawn to it by aromatic substances contained in the droplets washed from leaves and branches in the rain forest canopy? Does the rain forest canopy in this way somehow "feed" creatures of the lower depths of this forest? Had I not accidentally disturbed the ithomiines along the path, I would not have noticed the resettling butterfly and its apparent feeding on the water droplet.

Where the hill rises to the left of this trail, the cacao comes right up to within a few meters of the forest edge. Stepping into the forest on the crest of that hill, there is no margin of dense young secondary growth or "jungle." It is only here in the swale that you find such a transition, where a logging exploration trail was blazed several years ago by the owner of this property, Carlino Quesada, who lives in La Virgen. Don Carlino and his men thinned out the forest around this spot, creating, in essence, a large light gap at the edge of the rain forest. After the cutting, the place was left alone, allowing secondary forest to develop on the thinned-out parcel. The trail they made through the forest still exists today, leading back about a thousand meters to another large light gap or cleared area well inside the forest. But none of this occurred on top of the hill. Farm hands chop away the grass and weeds that engulf the cacao trees here and throughout La Tigra. They use very long machetes, which they wield by stooping over very low to sweep the sharp blades as close as possible to the ground. The contrast between the forest and the cacao along this slope is especially striking because of this. The *peones* must work around several huge tree trunks, felled fifteen or twenty years ago, that lie on the open ground among the cacao trees, next to the rain forest. These very large logs are now deeply dark brown, rotted on the outside but, judging from my probing with a machete and knife, still very hard inside. Each of these logs is a microcosm of tropical nature. One in particular has a lace network of herbaceous vines growing over it, perhaps three or four species, and tiny ferns growing out of it. At certain times of the year, various mushrooms, some bright orange and others creamy white or sooty gray, festoon the logs. One of these mushrooms, about fifteen centimeters across, has a whitish fruiting body with leaflike projections from its otherwise flat fruiting body on the log. The undersides of the lamella-like projections are often coated with many tiny flies, including Drosophilidae and Mycetophilidae. The mushroom is a breeding site for many of these flies, which consist of several dozen species as I watch them. Under a hand lens, some of these flies are marvelously fashioned creatures, with tiger-striped compound eyes, mottled wings, and sculpted body cuticle. I suspect many species oviposit in the soft tissues of the mushroom, and that their larvae feed on it.

There are also many kinds of tiny beetles present on the fresh tissues of the fungus, some harlequin-colored in orange and brown under the lens. There is much life to be found here, packed onto and inside a single mushroom. In death, the fruiting body and the exudates left behind by these insects and other creatures become food for worlds within worlds of protozoans and other microorganisms. Inside these rotting logs, life is drumming on as well. The larvae of buprestid, scarab, and passalid beetles gnaw their way slowly through this corpse of a once giant rain forest tree. Even in its death, enforced at the hand of men, this tree is sprouting new life, a thousand-strong legion of creatures, most of which are invisible to the naked eye. What the mushrooms attached to the log do to the wood is what the insect grubs, even the grubs of giant flies, are

When encountering a rotting log embraced by ghostly white bracket fungi in the rain forest, it is compelling to see the bigger picture. Fungi and wood-chewing beetle grubs in the log garner energy from the log, allowing their own survival. Many kinds of rain forest insects, including morphoes, may disperse the spores of such fungi, the rain forest's agents of decay.

doing on the inside of it—returning its locked nutrients and minerals to the fragile soil. New life yet to be born, and ancient life, giant trees that exist closely by, may suck their sustenance from this cycle of slow decay. In the rain forest, some trees rot quicker than others, imposing a heterogeneity upon the availability of such energy for other creatures. Heterogeneity in growth, form, and life style is the binding secret of the tropical rain forest's existence.

Behind these fallen tree trunks, blackened now with many cycles of tropical heat and rain, the rain forest begins as a majestic curtain.

Near the apex of the hill, a giant tree fern, its huge fronds jutting out into the open space of the cacao, competes in height with a six-meter-tall tree trunk, snapped off, encased in huge philodendrons. Several species of large trees, their identities unknown to me, form an almost even row along the slope. Metallic-sheen hummingbirds dart in and out of a large patch of blooming *Heliconia* when the sun is bright. "Zip, zip, zip," they go, a pleasant sound against the thudding of machetes in the brush, wielded by *peones* hidden by the cacao foliage. Human life is juxtaposed ever so close to nature along this margin of the rain forest. When I try to enter the forest along the slope, rather than on the trail, I encounter a wiry, nettled mass of brambles—a mix of fallen palm tree fronds and understory plants that form a threshold of vegetation one must cross. Many times, when I do this, my pants become covered with some kind of seed stickers—an effective seed dispersal mechanism adapted to roving mammals such as tapirs and peccaries. As I walk along the edge of the forest, without entering it, sometimes I flush up from the brush thousands of tiny brownish moths of unknown species. If I turn around and face out over the cacao, from one particular open spot where a couple of these trees have succumbed to disease, I see an expanse of reddish green canopy leaves for as far as the eye can see, the La Tigra cacao *finca*. I am standing on one of the highest points in the *finca*. In the late afternoons, I can see from here the rain clouds building in the east, heading this way.

There are certain places along the border between the cacao and rain forest where the cacao trees are quite old, their blackish branches twisted and gnarled, seemingly overburdened with an interlocking lacework of epiphytes and parasitic plants. Here, under these partic-ular patches of trees, you encounter a springy, squishy leaf mulch, its reddish earthtone hues highlighted here and there by a dabble of sunlight struggling down through the "canopy" only a meter or two above your head. The sun catches a smorgasbord of scattered seedlings, a carpet of broken verdancy superimposed on earthtones of soft brown. Many of these little plants, struggling upward to reach the sunlight, display succulent heart-shaped leaves. This cacao understory at La Tigra, especially near where the plantings skirmish with the rain forest, is a rich salad of baby philodendrons, pipers, cucurbits, and Dutchman's pipe vines. It is the latter that are of particular interest.

Even at a relatively short distance, the Dutchman's pipe, seedlings of rain forest woody lianas belonging to the large family Aristolochiaceae, catch my eye. I have seen many times that butterflies are drawn to these *Aristolochia* vines, but only a particular kind of butterfly. It is a creature of the neighboring rain forest, one that appears very swiftly, descending or swooping low into this mock understory of cacao trees, then exits just as quickly. The butterfly navigates exquisitely through this maze of upright black sticks, guided by a complex, sophisticated sensory apparatus, a repertoire of keen visual perception and responsive motor skills. This is one of Sarapiquí's most beautiful creatures, a *Parides* butterfly. The flecks of sunlight illuminate its moving patchwork of vibrant colors, a stark contrast to the muted earthtones of everything else around it. What I see here is the female butterfly, easily recognizable by the very distinctive colors of its full, expansive wings. This medium-sized butterfly seems bigger than it is every time I watch one glide along. In both sexes, the ground color of the wings is a satiny black, adorned in the female with a vibrant crimson splotch on each hindwing and a large, roundish cream spot on each forewing. In males, the cream patch on the forewing is replaced with a triangular splash of vivid, sometimes iridescent green. *Parides*'s colors, including its black body sporting red dots, speaks of darkness and lightness, a medley of foreboding and optimism. And *Parides* has a special story to tell, chapters of which I have learned in Sarapiquí over many years.

Because this *finca* is crisscrossed with many little dirt roads and homesteads, it is not uncommon to find butterflies of the rain forest, including *Parides*, flying through these human-generated habitats. But to study the biology of these butterflies, one must seek them out inside the forest and along its margins. These are the places where most of the adult food sources and caterpillar food plants of many Sarapiquí butterflies are found. In the cacao I see only a few male *Parides*, but females come and go very frequently—fervent transients looking for egg-laying sites. *Parides* is in the cacao because *Aristolochia* is the sole food plant of its caterpillar, a purplish brown or maroon larva studded with fleshy tubercles. These vines grow along the margins of the rain forest and in its light gaps. Here these butterflies also find various nectar sources, giving them the energy and sustenance needed to court, mate, and lay their eggs.

Parides and a closely related genus, *Battus*, belong to the troidine swallowtail butterflies, a globally distributed but chiefly tropical (excluding Africa) group whose caterpillars feed solely on Aristolochiaceae. In Sarapiquí live two species of *Battus*, both large butter-

A pharmacological swallowtail, *Parides* species, adult stage, at Finca La Tirimbina.

flies, the widespread familiar *B. polydamas* with its expansive black wings decorated above with rows of yellow dots, and *B. belus*, with greenish, powdery blue markings on the upper side of its hindwings and a light blue or greenish white hue to its abdomen, especially in the male. The *Parides* of Sarapiquí are a complex of four or five taxonomically somewhat confusing species, all of strikingly similar appearance (especially the females), of which I have seen *P. arcas, P. iphidamas, P. childrenae,* and the seemingly rare *P. erithalion.* The first three of these are familiar citizens at my La Tigra and Padre Núñez study sites. With their bold wing colors, their good size, and their habit of thriving in rain forest clearings, *Parides* seem to be archetypal residents of the tropical rain forest.

To begin to understand these butterflies, you must consider their caterpillar food plant. Rain forests in Central America and South America provide animals with many kinds of resources. In some cases

Final-instar caterpillar of *Parides iphidamas* on its food plant, *Aristolochia constricta.*

the relationship is a never-ending tug-of-war between herbivorous species and their food plants, in others a cooperative, often mutualistic partnership between flowers and pollinators, seeds and dispersal agents, plants and symbionts—ecological interconnections evolving over very long periods of time. This is the evolutionary interplay that has graced the edges and light gaps of Sarapiquí's rain forests with the beauty of *Parides*. These creatures have helped me understand the basic principle of life's great diversity in the tropical rain forest, that of tightly woven links of plant-animal interdependence that shapes the living infrastructure of this habitat. These butterflies are among nature's catalytic agents, channeling biologically reactive substances through the rain forest's food chains.

Consider the following axiom. While virtually all living green plants are basically nutritious in terms of their profiles of carbohydrates, fats, and proteins, different groups of plants, and different species or other taxa within these groupings, are not at all equally edible. For the largest segment of the insect herbivore community in tropical forests, the Aristolochiaceae are essentially inedible. This is due to the fact that aristolochias are vastly pharmacological, their living tissues loaded with formidable titers of noxious substances, called "secondary plant substances" or "defensive compounds" because they have virtually nothing to do with the primary metabolism of the plant and everything to do with how plants protect themselves against herbivore attack, especially from the most ubiquitous herbivores, the insects. Many kinds of plants, especially those of the tropics, synthesize and store such substances, and more than 10,000 of them, all with varying pharmaceutical complexions, have already been identified by biological chemists.

The aristolochias are especially unique in this regard since their chief toxic elements, the "aristolochic acids," are found only in them. Because of plant secondary substances in particular, it is no wonder that the tropical forest is often referred to as a vast library of natural chemical diversity. Because green plants are sitting targets for animals to eat, and since virtually nothing in nature is spared from becoming food for other creatures, noxious defensive chemicals, mostly synthe-sized *de novo* by the plant rather than obtained from the environment, play significant roles in helping plants survive the onslaught of herbi-vore attack. *Parides*, *Battus*, and the other troidine swallowtails else-where in the world have won this ecological contest with their *Aristolochia* caterpillar food plants. But most of the many millions of other herbivores in the tropical rain forests of Central America, South America, and the Caribbean basin have failed to do so.

"Aristolochia" is derived from the Greek *aristos* meaning "best" and *locheia* meaning "childbirth"; ancient people used pulverized dried leaves of these vines as the "aristocrat" of medicines adminis-tered during childbirth. Common names of *Aristolochia* such as "pipevine" and "Dutchman's pipe" refer to the twisted brownish or purplish flowers oddly curved into the profile of smoking pipes. The potent chemical substances found in these vines, including volatile sesquiterpenes and an isoquinoline alkaloid, in addition to aristolochic acid, have prompted a broad range of folk medicine uses over the centuries, including as a remedy for snakebite, bacterial infections, arthritis, malaria, internal parasites, scabies, ulcers, pneumonia, ty-phoid fever, typhus, and menstrual cramps. Ingestion of *Aristolochia* by humans leads to nausea, vomiting, distention of the abdomen, salivation, and headaches. It has even been reported that extracts of aristolochic acid alone significantly reduce the growth of certain kinds of cancer in laboratory mice. "Aristolochic acids" have been used in medical research to explore the physiology of cardiac arrest and respiratory failure in mice, and their potential as biological insecti-cides has also been studied. *Aristolochia* leaves are brewed by South American Indians to make curare arrow poisons used in hunting.

The unusual flowers of *Aristolochia* also point to these vines being different from many other kinds of plants. The flowers generally exude a musty fragrance that attracts various kinds of small flies, including ceratopogonid midges, phorids, muscids, and otitids. These insects include the pollinators of *Aristolochia*. Pollination is effected by sapromyophily, involving deceit since *Aristolochia* flowers do not produce an obvious nectar secretion. The flowers are designed to lure and trap pollinating flies by deception. The outer portion of the flower in some species of *Aristolochia* resembles the ear of a small-sized mammal, thus attracting blood-sucking species of ceratopogonids, the so-called "biting midges." Some kinds of biting midges are attracted to mammalian ears, homing in on the gradient of warmth exuded into the air from tufts of capillaries just under the surface of the skin. In many species of *Aristolochia* the flowers are richly streaked and splotched in shades of brown, deep red, and pink—somewhat reminiscent of mammalian blood. Duped midges, lured by visual illusion, land on the floral tube rather than on a mammalian epidermis carpeted with fine hairs. The midge or other fly tumbles down into the flower, and its escape is prevented by dense rows of strategically placed, downward-pointing hairs lining the lower reaches of the inner surface of the twisted floral tube.

Typically *Aristolochia* flowers are protogynous, that is, their stigmas mature two or three days before their anthers. Thus the hermaphroditic flower is functionally female first and later functionally male; during the female stage the flower becomes a fly trap. During this time of captivity trapped midges or flies bite through tissues in the basal chamber of the flower and feed on a nectarlike exudate. In some species of *Aristolochia* the flowers have translucent, windowlike areas in the basal chamber wall that help attract midges to the stigmas and stamens. Flies crawl over the stigmas during their prison time, and a couple of days later the anthers dehisce and the trapped insects pick up pollen grains on their stout bristles. At this time the "prison bars," those downward-pointing hairs, wilt as a result of hydrostatic changes in the floral tube tissue, thus allowing the pollen-caked flies to crawl up the tube and fly away. From this brief and sketchy account, distilled from a handful of studies chiefly on temperate-zone species of *Aristolochia*, it is clear that a pollinating insect must fall into not one, but two different flowers in order for successful pollination to take place. The protogynous habit of the flower prevents self-pollination and promotes outcrossing, since the stamens of a flower do not become functional until after the stigmas have already been fully receptive and the pollen tubes, the result of successful pollination, have already begun growing toward the ovaries. The elegant studies of B. J. D. Meeuse have elucidated the most fascinating physiological aspects of dipteran-pollinated flowers, including *Aristolochia*. For example, Meeuse discovered that tiny pores in the basal chamber wall of the flower permit the timed release of water vapor from tissue cells into the chamber, the "midge prison," to keep midges at an appropriate level of humidity needed for their survival!

Luko Hilje reported in the Museo Nacional's natural history journal *Brenesia* in 1984 that the huge flowers of *Aristolochia grandiflora* in Costa Rica are pollinated chiefly by muscids, otitids, and phorids, and that withering flowers encourage a succession of other arthropods, akin to what is found in the decay of vertebrate carrion. Very little is known about the degree to which individual species of these midges are specialized pollinators of certain kinds of rain forest plants including aristolochias. My hunch is that many species of ceratopogonids and other floral diptera are more generalist than ecological specialist in their floral associations. But one thing is certain, *Aristolochia*-specialist herbivores such as *Parides* and *Battus* depend on ceratopogonids and other floral dipterans for their survival, for without adequate levels of successful pollination, there would not be sufficient local supplies of their caterpillar food plant. Where the vines are absent, so are these butterflies. To know the butterflies is to appreciate the tiny midges or gnats and small flies that intermediate the sex habits of *Aristolochia* vines.

Stated differently, ceratopogonid midges and other diptera ensure the genetic integrity of *Aristolochia*, for it is through the vehicle of pollination that each kind of plant, particularly those with outcrossing, continually adapts to the changing environment, of which herbivore pressure is a very large component in the tropical rain forest. *Aristolochia* vines in Sarapiquí occur as scattered individuals, not big clumps, necessitating further the movement of pollen from one vine to another some distance from the first one, by tiny midges and small flies, which can be very strong fliers. The mature seeds of *Aristolochia*, each one a remarkable flattened, feather-light tiny disc, are blown about by the gusts and winds coming in from the Caribbean. These rain forests, and all that dwell in them, that comprise them, are constantly being shaken by the wind and rain: giant trees toppling, light gaps appearing and disappearing, *Aristolochia* vine seeds being jostled free of their thin-walled pendent fruit capsules to start new vines. These are processes shaping too the destiny of *Parides* and *Battus*, *Aristolochia*-specialist predators or parasites whose stout, tentacled caterpillars have evolved to know that theirs is a world of only one thing, the taste and touch of *Aristolochia* tissue, be it leaf, flower, or green developing fruit (seed capsule).

It is along partially shaded paths, rain forest borders with young secondary growth, or where a path cuts through dense, older secondary forest, that one finds the parent *Aristolochia* vines. They hang down, draped over taller trees, their presence almost indistinguishable from the riotous pattern of foliage cascading down. You have to look closely and patiently to detect their foliage. The aristolochias here have big heart-shaped leaves, dark green and splotched above the lichens and mosses. You might be lucky enough to catch a glimpse of the vine's newest growth, beautiful lemon-yellow greenish leaves. When viewed from behind and with the sun illuminating their top sides, these new-growth leaves show off a delicate network of veins sticking out like little crisscrossing ridges, giving the undersides of both new leaves and mature ones a slightly dull silvery luster. The upper sides of the leaves are smooth and glossy, almost platelike. I often spot the woody adult vines, amongst the dozen or so other species of vines they grow with, by the unusual, unforgettable seed capsules. These roundish, somewhat ellipsoid structures, each one filled with hundreds of small flattened, paper-thin seeds (each one about 15 x 9 x .05 millimeters in *A. constricta*) stacked like potato chips, are dark brown when mature, splitting their lengthwise seams in several places. When young and not yet ready to shed their seeds, the capsules are green. The splitting process retains the general profile of the seed capsule while creating wide spaces allowing ready dispersal of the packaged seeds inside, no doubt aided by wind and rain. While the seeds look unattractive to animal dispersal, ripe seed pods kept in my field station room at La Tirimbina have been eaten by rats on occasion. The flowers of *Aristolochia*, especially the huge ones of *A. grandiflora*, are a rare treat when discovered in the wild. I have not seen them many times at all. No doubt I might have missed the green and purplish flowers of species such as *A. constricta* and *A. pilosa* dangling in the muted shade of the rain forest, but not the reddish, purple, and green flowers of the impressive *A. grandiflora*.

Because *Parides* and *Battus* caterpillars feed on plants highly repellent to most insects and collect and store (sequester) these plants' potent chemical weaponry in their own body tissues, they are rightfully called "pharmacological" or "pharmacophagous" butterflies. In storing the plant's poisons, snagged, tagged, and shunted by the insect's digestive chemistry, they cloak themselves in their own veil of acquired repellency (even though at a high metabolic cost), which is then passed along the life cycle to the insect's adult stage.

It was at La Selva in 1968 that I first became interested in pharmacological butterflies such as *Parides*. Not long after first arriving there, I walked down the trail from the old building with Daniel Janzen, who pointed out *Parides* as we approached an opening filled with dense vegetation. At the time he mentioned that a great discovery in science would be to determine whether or not these butterflies obtained their supposed distastefulness to predators from their *Aristolochia* caterpillar food plants. At that time I also received information on these butterflies from Woodruff ("Woody") Benson and Thomas Emmel, two butterfly ecologists who were already familiar with these species.

Several years earlier, in a now classic research paper published in *Zoologica* (1964), Lincoln P. and Jane Van Zandt Brower reported the unpalatability of adult *Parides* butterflies in Trinidad to captive blue jays, arguing that this strong distastefulness derived from the caterpillars being specialist herbivores on the toxin-rich leaves and

Aristolochia constricta, with pendent heart-shaped leaves, at Finca La Tigra.

stems of their *Aristolochia* food plants. This research by the Browers was built in large part upon their earlier discovery that the North American troidine swallowtail *Battus philenor* was also highly distasteful to captive blue jays. Later, the Browers and Phillip Corvino reported in the 1967 *Proceedings of the National Academy of Sciences* that cabbage-reared monarch butterflies (*Danaus plexippus*) lacked the distastefulness of milkweed-fed monarchs when both groups were offered as food to captive blue jays. The birds readily ate the cabbage-fed butterflies and rejected the ones reared on milkweeds, the monarch's natural caterpillar food plant. The natural phenomenon of a living creature deliberately feeding on something poisonous is quite uncanny, when you think about it. Even more startling is the fact that this unusual feeding behavior actually enhances the survival of the species in its natural environment!

Creatures such as *Parides* butterflies provide some outstanding examples of how chemistry binds together the webs of life here. Research studies on Old World troidine butterflies in particular, such as *Ornithoptera* (the "birdwing butterflies"), *Troides*, and *Pachlioptera*, by J. von Euw, T. Reichstein, and M. Rothschild, have revealed that aristolochic acids, benzylisoquinoline alkaloids, sesquiterpenes, and other defensive substances are the principal pharmacological agents in *Aristolochia* that are taken up by the caterpillars of troidines. In clinical studies, aristolochic acids have been shown to have pharmacological effects on vertebrates and to inhibit feeding in some insects. Yet *Parides*, *Battus*, and other *Aristolochia* specialists among the troidine swallowtail butterflies utilize these substances as feeding stimulants and as a powerful chemical weaponry against some kinds of natural enemies.

A highly simplified account of what happens in the digestive system of a *Parides* caterpillar feeding on *Aristolochia* is as follows. The ingested, shredded leaf tissue is mixed with digestive tract juices under the proper conditions of alkalinity or acidity to allow digestion to proceed. Digested nutrients are absorbed through the gut wall into the haemolymph (blood) cavity and eventually stored in body tissues, where they are drawn upon to fuel cellular metabolism, the basis for growth. From the standpoint of the remarkable dependence of these pharmacological butterflies on the poisonous Aristolochiaceae, an exciting drama unfolds in the digestive tract having nothing to do with the uptake of nutrients. Specialized catalytic agents called "detoxification enzymes" work over and modify the aristolochic acids and other secondary substances, rendering the caterpillar immune to their inherent toxicity while mobilizing them into forms that can be passed through the gut wall to be stored in body tissues. It is this sequestration of plant poisons in the caterpillar's body tissues that renders the insect potentially distasteful to certain kinds of predatory animals. As these substances are carried forth through the life cycle into the adult butterfly, this noxiousness, derived directly from the food plant of the caterpillar, is advertised in the adult through warning or aposematic coloration—usually some gaudy combination of red, yellow, orange, green, etc., in various groups of insects. *Parides*'s striking wing colors are classically aposematic in this regard.

Because plants, particularly those in tropical forests, have evolved a broad array of toxic chemical defensive substances against insects, including alkaloids, cardiac glycosides, phenolics, and mustard oils, insects, in response, have developed different kinds of detoxification enzymes, "midgut oxidases," to modify and sequester particular kinds of plant chemical defenses. Some insects, capable of feeding on several different kinds of plants, are equipped with "jack-of-all-trades" mixed-function oxidases, whereas specialist insects restricted to one kind of food plant have a certain midgut oxidase to handle the chemical defenses of that plant.

Having the physiological talent of being able to feed on a toxic plant does not necessarily lead, ipso facto, to an insect being distasteful to predators. While some species of heliconiine butterflies most certainly sequester potent alkaloids from their passifloraceous caterpillar food plants, others do not, even some that share the same food plant species. In these instances, the noxious elements from the food plant, while undoubtedly functioning as important gustatory cues for caterpillar feeding, are not detoxified and absorbed (sequestered) into the body tissues but rather excreted as waste material—usually because the detoxification enzymes required for sequestration are either absent from the caterpillar's gut or not induced into action. In the troidines, however, all species apparently sequester the powerful toxins from their *Aristolochia* food plants. Because the sequestration of plant poisons by butterflies represents a highly adaptive ecological pharmacology, most elegantly expressed in many of the myriads of herbivorous insects in the tropical forests of Central America and South America, its role in the survival of butterflies must outweigh the loss of energy needed to fuel it in relation to other life processes. Rain forest ecological specialists such as the beautiful *Parides* constitute an elegant example of how to cope with the imminent threat of becoming food for other creatures in this species-saturated habitat. In the truly pharmacological insects, energy that would otherwise have been used for speeding up the growth rate of immature stages of the life cycle, or for producing greater numbers of eggs, has been evolutionarily redirected toward chemical protection against natural enemies. By contrast, more palatable insect species may exhibit speedy growth rates and larger clutches of eggs as an alternate survival tactic.

In a further ecological twist, *Parides*, especially the females, are classic models for mimicry complexes in tropical rain forests. In Batesian mimicry, palatable species, through convergent evolution, evolve a visual resemblance to one or more distasteful "model" species. Early naturalists such as H. Bates (1862), F. Müller (1878), and A. Wallace (1889), observing different kinds of butterflies and other insects displaying similar patterns of color, developed intuitive insights into the existence of mimicry in the tropics. The central idea behind both Batesian mimicry and Müllerian mimicry is that the risk of being detected and eaten is shared among more than one species, the palatable ones resembling and behaving like the unpalatable model (Batesian) or more than one model resembling and behaving like one another in a "ring" of cooperative reinforcement (Müllerian). Such ideas are difficult to assess in nature, as it is very difficult to measure relative rates of predation on models and mimics in the wild or to really evaluate the extent to which mimics behave like their supposed models. Yet in tropical rain forests, where there are many different kinds of butterflies and other insects that resemble each other very closely, it is difficult to imagine that mimicry is not operative.

Thus in Sarapiquí, it is not unusual to consider female *Parides* at the center of mimicry rings or complexes involving several different Lepidoptera, including *Papilio anchisiades*, the heliconiine *Heliconius doris* (red morph at La Selva), the pierid *Archonias tereas*, and the day-flying pericopid moth *Dysschema tricolor*. The degree to which any or all of these other species are actual mimics or co-models of *Parides* awaits further field study. Sarapiquí's rain forests are filled with many kinds of pharmacological or aposematic herbivorous insects, including lygaeid bugs, pyrgomorphid grasshoppers, arctiid and ctenuchid moths, and acraeid butterflies—groups associated with different kinds of toxic plants found there.

Parides, like other butterflies and many other herbivorous insects, locates the correct food plant of its caterpillars by visually recognizing the general growth profile of the plant (vine versus shrub versus treelet), its leaf shape, and perhaps leaf size, leaf texture, leaf smell, and approximate age of the plant tissues close at hand (meristem versus older, mature leaves), assessments mediated by tactile and olfactory cues perceived by the butterfly. Imagine that from a butterfly's vantage point, the margin of a tropical rain forest is a rich but complex range of visual and chemical signals issuing from the many species of plants found here, including several different kinds with similar overall appearance and leaf shapes.

At various times between 1972 and 1978, I studied the natural history of *P. iphidamas, P. arcas mylotes*, and *P. childrenae* at Cuesta Angel and La Tirimbina, particularly at the latter site. At La Tirimbina and along the edges of the La Tigra cacao, I discovered that a prime caterpillar food plant of both *P. arcas* and *P. iphidamas* is the fairly common *Aristolochia constricta*. Along roadcuts and paths, at the borders of the rain forest, this woody liana is kept in a virtual herbaceous state by repeated, frequent cutting away of dense brush with machetes by the *peones* who work here. This unrelenting pruning of everything in sight paradoxically tends to encourage the proliferation of *A. constricta* vegetatively. Having spotted this species out here for many years, I can now readily recognize it by the latticework fine leaf veins and posturing of the regenerating vines as they droop themselves over decaying fenceposts, barbed wire, mammoth logs, and plants. In these open, exposed habitats skirmishing the shrinking rain forest, vines such as *Aristolochia* are unusually lush and exuberant, conveying at once a distinct sensation of being in the tropics.

I place fresh cuttings of *A. constricta*, their cut ends pushed into florist's water piks, into a plastic bag along with a wild-caught female butterfly to obtain eggs. *Parides* readily lay eggs on the leaves of the vine cuttings, and within a week's time it is not unusual to have two or three dozen eggs from one female. I fashion a loose nest of the cut vines in the bag, positioning them up against the plastic, so that the captive butterfly, which I assume is already fertilized, does not have a clear view of open space and the sky. Doing this helps reduce the predisposition of the butterfly to flutter nervously against the bag, which I keep inflated as much as possible, providing the butterfly with a lot of space in which to maneuver. The trick here, as with *Morpho* and other species I have reared under these conditions, is to provide the captive butterfly with enough sunlight to stimulate fluttering and oviposition, and at the same time to minimize its preoccupation with escape, often induced by a clear unobstructed view of the sky. Given these limitations, *Parides*, fed once a day with a 5–10 percent sugar water solution, does fairly well. The culture bag is kept in the field house, on the bed, in direct sunlight, but not near a window. In this manner I obtained viable eggs from *arcas mylotes*, *iphidamas*, and *childrenae* at La Tirimbina intermittently over several years. A freshly mated young *P. iphidamas* held captive in a clear plastic bag bloated with air and containing a fresh sprig of *A. constricta* can lay usually between ten and thirty viable eggs in a couple of days, once the butterfly has settled down to the confines of this nursery. Many captive butterflies, of seemingly equal condition, may lay no eggs. Inducing captive butterflies to lay eggs is an imprecise system, at least for the technique I have used in Sarapiquí. This material has been used to study the early stages and habits of *Parides*.

Typically a *Parides* egg hatches, if it is going to hatch at all (this is by no means a sure thing), within six or seven days after being oviposited. The caterpillar stage lasts about twenty-five to thirty days in the species I have reared in Sarapiquí, and the chrysalis a lengthy thirty days. In the wild I have tagged *Aristolochia* vines where I have seen *Parides* eggs and young caterpillars, only to discover a few days later that they have disappeared. From seeing this pattern many times, I infer that the mortality of the immature stages of these butterflies, food plant poisons notwithstanding, is very high in the wild.

Because eggs are frequently placed on food plant seedlings by *P. arcas*, I can only further surmise that partly grown caterpillars, crawling off one vine and searching for another in response to hunger, fall victim to many kinds of predatory arthropods, especially ants and spiders.

From observing tagged *Aristolochia constricta* seedlings to estimate their rates of growth, I have concluded that these vines, given their initial small size as seedlings, do not grow quickly enough to keep up with the voraciousness of their caterpillar parasites, a condition that escalates almost exponentially as the caterpillars mature. Nonetheless, I believe that browsing by *Parides* and *Battus* caterpillars imparts a sizable source of selection pressure on *Aristolochia* vines in Sarapiquí. It is doubtful if these insects actually regulate the abundance of these vines, as best evidenced by the evolution of a powerful defensive chemistry by *Aristolochia* species.

Why is it that some plants are highly repellent or toxic and others not? Why are there so many diverse kinds of antiherbivore defensive chemicals in the plant world, and why especially in tropical rain forests, nature's highly complex theaters of evolutionary innovation and experimentation? There are no easy answers to such compelling questions. Certainly all green plants express ways to minimize the chances of being discovered and eaten, since less leaf tissue surface area, for example, means reduced sun-trapping panels, which dampens the plant's ability to use light to set into motion the energy cycles feeding all life. Living plants trap the sun's furious power to feed themselves, inadvertently setting themselves up to become prized energy sources for other creatures incapable of photosynthesis, of which the insects surely rank the highest. For what is a butterfly or moth but disguised plant flesh—a remaking of life's energy into shapes molded by genetics? The caterpillar edits, by its physiological machinery governed in large measure by the insect's own code of genetic ingenuity, the life already encoded in the plant's tissues. Is not the butterfly, therefore, made of the sun through its mirroring of its power in the plant's chemistry and succulence? Is not the Earth's nature forged by events in the universe from many millions of miles away? Is not this realization that special message of a star-studded sky enjoyed from a hilltop at La Tirimbina when the rain clouds suddenly break apart and the celestial light show, itself a grand illusion prompted by the sun, illuminates the land's carpet of greenery, its ghostlike outlines of leaves, so many sizes and shapes, almost as bold and striking as the wings of *Parides* caught in a spot of sun earlier this day inside the rain forest? Is not all of this, all of nature, one continuum? Yes, but there are exciting boundaries to discover! What defines the boundary of a living plant in this vast continuum is pharmaceutical agents establishing barriers as to what can and what cannot be eaten. This is what separates *Parides* or *Battus* from its *Aristolochia* caterpillar food plants.

I view plant-feeding insects as extensions of the sun's energy fixed in the green tissues of plants here. This rain forest is a finely balanced network of animal-plant interrelationships, connections that require thousands, perhaps millions of years to evolve and be expressed as the myriads of life forms dwelling here. And I must caution you that much of the biological "action" driving the rain forest's proliferation of species occurs among small creatures such as insects and microorganisms. All species count, of course, but much of the foundation for life is built upon the insects and the highly varied ecological scripts they enact across this living theater. To understand just glimpses of these creatures requires years of patient study.

Here, as I see the butterflies and watch an *Anolis* lizard or a striking black and orange jumping spider spring from one leaf to another at my eye's level, the unity of all flesh, compartmentalized as distinct organisms along nature's continuum, comes to mind. The butterfly is in large measure its caterpillar food plant, since much of the energy needed for metamorphosis and the tissues of the adult insect come from nutrients mobilized from plants. The lizard is the butterfly and all of the many other insects it feeds upon along the margins of the rain forest, where insect diversity is well matched with plant diversity and the luxuriance of greenery everywhere you look. In the cream-colored wafers of bracket fungi I see jutting out from a reddish brown mammoth log, I see the huge ghostly pale grubs of rhinoceros beetles (*Megasoma* and *Dynastes*) chewing away deep inside the log. Are not both sets of these creatures essentially doing the same thing from the standpoint of the rain forest? Is not the bracket fungus reworking the external crust of this log into decay products enriching the leaf litter and topsoil, and the beetle grubs redesigning the log's soggy interior with the same or similar result? Is not this entire rain forest the reworked broken flesh of plants and animals, exposed and made available as food by the action of arthropods, bacteria, and other animals, visible and subvisible? And are not the little nitidulid beetles, drosophilid "fruit" flies, and mycetophilid flies breeding in the spongy flesh of the fungus the mobilized energy of the log? Are not, in their barest essence, the leg bristles of a *Morpho* butterfly, uncanny in their snaring of fungal spores as the insect feeds on the forest floor, the same as the stickiness of a *Heliconius* butterfly's proboscis collecting pollen grains from *Anguria* flowers along the narrow footpath leading from the cacao into the rain forest? And is not the striking beauty of *Parides*, decked out so prominently in "nasty taste" overtones of red, cream, and green on black, the marriage of its *Aristolochia* caterpillar host's tissue-locked nutrients and plant poisons? Is not *Parides* too the nectar of its floral hosts? So what if life's many forms are disjunctly coded alphabets of the nucleic acids, for what significance are nucleic acids, life's masterprint, without the sun's glow and a cradle of water—circumstances particularly germane to this tropical rain forest where butterflies swing low through light gaps and the concerted calls of cicadas make our heads ring?

Parides and the orchid bees tease me into taking note of the total exquisiteness of life in the tropical rain forest, a phenomenon that only appears at certain times. I have come often to this place where the cacao borders the rain forest, but on certain days I am compelled to stand motionless for many minutes and simply see things going on around me. The collective beauty of this place sometimes catches up with me, releasing me from thinking about hunting down this insect species or that one. These are moments for imbibing the big story, for realizing that an iridescent blue butterfly imbibing fermenting juices from a moldy sap wound on a tree, or a cicada squawking wildly with a bird in hot pursuit of it, are pieces of this rain forest's very ancient, complex saga. There are appropriate moments to consider the details, and there are others when nature's living accent marks, like silently gliding *Parides* in and out of a lush light gap gently flecked with the sun's gold, or the swift buzz of a dazzling bee just inches from your nose, encourages you, the visitor to this land, to absorb the staggering big picture. Only in passing through such special moments, recognizing them and embracing them, does one feel refreshed to pick up the insect net and other tools of the trade to unravel the details of what is happening here. One does not tire or become numb to such occasions, even after many years of going to and from the same spots in the rain forest.

Where I have watched *Parides* patrolling blooming patches of *Cephaelis* in the Padre Núñez rain forest patch at La Tirimbina, I have seen other very attractive butterflies sharing the same air space. Most prominent is the orange-, yellow-, and black-winged *Heliconius hecale*, a very impressive butterfly, which, like *Parides*, comes here to soak up nectar from the lady's lips. And then there is *Heliconius cydno*, its wings sporting bands of white and steel-blue, doing much the same thing as *H. hecale*. Flitting through the shaded understory along the edges of the clearing are several *Mechanitis isthmia*, their vivacious orange, yellow, and black wings convincingly suggestive of warning coloration. Both the heliconiines, to which *Heliconius* belongs, and the ithomiines, to which *Mechanitis* belongs, are richly represented by many species in the New World tropical forests, and this is certainly so in Sarapiquí. Like *Parides*, they too have impressive stories to tell about other avenues of pharmacological insect ecology, stories recorded in research by various tropical biologists, but most notably by Drs. Lawrence E. Gilbert and Keith S. Brown, Jr., and their associates.

Heliconius butterflies, of which there are several dozen species, lay their eggs on passionflower vines, the sole host plants of their caterpillars. Although there are about 500 species of passionflower vines in the American tropics, each species of *Heliconius* is specialized to feed on only one or a couple of these. A chemical dependence, mediated by alkaloids in leaves, drives this food plant specialization. Furthermore, feeding pressure by *Heliconius* has played a key role in the diversification of the passionflower into many species. The passionflower's chemical weaponry, while ineffective against *Heliconius*, prevents many other kinds of insects from attacking. To deter attacks from *Heliconius*, some species of these vines possess "fake eggs" on leaves, tiny structures resembling the butterfly's bright yellow eggs, which discourage a butterfly from placing its eggs on the plant. The leaves and stems in some species of passionflower are clothed in tiny hairs that snare and kill the baby caterpillars of *Heliconius*. Some species of these vines possess nectar-filled tiny cups, "extrafloral nectaries," attracting highly pugnacious ants that chase away egg-laying butterflies. Adult *Heliconius* benefit from plants in another remarkable way. They mulch pollen for "wild cucumber" vines abundant along openings in the rain forest, digesting the pollen and incorporating its protein fraction into their own eggs. In doing so, the butterflies pollinate the vivid orange flowers of these plants, unrelated to the passionflower vines.

The ithomiines interact with plants in a markedly different way. Some of these butterflies have delicate, translucent wings, rendering them almost invisible as they glide along within inches of the forest floor. Others, such as *Mechanitis*, have vivid tiger-striped wings, making these animals stand out boldly along sun-drenched paths and river banks. What the hundreds of species of ithomiines all have in common is that most feed as caterpillars on Solanaceae, a huge group of tropical plants known for powerful insecticidal alkaloids (different from those in passionflower vines) in their leaves, stems, and fruit. Crude extracts of nicotine-containing leaves of Solanaceae have been used to hunt animals by Indians, who recognize the paralytic effect of this substance on wildlife. A handful of species of these plants has been cultivated by humankind, among which are tobacco, egg-plant, tomato, and potato. Some of the poisonous and narcotic alkaloids from these plants have been studied as clinical depressants.

Research has shown that ithomiines are generally avoided as prey. Giant orb spiders, such as the familiar *Nephila clavipes*, gingerly cut trapped ithomiines out of their sticky webs rather than eating them. Apparently the big spiders recognize these butterflies as being very distasteful. While the poisonous alkaloids of the plants are used by the butterflies as cues for egg laying and by caterpillars as cues for feeding, these substances are not deployed as a chemical arsenal by the adult butterflies. What makes the butterflies distasteful?

The answer resides in yet another way in which these butterflies interact with plants. Recent experimental studies by Keith S. Brown, Jr., have demonstrated that the adult butterflies visit dead inflorescences of various compositae from which they collect pyrrolizidine alkaloids, substances very different from the alkaloids found in their caterpillar food plants. These they use to synthesize a courtship pheromone or mating signal. Without the pyrrolizidine alkaloids, the butterflies would not be able to mate and reproduce. In the process of visiting the blooms, the butterflies pollinate the flowers. Such observations show that these plants and the ithomiine butterflies are obligately coevolved with each other, that is, neither one can survive without the other.

Monarch and queen butterflies, and their dozens of tiger-striped wild cousins such as *Lycorea*, illustrate another dimension to the diversity of ecological interactions between plants and animals in tropical rain forests. Monarchs and queens are also familiar butterflies in the U.S., best known for their gaudily striped caterpillars feeding on milkweeds. Both species originated in the American tropics, and the migratory habits of the monarch attest to this heritage, for this species cannot overwinter in temperate North America. Although many species of milkweeds occur in North America, the family to which they belong reaches a zenith of diversity in the rain forests of Central America and South America, home also for many species of "milkweed butterflies." These butterflies lay eggs exclusively on plants in the milkweed-dogbane family, and their caterpillars feed only on these plants, whose leaves are rich in natural poisons known as cardiac glycosides. These substances, while noxious to most insects, are feeding stimulants to the caterpillars of milkweed butterflies, and become incorporated into the body tissues of these insects without harming them. Like *Parides* and *Heliconius*, the butterflies are distasteful to predators, although the chemical basis for this line of defense is quite different among the three groups. Adult milkweed butterflies often pollinate the food plants of their caterpillars, unlike *Parides* and *Heliconius* which almost never do. As the name suggests, cardiac glycosides and synthetic mimics thereof have been useful in biomedical research studies of heart muscle tissue.

Chemical exquisiteness in the modes of adaptation by insects to their environment is not limited to the binding of volatile and bitter substances in food plants. In particular, biochemicals encode the means by which butterflies recognize their own species and other resources in their environment. No one knows for sure just how a butterfly recognizes an individual of the opposite sex belonging to the same species. There are many views on the matter, and certainly it suffices to say that visual and chemical cues are most likely involved in most species. Species-specifc signals in butterflies, moths, and a fanfare of other insects represent a chemically diverse and complex repertoire of coded communication, a sort of biological language that ensures the survival of each species. No doubt the slight to moderate differences in wing-spotting patterns between the males of *Parides* species, coupled with alleged differences in their sex-related body scents issuing from their fluffy wing folds, synergistically preserve the biological integrity of each species, minimizing or erasing chances for cross-species confusion during courtship and eventual copulation. Seeing mixed cohorts of females belonging to two or three species of *Parides* at *Hamelia* blossoms, a very typical situation in Sarapiquí, I am often unable to confidently differentiate the species. But I have no doubt that the courtship-receptive females of each species aptly direct themselves toward the appropriate patrolling male, guided by species-specific wing colors and male sexual scent.

Philip J. DeVries, in his book *The Butterflies of Costa Rica* (Princeton University Press, 1986), reports finding newly eclosed female *Parides* bearing white "scent wool" on their antennae and heads—the androconial scales from the inner fold of male butterflies' hindwings, transferred during courtship. A male *Parides* displays the perfume-impregnated fluffy white inner fold of its hindwings, a structure absent or reduced in the female, as it hovers over a perched female, almost brushing the sex-scented fold over the female's antennae. One can readily imagine that the pheromone exuded from the androconial fold of the male's hindwings varies among the species to ensure proper pairings in the wild. But the chemistry of these scents in troidines has not been studied, to the best of my knowledge. DeVries mentions that the male *Parides* plugs up the genital opening of the female following sperm transfer, thereby preventing the newly mated butterfly from mating again soon. Eventually this plug, called a sphragis, disintegrates, freeing the female to mate again once the sperm of the first male has been used up. Sphragis-plugged female *Parides* disperse over large areas of habitat looking for egg-laying sites, and mated females are generally transient visitors to floral patches patrolled by their male counterparts.

Perhaps too species differences in male wing color patterns function to facilitate intraspecifically individual male butterfly patrol areas in the rain forest? There are no clear answers at this point, only more questions and much more field work needed to elucidate the answers.

In their long since classic book *The Principles of Animal Ecology* (Saunders, 1949), Drs. Warder Clyde Allee, Alfred E. Emerson, Orlando Park, Thomas Park, and Karl P. Schmidt, the pioneering founders of what is known as the "Chicago school of ecology," reported that the breeding structure of an animal population is shaped in sizable measure by both the abundance of individuals and the spatial use of the habitat. Patrolling, as certainly done by *Parides* and many other tropical rain forest butterflies, is viewed as a behavior that might originally have evolved for the purpose of food acquisition but has become a mechanism for the acquisition of mates. Patrolling, a frequently observed feature of butterfly species within and at the edges of primeval rain forest in Sarapiquí, allows butterflies, especially males, to become familiar with the habitat, thereby reducing dangers while enhancing the prospect of finding food and mates. While *Parides* species such as the strong-flying *childrenae*, the males of which are quickly distinguished from those of smaller-sized species in the same pockets of rain forest by their very large iridescent forewing patches, move about a lot in the rain forest, my impression from Sarapiquí is that the populations of each species tend to be disjunct, that is, having subunits or gatherings of individuals associated with certain preferred sites in the habitat. I believe that the observed generally low density of *Parides* populations, as with those of many other tropical butterfly species, is consistent with the generally held notion that tropical species, especially herbivores, are largely "biologically accommodated" in the major aspects of their interaction with the habitats. The well-known Spanish theoretical ecologist Dr. Ramón Margalef, in a paper published in 1968 in *The American Naturalist*, predicted that many species in tropical rain forests exhibit very specialized forms of behavioral defenses, including sophisticated symbiotic associations, environmentally acquired or *de novo*-synthesized protective poisons, and mimicry associations, due to lengthy evolutionary opportunities in ancient, mature ecosystems that developed over thousands or millions of years in climatically benign (such as abundant monthly rainfall and stable warm temperatures) geographical conditions.

Walking along the footpath into the rain forest from the La Tigra cacao, it is easy to spot various species of butterflies. Orchid bees also appear in the light gaps here, swift-moving blurs of metallic green or bronze, or combinations of black, orange, and yellow. They and their chemical ties to the rain forest are more difficult to study than the butterflies because of their elusive habits. I notice a sudden distraction not of color and movements but of sound, a distinctly curt and loud buzz coming from the shadows on the path ahead of where I stand. It seems to be a protest to my presence, communicated crisply across a few meters of heavy, stagnant air. Then I see it, a huge fat bee with calico stripes of black, yellow, and orange alighting on the muddied path, then hovering above it, and then back again on the mud. I know from what I have read and experienced before that this startling creature is a female orchid bee, *Eulaema meriana*, called locally *chiquiza*. The bee is collecting mud from the soft wet clay on the path, a construction paste it will use to build a nest somewhere off in the rain forest. Its modest nest consists of a couple or several large cells concocted of mud, plant debris, and resin, usually found in a preexisting hollow cavity such as a rotten tree stump. Each completed cell is then provisioned with a pollen and nectar paste and a single egg. The cells are sealed and this is the end of parenting. New bees emerge from these brood cells tucked away in the moist darkness several months later.

As usual, I scarcely get a good look at this very wary bee before it is swiftly gone. What was a smart, crisp-lined bee sporting its own version of vibrant warning coloration (for the female has a very painful sting) is now a rapidly fading blur, whose only proof of presence is a loud buzz, the beat of powerful wings and muscles, which fades away almost as rapidly as the creature shoots off in a straight line into the rain forest. This is one of about two hundred species of orchid bees, important pollinators of many kinds of rain forest plants that would not survive without these insects. But unlike the easily spotted pharmacological butterflies in the light gap and the monotone droning of cicadas overhead in the feathery crests of the *gavilán* trees, the orchid bees, known as the tribe Euglossini of the subfamily Bombinae, or as the subfamily Euglossinae of the family Apidae (which also includes bumblebees, stingless bees, and the "true" or stinging bees of the genus *Apis* such as the familiar honey bee), comprise an elusive, difficult to study slice of the biological diversity of American tropical forests. Orchid bees are unique to the American tropics, and the males are essential pollinators for many kinds of the more than eleven hundred species of orchids found in Costa Rica alone.

The euglossines systematically consist of five genera (*Eulaema, Eufriesea, Euglossa, Exaeretes,* and *Aglae*). *Euglossa* is the largest genus, comprising seventy-five described species and perhaps another thirty or so awaiting description. *Eufriesea* has sixty described species and *Eulaema* thirteen. While the larger bees such as *Eulaema* can be up to about thirty-five millimeters in body length, *Euglossa*, the most diverse genus of the group, generally consists of small to medium-sized bees (eight to twenty millimeters long). The euglossines represent both a systematically and an ecologically diversified group of organisms enjoying specialized associations with a very diverse subset of the plant life in the tropical rain forest. The bees occur from sea level up to sixteen hundred meters of elevation. The Sarapiquí district, with its patchwork of rain forest habitats from the lofty heights of La Cinchona and Cuesta Angel to the hot, humid lowlands of the La Selva Biological Station near Puerto Viejo, has been an ideal evolutionary testing ground and ecological theater for the expression of diversified species of orchid bees interacting with their floral hosts, both orchid and non-orchid. I consider myself fortunate to have studied them for a brief while, to have entered into a collaborative research project on their still much to be charted chemical behavior, and to have accidentally stumbled across a nest or two of the orchid bees. My acquaintance with them has heightened my appreciation of the elegant study already devoted to the orchid bees, and of what they can teach us about the pharmacology that binds all of life in the tropical rain forests.

Orchid bees, as a group, do not resemble any of the bees found in the temperate zone. They are distinctly tropical in appearance. Once you have seen an orchid bee, I can almost guarantee that you will not forget what it looks like—especially one of the stunning, jewel-like flashy bronze or metallic *Euglossa*. But finding them to see can be quite a challenge. Researchers often set out pieces of blotter or filter paper to which an appropriate scent has been applied, and then wait for bees to arrive. The lure is typically tacked to a tree, allowing for capturing of the bees with an insect net. Once, not too long ago, just to satisfy my curiosity, I set out some scented traps to lure orchid bees. In my case, I used a McPhail trap, a glass, bell-shaped vessel open in the middle and having a trough of water forming the bottom. A cotton ball, impregnated with the scent, is suspended from the top, beneath a foam stopper. The trap is suspended in a tree, and the bees attracted to the scent fly up into the opening and fall into the water. Scented traps were a familiar technique to researchers exploring the ecology of orchid bees, one still used today. But for me it was a new facet of my field study in Sarapiquí. The technique is simple in one sense, but based upon some very complex, sophisticated research in the underlying context.

Researchers of orchid biology have both distilled and air-trapped the floral fragrances from orchids in blossom, capturing a sample of their essence, which through the laboratory techniques of gas chromatography and mass spectrometry have provided a chemical fingerprint of the orchid's fragrance. Of particular interest are the volatile substances found in the "floral oil." Biologists perform such analyses for a number of reasons, usually related in one way or another to understanding the unique properties of the floral fragrance emitted by a certain species, how it compares with other species (usually closely related), and what components of the fragrance might be the most biologically active in terms of regulating or mediating pollinator behavior. In the tropics, the vast majority of plant species are pollinated through the action of animals; orchid bees comprise one major group of orchid plant pollinators in Central America and South America. Once the major floral fragrance components have been determined, synthetic analogs or copies of them, many of which are commercially available from chemical supply houses, can be tested in the wild individually, or in predetermined mixes, to examine their relative or combined capacity to attract pollinators. Much of the current understanding of orchid bee biology stems directly from the use of this approach. The pioneering research of Dr. Calaway Dodson, Robert Dressler, Norris Williams, and others within the last thirty years, developing and using this important technique, have made it generally common knowledge that certain substances are reliable chemical baits for trapping orchid bees—a font of information taken directly from the analyses of orchid floral fragrances.

In all of my years of field work in Sarapiquí, I had not seen *Euglossa*, perhaps because I was not looking for them. But these bees must have been all around me, flying very swiftly through the rain forest and along its margins. What impressed me most about my trapping experience was the large number of orchid bees that showed up so quickly in response to the series of chemical baits. In a brief period, I obtained a modest sample of orchid bee species that I had no idea existed in this habitat. It was as if some invisible or hidden component of this rain forest's wealth of species was suddenly exposed for me to see. Just gazing at the bees, their beautiful metallic colors a dazzle of reflected spots of sunlight, reinforced in me how challenging it surely is for biologists to fully understand the webs of life in the tropical rain forest. Robert Dressler, in his 1981 book *The Orchids: Natural History and Classification* (Harvard University Press), mentions that as many as fifty species of orchid bees have been collected from a single area, clearly suggesting an impressive, if not staggering, level of bee diversity over small regions of the tropics.

I knew that all of the bees I had trapped in that brief period one sunny morning in Sarapiquí were males. Thanks to a lot of elegant research by Dodson, Dressler, Williams, Mark Whitten, and others over many years, much is now understood about the biology and behavior of euglossine bees. Although it had been known for more than a century that male euglossines visit and pollinate many kinds of orchids exclusively in the American tropics, it has only been in the past thirty years, or thereabouts, that the interaction between male orchid bees and their floral hosts has been studied in great depth. While euglossines specifically pollinate certain kinds of orchids, many other orchids are pollinated by fungus gnats, mosquitoes, moths, and wasps. As a family, the orchids, which comprise an impressive ten percent (about 20,000 species) of all flowering plants, exhibit a tremendous range of floral diversity representing many special adaptations for pollination by animals, chiefly insects. About 650 species of orchids in the New World tropics rely exclusively on euglossine bees for pollination.

Female euglossines frequently collect nest-building resins from *Dalechampia* (Euphorbiaceae) flowers and pollinate them in the process, as studied by Dr. Scott Armbruster in Ecuador. Female orchid bees representing several species pollinate the flowers of *Calathea* in Sarapiquí and elsewhere in Costa Rica, and harvest nectar and pollen from many different rain forest tree species as well. Although orchid bees, especially females, work flowers at different levels in the rain forest, many species are active in the forest canopy at certain times of the year, where many orchids occur. Female orchid bees may live three to six months, perhaps up to a year, gathering nectar, pollen, and resins from plant species bearing tubular flowers, such as arrowroot, gloxinia, solanums, and verbenas, to name a few. What seem to work best for female euglossines are flower types having a wide opening but an elongated narrow tubular access to nectar, which is the floral reward available to these very long-tongued bees. Female orchid bees collect pollen for nest provisioning either by brushing exposed anthers or by "buzz-vibrating" tubular anthers to shake free pollen lodged within. Dan Janzen and others discovered that female *Eufriesea* bees "trap line" over large areas of rain forest in Costa Rica, visiting both nectar source and pollen source tree species along the route, and that the bees' route over several weeks and months changes in accordance with the flowering regimes of host tree species. The bees learn the foraging routes in the rain forest and modify them as the spatial pattern of flowering trees changes. Such trap-lining behavior by female euglossines, and probably by males (see below) and by other groups of floral-visiting animals in the rain forest such as hawk moths and some butterflies, undoubtedly has a great evolutionary impact on tree species by promoting pollen flow over large distances (up to twenty kilometers or more in Janzen's study).

Male orchid bees appear to be highly chemically dependent creatures. Orchid fragrance substances that have been identified and then used in the form of commercially available analogs to successfully trap euglossine bees in Central America and South America include both monoterpenes and simple aromatic compounds such as alpha and beta pinene, cineole, p-cymene, citronellal, linalool, geraniol, methyl benzoate, alpha-terpineol, benzyl acetate, citronellol, methyl salicylate, nerol, methyl cinnamate, skatole, myrcene, vanillin, and eugenol. Bioassays are done by tacking to tree trunks five-centimeter squares of blotter pad paper saturated with these test compounds and then standing back to see what comes to them. Calaway Dodson and Norris Williams between 1969 and 1972 screened many of these substances for orchid bee activity in Mexico, Guatemala, Honduras, El Salvador, Costa Rica, Nicaragua, Panama, Colombia, Ecuador, Peru, Venezuela, and Brazil. Specificity in attraction by bees can be very fine-tuned. For example, Williams and Dodson discovered in one test that more than three hundred male euglossines were attracted to eugenol and only one bee to this substance's mirror image, isoeugenol! What finicky field chemists male orchid bees can be!

For male orchid bees, the floral fragrance of an orchid "host" is both the attractant and the reward, since euglossine-pollinated orchids generally lack nectar, and pollen is contained in a capsule called a pollinarium, inaccessible to the bee. It was Cal Dodson who reported the first complete, accurate account of euglossine bee pollination in several species of *Stanhopea* orchids in 1961, opening an important door for subsequent research by Dr. Stefan Vogel, Robert Dressler, and Norris Williams. Basically, euglossine-pollinated orchids express specialized adaptations that exclude pollination by other kinds of bees and other insects. These orchids are very fragrant and lack nectar. The act of pollination in these orchids depends directly upon the behavior of male euglossines as they collect floral fragrance from their orchid hosts, substances needed for their own use and survival.

Norris Williams, in a chapter in the book *Orchid Biology—Reviews and Perspectives* (Cornell University Press, 1982), summarized the "euglossine pollination syndrome" as consisting of these sequential steps: (1) the male bee is attracted to the orchid's floral fragrance, being capable of deciphering it from the rich array of floral fragrances issuing through the rain forest; (2) the motivated bee alights on the flower and quickly moves to the floral area having the strongest fragrance (the base of the labellum or lower lip of the flower); (3) the bee brushes the labellum surface, using specially modified bristles on its forelegs (called "tarsal brushes") to sweep across specialized glandular structures called osmophores (discovered by Stefan Vogel in Germany in 1966 to be the orchid's scent glands), picking up a unique oil from them by capillary action of these bristles; (4) the bee hovers in the air, during which time the collected fragrance oils are then shunted, by leg action, to specially designed inflated slits or pouches on the hindleg tibiae (structures corresponding somewhat to the pollen baskets (corbiculae) of honey bees, although having unique properties for their specialized function; in fact, this unique orchid fragrance storage and processing structure on the male bee's hind tibia is absent in the female, replaced with a more conventional pollen basket for transporting pollen associated with nest provisioning for brood); (5) the bee returns to the flower to collect more fragrance oil. It is during the hovering that the bee inadvertently removes the pollinarium from the orchid flower, which ends up being affixed to the back of the bee's body. When the bee visits another flower of the same orchid species, the pollinarium is cleverly dislodged and deposited in the flower, completing pollination.

Because male orchid bees do not participate in nest building and brood provisioning, they are nomads, sleeping around in the rain forest, and therefore likely candidates for considerable long-distance movement of orchid pollinaria, thus helping to maintain a viable level of gene flow within various species of orchids. Male orchid bees may also have a greater evolutionary impact on non-orchid plants as well, since they do visit other kinds of flowers such as those of Araceae. Both male and female orchid bees forage at non-orchids for nectar as their prime source of energy. Major nectar (food) sources for adult bees of both sexes include the Costaceae and the Marantaceae in the monocots, and several families of dicots as well. Dr. Douglas W. Schemske of the University of Chicago recently discovered that just one species of orchid bee, *Euglossa imperialis*, is responsible for ninety percent of the pollination of *Costus laevis* in central Panama. Males also visit and pollinate the flowers of other plant families well represented in tropical rain forests, such as the Gesneriaceae and Solanaceae.

The Gesneriaceae indeed comprise a very special case. The family includes species bearing two different kinds of flowers, both types of which are pollinated by euglossines. One type of flower attracts males, and the other kind attracts both male and female euglossines that feed on nectar. Female bees also collect pollen from this second kind of flower. It is believed that because there is a lot of floral specificity within the Gesneriaceae for certain species of orchid bees, this plant group has been capable of substantial diversification into many species, many of them bearing unique floral adaptations. Another fascinating example of male-female bee divergence in the pollination of non-orchids was uncovered in the late 1970s by Drs. Scott Armbruster and Grady Webster in Panama, in which male euglossines pollinate *Dalechampia spathulata* and female euglossines the closely related *D. magnistipulata* (Euphorbiaceae). The males of three species of *Eulaema* inadvertently pollinate *D. spathulata* while collecting a wintergreen-like fragrance compound by brushing a specialized gland situated on the inflorescence.

Non-orchid floral hosts for both male and female orchid bees might be more significant in the overall biology of these insects than formerly envisioned or even considered. Rather, bee survival, as studied particularly by Dr. James D. Ackerman in central Panama, may be more linked to the overall cycle of nectar host flowering in the tropical rain forest. Ackerman discovered that the euglossine bee nectar hosts displayed "steady-state" flowering phenologies, blooming primarily in the middle of the long rainy season when bee species richness and abundance is lowest. About 69 percent of all euglossine steady-state bee nectar hosts in central Panama belong to the rain forest chiefly understory plant families Marantaceae, Zingiberaceae, Rubiaceae, and Apocynaceae. The euglossine bees that peak in abundance and species number at the time of peak flowering for these plant groups are the long-tongued species, well adapted to penetrating the long, narrow corolla tubes of these nectar hosts. Other euglossines peak at times of the year when upper-layer tree species in the rain forest undergo mass flowering, and male bees actively patrol these for nectar. Mass-flowering tree species tend to eliminate the need for bee trap-lining since there are abundant floral sources close at hand, generally in one relatively compact area. Bees find ample nectar food under conditions of seasonally related mass flowering, most notably in this case in the middle of the dry season and early into the rainy season.

Mass-flowering species such as the Bignoniaceae tend to have unspecialized flowers that readily attract euglossines, specialists on orchids and a few other groups of plants. At other times of the year, according to the Ackerman study, when mass flowering is reduced, male euglossine bees switch to various rain forest understory plants for nectar foraging. Some of these species have scattered, highly disjunct spatial patterns in the rain forest, thereby compelling euglossines to exhibit trap-lining behavior in order to feed themselves.

Such discoveries elegantly point again to the interconnectedness between the strata of life in the tropical rain forest. We must view orchid bees as facultative users of what nectar sources the rain forest habitat offers at different times of the year, since these insects cannot obtain energy from their orchid hosts, and in fact may not interact very frequently with orchids. What Ackerman's timely study helps us appreciate is the fact that euglossine bee species require different strata of the rain forest at different times of the year in order to survive. They switch around to different parts of the habitat in accordance with what nectar sources are blooming and the degree to which they can extract it. My hunch is that what applies here for orchid bees might also be true for many other groups of insects and other animals in the rain forest—each species, within certain limits, switches on and off different resources depending upon their annual cycles of availability. The tropical rain forest, therefore, is a somewhat fluid system of life.

A central question regarding orchid bees is why male orchid bees collect fragrance compounds from orchids. It is easier to understand the orchid's benefit in attracting the bees, since pollination is necessary for the orchid to reproduce sexually. The most plausible explanation to date for the other side of the story, based upon research chiefly by Norris Williams at the Florida State Museum, is that male orchid bees collect and store these substances in their hind tibial organs, modify them through a not yet fully understood process, translocate the modified compounds to the mandibular glands in the head, and then use mandibular gland secretions involving these substances to mark courtship sites to which unmated female bees are attracted. Norris Williams and Mark Whitten are using radioactively labeled compounds to chart the metabolic pathway inside male orchid bees, such as *Eulaema cingulata*, after these substances, such as tetradecyl acetate, are introduced into the bee's hind tibial organ. The object is to determine when and how orchid and other substances collected in nature and stored in the hind tibial organs become modified and possibly shunted to the mandibular gland in the bee's head. The fact that, with a few exceptions, only male euglossine bees visit orchids, pollinate them, and collect their fragrances, clearly indicates a sex-related function for these compounds by male bees; but the challenge is still to uncover precisely how the male bees use them, to what end in their own sexual habits.

It may not be very easy for male and female orchid bees to locate one another in the tropical rain forest. These are large powerful bees capable of moving about over very large areas. Coupled with what is most likely a low-density population structure for most species in a particular area of habitat, these creatures may have to rely on courting cues other than vision, at least in the initial stages of courtship. Pharmacological chemistry may again be the answer. When I am inside the La Tirimbina rain forest, or the steep ravine at Cuesta Angel, I cannot in any way sense the wealth of airborne chemical signals issuing from flowers, leaves, fruits, insects, and many other creatures that live in these habitats. What I tend to perceive most of all is the smell of decay, humidity, and the fragrances from perhaps one or two flowering species at a time. But this rain forest is a chemical dictionary for creatures like orchid bees.

In the light gap in the rain forest behind the La Tigra cacao where *Parides childrenae* can be seen frequently on sunny mornings, before the day becomes too hot, occasionally I see a single *Eulaema meriana*. The big bee passes through the open space in a single shot, one way and then the other. Often as it whizzes back and forth, the bulky bee, easy to spot even from several meters away where I stand in the shadows off to one side, alights on the smooth gray bark of the tall, straight trunk of one of this rain forest's oldest citizens, an immense canopy tree. The bee alights fully exposed in the sunlight, launches backward into the air, hovers, and then lands again. This behavior is repeated several times, especially over the morning hours. Its greatly enlarged, swollen hind tibiae, dangling free as the big bee perches on a mammoth tree trunk, tell me right away that this is a male.

The male bees certainly make themselves quite conspicuous by positioning themselves on light-colored mammoth tree trunks, often in very good light as well. Seeing this behavior, I wonder what works first for such an orchid bee presumably in search of a mate—vision or perfume? Or both? Since these creatures are highly visual, with large compound eyes, perhaps a male bee postures itself in the spot in the rain forest where it is most likely to be visually noticed by a newly hatched virgin bee of the same species? By displaying themselves in the sunny openings of the rain forest, the male *Eulaema*, and males of other orchid bees, incur much less of a problem from dense foliage and branches in the forest canopy, or from the deep shade of the understory for that matter?

One quickly gets the feeling, from watching pharmacological butterflies, orchid bees, and many other insects thriving in forest light gaps and along the borders of the forest, that these places are evolutionary hot spots for the overall healthiness and maintenance of biological diversity in tropical rain forests. Perhaps the male orchid bee deploys its perfume aphrodisiac, gleaned from orchids or other substances and metabolized into a sexual potion inside its own body, when an "interested" female counterpart is within close (sexual scent) range? Or perhaps visual display and chemical signaling work hand in hand to provoke courtship in orchid bees? Perhaps, too, vision has little to do with juxtaposing the male and female, the male choosing a light gap because this is a suitable spot for disseminating an airborne chemical sex signal in an area of high insect activity (and, therefore, a good likelihood for encountering a female bee)? Just how the chemical signal is given off is also an area of promising study. Does the male bee "mark" the tree with his own particular signal?

Dr. Lynn S. Kimsey, an orchid bee biologist, has determined that males of *Eulaema meriana* and *Euglossa imperialis*, two familiar Central American species of orchid bees, form "leks" in rain forest light gaps. Each male has a territory perching site, such as a tree trunk, and a particular display route that it flies to and from the perch. In this situation, one might expect to discover several male orchid bees of the same species occupying a sizable light-gap area, and the cruising females to have a choice from among them. If there is a causal relationship between a male bee's genes and the quality of its perch site and territory, under the auspices of the lek model borrowed largely from bird studies, then natural selection might well favor an orchid bee breeding system in which unmated females assertively choose males for courtship and sexual intercourse based on the quality of their displayed goods. This is an idea well worth pursuing in the Sarapiquí rain forests, where light gaps and many species of orchid bees exist. It seems to me that such research should be done very soon. What strikes me too as particularly fascinating about this line of research is that the male orchid bee's chemical signal used in either establishing leks and/or attracting females must vary among the many species that cooccur in the tropical rain forests of a place like Sarapiquí or Costa Rica's Corcovado National Park in the southwestern region (Osa Peninsula) of the country.

Given the obvious importance of chemical scents in the mating of orchid bees, it would follow that male bees synthesize species-specific scents in order to prevent accidental cross-matings that would likely result in infertile or unviable offspring—a major violation of nature's consistent code of the biological integrity of the species. Iso-lating mechanisms in orchid bees have not been studied very much. But considering what I found in just twenty minutes of trapping for male bees in the rain forest behind the La Tigra cacao not long ago, I am impressed by what surely must be effective species-isolating mechanisms in this rain forest. What separates the courtships and reproduction of a dozen or so species of orchid bees all coexisting within the same stretch of forest? I have read too that as many as thirty or thirty-five species of orchid bees arrive at chemical baits in Costa Rica, and that roughly a third to a half of the species thus collected at a given site tend to be species unique to that site!

Little did I know when I first started taking notice of orchid bees that I would find myself involved in a collaborative study of these insectan chemists, a project that would help me understand how the orchid bee–orchid interaction may have evolved in the first place, and why it is that orchid bees may not need orchids to survive and reproduce. This saga started in La Lola in 1983. Finca Experimental La Lola is a cacao plantation in the Caribbean lowlands south of Sarapiquí, in Limón Province. In spite of its extensive area of culti-vated land, La Lola and surrounding areas are unusually rich in insect life, including orchid bees. Beginning in 1978 and extending annually to the present, I have been engaged in a field study of insect-mediated pollination in cacao (*Theobroma cacao*) in Costa Rica, funded by the American Cocoa Research Institute (McLean, Virginia). For this project, La Lola was one of my principal research sites; since 1980 I have stayed periodically in the field station building located on its premises. La Lola, which belonged to the United Fruit Company many years ago, is now owned and operated by the Centro Agronómico Tropical de Investigación y Ensenanza in Turrialba. It is the place I recommended to the producers of *Indiana Jones and the Temple of Doom* as a good place to collect giant beetles that they wanted to use in certain scenes.

One fellow, a seasoned cacao worker named Moya, who lives in nearby Madre de Dios and who has worked in La Lola for many years, knows something about the habits of one kind of orchid bee found here. When I first began to observe orchid bees at La Lola, Moya shared with me a bit of information that proved to be very helpful. His comment had taken me by surprise. "*Pues sí, doctor, las chiquizas siempre vienen a este árbol, por lo menos hace veinte años que yo estoy trabajando aquí en esta finca.*" ("But of course, the orchid bees [*Eulaema*] always come to this tree, at least for the twenty years that I've been working on this farm.") I had noticed several times that large bees, later identified as *Eulaema cingulata*, regularly visited tiny sap flows exuded from the trunks and exposed roots of several *Dalbergia cubilquitenzis* trees, planted thirty-odd years ago as a leguminous shade cover in one small sector of the cacao at La Lola. Both the bees and the tree were identified by my collecting of voucher specimens, in the case of the *Dalbergia* including leaves, flowers, and seed pods. Because the branches were quite high, I had to lasso one with a rope and pull it off to get flowers and leaves. The pods I collected when they fell to the ground.

Walking along the main gravel road leading to the La Lola field station building, I noticed on several occasions, especially during the sunny morning hours, loud buzzes coming from the cacao grove off to one side, and always at the same spot. The sound reminded me of *Eulaema meriana* on the muddied path in the rain forest behind

La Tigra, yet it was different. This was more the droning whine of a large insect flying around than the more abrupt, almost squawking buzz of a mother bee I had inadvertently disturbed. One day I decided to check out the mysterious buzzing. Crouching down low and looking through the cacao trees in the direction of the sound, I could see, about ten meters away, two large blackish bees flying around the lower section of the large tree trunk. This tree trunk is swathed in the climbing stalks of *Philodendron* and I had no idea at the time what it was that was attracting the bees. My first thought was that I had discovered their nesting site, and that the bees were searching for a crevice in the bark, the entrance to a nest. The bees were acting very warily too, for as I approached, they flew off into the cacao and quickly out of my sight. I counted several similar-looking trees in one small area, and from one spot I could make out the trunks of all of them just by ducking low again and peeking through the cacao. It was then that I noticed several bees swirling around two other trees. Looking at the foliage of these trees, I could tell that they were all the same species, which later turned out to be the *Dalbergia* legume. The canopy of these half-dozen or so trees, which all appeared to be the same age and height, is about twelve meters, towering over the cacao.

Eventually I was able to stalk the bees being lured to the trees and discovered that they alighted individually on different discolored wounds issuing from the trunks and exposed roots. The bees did not exhibit such interest in the neighboring cacao trees, or, as I discovered later, in several other kinds of shade-cover, canopy-size trees, including other leguminous species such as *Inga* and *Erythrina*, the latter especially prevalent at La Lola. Some of the tree wounds attracting *Eulaema cingulata*, which looks very much like a smaller version of *E. meriana* (which also occurs here, but which I have not seen visiting the tree wounds), were old machete cuts made by *finca* workers cleaning brush and pruning the cacao trees. Others appeared to be made by animals.

Moya had used the word "*chiquiza*" in referring to these bees, even though this popular local name usually refers to *E. meriana*. Perhaps the Costa Ricans use it for both these bees. *Eulaema cingulata* closely resembles *E. meriana*, although in addition to relative body size (which is not all that different but noticeable when specimens of the bees are held up side by side), the striping pattern of the abdomen is somewhat different. I noticed too that the sap wounds visited by the bees are deep red in color and appear mildly and pleasantly fragrant when sniffed closely. Typically a bee would fly around the tree many times, apparently home in on a wound of appropriate condition, hover next to it, land, and then hover some more. During the second hovering, I noticed the bee moving its legs, as if transferring something from its forelegs to its hindlegs in rapid motion. By crawling slowly through the cacao understory, which gave me an unobstructed view of what was going on, I was able to get close enough to a bee already engaged with a tree wound. I was even able to capture with my net some bees as voucher material. These bees are very wary, and I noticed that they were active on the lower portion of a tree, for the most part.

Seeing the bees and hearing Moya's remark about how long he has noticed them at the *Dalbergia* tweaked my interest. I began observing the *Eulaema* and contacted orchid bee specialists who knew much more about these organisms than I did. Up to this point, I had a very general acquaintance with the orchid bee literature, knowing that it was the male bee that visited and pollinated orchids and that the males obtained fragrant compounds from the orchids in the process. In *Costa Rican Natural History* (University of Chicago Press, 1986), edited by Daniel Janzen, I had read that Norris Williams on the University of Florida campus was doing pioneering studies that would explain just how male orchid bees utilize orchid fragrances. Williams and his associates were on the cutting edge of euglossine bee research; I decided to contact him about what I had been observing with *Eulaema* at La Lola.

I had read that it was well established that male euglossine bees collected fragrant compounds from sources other than orchids, including aromatic exposed tree roots. Norris Williams and Robert Dressler had reported seeing *Euplusia* and *Euglossa* species "brushing" on tree trunks, rotten logs, even boards, in Peru, and *Euplusia* males brushing on tree roots in Panama. It was also known or suspected that perhaps volatile substances produced by fungi associated with rotting wood or sap wounds, such as monoterpenes or sesquiterpenes, are attractive to male orchid bees. Perhaps the attraction of male orchid bees to fragrant wood and sap wounds in the wild, I speculated, might represent a clue to the evolution of the relationship between these bees and orchids in tropical forests.

Could it be that certain kinds of fungi associated with tree sap wound fermentation and with rotting aromatic wood were important sources of fragrance substances required by certain kinds of insects, including male orchid bees? I was tempted to draw a parallel with the *Morpho* and other butterflies that visit rotten fruit and rotting fungi in Sarapiquí's rain forests. Morphoes and related butterflies may obtain more than nutrients from decaying fruit and soupy fungi—perhaps they too are retrieving aromatic compounds? This intriguing idea would help explain, if verified by research, why it is that male butterflies are more abundant at these unusual rain forest resources than females. Perhaps there is a sex-related substance or substances collected from microbial and fungal metabolism, especially as this recycles the forest's sugar-rich resources? It is not too difficult to imagine how such behaviors could have evolved early on in the establishment of the rain forest's intricate webs of life, and become ecological stepping stones to other kinds of insect-plant associations, including male orchid bee pollination syndromes.

But the male eulaemas at the tree wounds in La Lola provoked a more immediate need—to explore this particular aspect of orchid bee biology in a manner that had not been done before. It is the kind of project that clearly necessitated the expertise of euglossine bee biologists. In the meantime, I had begun simply keeping field notes on the number of bees I saw at tree wounds each day, and as much anecdotal information as possible on bee behavior—not knowing for sure what I was actually looking for. By doing this at intermittent intervals, whenever I was at La Lola over a couple of years, I began to see a pattern of bee abundance at the *Dalbergia* trees. Bees were most numerous during the rainy season.

In correspondence with Norris Williams, it became clear that there could be an interesting story behind the *Eulaema* brushing the discolored sap wounds on the *Dalbergia* trees in La Lola. We were both impressed by the high abundance of the bees in the cacao *finca*, well removed from expansive rain forest habitats. Dr. W. Mark Whitten, at the time a postdoctoral research associate in Williams's laboratory, contacted me about the eulaemas, and I shared with him what I had found out to date. At Mark's suggestion, I began collecting samples of *E. cingulata* from the tree trunk wounds in 1984 and 1985.

The heads, forelegs, and hindlegs of bees were individually collected and stored in a hexane solvent, for subsequent extraction of volatile substances and analysis by gas chromatography–mass spectrometry (GC–MS) in Norris Williams's laboratory in Gainesville. Mark supplied me with the vials of hexane and instructions on how to prepare the samples of bee parts. When I returned to the U.S. I shipped the samples to him. I must admit that at first I was a bit hesitant to decapitate the bees and cut off their legs. This bee is a large, strong insect and cutting off its head produced a loud cracking sound as the razor blade went through the tough cuticle. Mark's idea was to extract and analyze separately the substances found in these different parts of the bee's body, since all three are key players in the processing of environmentally collected fragrances. Eventually we built up enough samples of the bee parts and their analyses to encourage Mark and Norris that further study was warranted. Through the GC–MS analyses of my La Lola samples, Mark found similar and identical substances in the hind tibial organs and the heads of the bees, suggesting a possible movement of substances from the bee's hindleg to its head. Samples of deep wood and surface tissue from the discolored tree wounds through GC–MS also revealed substances found in the bees.

While they were attending an orchid conference in San José in 1985, I had the chance to meet Norris and Mark face to face for the first time since I had initiated contact with them about *E. cingulata* a couple of years before. After the meetings I drove with Mark down to La Lola so that I could show him firsthand the bees brushing on the *Dalbergia* trees. As my luck would have it, there were not too many bees brushing the trees at this time, but there was enough activity to give the project the go-ahead. I also showed Mark a spot in a nearby abandoned cacao grove where I had seen *E. meriana* displaying on the trunks of *Huara* trees, all of which convinced Mark that La Lola would be a good site for various orchid bee studies. What was remarkably interesting about this strip of abandoned cacao adjacent to La Lola was that it resembled to some degree a dense tangle of old secondary tropical rain forest, with lots of plant life present besides the very old, gnarled cacao trees left unattended for decades. Inside this thicket I saw lots of butterflies, along with orchid bees. This forgotten cacao patch belonged to an eighty-year-old Jamaican black man named Amos Barker, who kindly gave me permission to conduct research studies on his land. Mr. Barker, as the locals called him, lived in a little pastel-blue wooden house along the railroad track running through La Lola, the line connecting Puerto Limón on the Caribbean coast farther east of here with the Meseta Central—an eight-hour train ride with fifty-two stops. Mr. Barker is a descendant of the Jamaican black population that settled in this area of Costa Rica when they were brought here from the West Indies to build the railroad in the last century.

In full swing, our research, especially work done in December of 1986 when Mark returned to spend time in La Lola and further field studies I was to do under his instruction in the following months, asked specific questions about the chemical ecology of male *E. cingulata* in La Lola. What hexane-extractable lipids occur in the labial glands (in the bee's head) and hind tibial organs of male *E. cingulata*?

Do male bees secrete these lipids onto the substrate (such as a discolored tree wound or orchid labellum region) from which they are collecting fragrance compounds? We believed the answers to these and related questions would have broader application to all orchid bee species. In our experiments, squares of filter paper baited generously with skatole were set out, this substance being a known powerful attractant for *E. cingulata* males. The heads and hind tibiae from bees collected at these baits were extracted in a milliliter of pure (high-grade) hexane for GC–MS analyses. To determine whether or not male *E. cingulata* secrete lipids onto a fragrance substrate during brushing, bees were allowed to brush a filter paper substrate suspended over skatole-impregnated filter paper squares. We accomplished this by cutting a four-centimeter square opening in the top of a plastic petri dish, and securing, between the lid and the bottom of the dish, a nine-centimeter round piece of filter paper perforated with many small holes to facilitate the diffusion of skatole vapors. A small pad of skatole-saturated filter paper was then attached to the bottom of the dish. The idea was that the assembled petri dish, suspended or tacked to the trunk of a tree in the wild, would allow the pungent skatole vapors to seep through the holes in the top piece of (dry) filter paper. Male bees, arriving at the bait, brushed the surface of the dry filter paper without coming into direct physical contact with the skatole. The brushed filter was then collected after specified lengths of time, extracted, and analyzed with GC–MS, without the interfering presence of the skatole.

During February and March of 1987, I set out a series of these dishes in both the abandoned cacao and a well-maintained area of the La Lola cacao not far from the *Dalbergia* trees. To test the idea that male bees might deposit greater quantities of lipids on dry substrates not saturated with attractive fragrances, we also set out two kinds of bait assembly dishes—one having "accessible" skatole, where the bees would have contact directly with the bait, and the other with the "inaccessible" skatole lure described above. By this time Mark's general line of thinking was that male bees deposit a lipid

Male orchid bees brushing fragrance volatiles from an experimental
petri dish lure, designed by W. Mark Whitten. The large bee in the center
is *Eulaema cingulata*, while the smaller, less noticeable bee hovering just
beyond the right side of the lure is most likely *Euglossa dodsoni*.

substance from their labial glands which is an aid in collecting the
fragrance substances in nature. Again, the two kinds of filter paper
from these baits were collected and analyzed by GC–MS in Gainesville. Mark also made samples of *Dalbergia* twigs, leaves, bark, and
wood core samples, the latter from "healthy" and "discolored wound"
areas. This was done to determine the distribution of fragrant compounds within the tree, and especially to see if these substances were
largely limited to the discolored wounds visited by male *E. cingulata*.
Wood cores, using a tree corer instrument, were made in three-
millimeter increments of wood depth and analyzed separately, like
the other tree materials, with GC–MS following extraction in hexane
of any volatiles present. Having discovered these substances occurring naturally in the labial glands of male *E. cingulata*, from earlier

samples of bee parts I had sent, Mark monitored bee activity in the presence of synthetic tetradecyl, hexadecyl, and octadecyl acetates, and all combinations of these, along with extracts of the *Dalbergia* wood.

The analyses of bee parts revealed that the same major compounds, such as tetradecyl, hexadecyl, and dodecyl acetates, and several hydrocarbons in the alkanes and alkenes, are present in both the labial glands and the hind tibial organs of male *E. cingulata*. Additionally the hind tibial organs contain other kinds of compounds including monoterpenes, sesquiterpenes, and various aromatics, the latter substances undoubedly giving the male bee's hindlegs a foul-smelling bouquet when sniffed in the field. There is much variation from one bee to the next in terms of the kinds, numbers, and quantities of these various fragrance substances in the bee's body. The discovery of the same acetates in both the labial glands and hind tibial organs of male orchid bees suggests that the labial gland secretion may very well be shunted back into the hind tibial organs as a key part of the fragrance-collecting mechanism of these bees. We also discovered, from the lipid secretion experiments, that many of the lipid compounds found in the labial glands, such as eicosenyl-1, 20-diacetate, and eicosenol, were also found in the greaselike, translucent film that gradually accumulated on the dry filter paper "barriers" over many hours of fervent brushing by male *E. cingulata*, and also male *Euglossa dodsoni*. Thus it appears that male orchid bees, which are most active at the skatole baits in the morning and early afternoon at La Lola, actively secrete labial gland lipids onto a fragrance substrate as part of the fragrance-collecting process.

Similar lipid substances were also discovered in the outer six millimeters of *Dalbergia* wood near the discolored wounds, but not elsewhere. Chemical staining, with lactophenol cotton blue, revealed the presence of fungal hyphal growths in the surface wood tissue of the wounds. Tree wounds three to six months old attract male orchid bees but not fresh wounds, lending further support to our idea that fungal action in the wounded wood tissue plays a role in attracting male *E. cingulata*. Healthy bark, wood from *Dalbergia*, and the head extracts of *Eulaema* male bees do not attract *E. cingulata* in the wild. Yet both surface and deep core wood samples of *Dalbergia* attract male *E. cingulata*, most likely due to sesquiterpenes being found throughout the wood. The major sesquiterpenes found in the *Dalbergia* wood tissues, interestingly enough, also occur in one species of euglossine-pollinated orchid, *Polycycnis gratiosa*.

Our efforts in La Lola with the study of male *E. cingulata*, which had started with a fairly straightforward observation of these orchid bees being attracted to sap wounds on *Dalbergia* trees, culminated in the publication of a research paper describing the above studies and their results, in the *Journal of Chemical Ecology* in 1989. From watching bees and from work done by Lynn Kimsey, we found that male *Eulaema cingulata* and *Euglossa dodsoni* land on the fragrant substrate, touching it rapidly with partly open mandibles, followed by intense brushing with the front leg tarsal brushes as the bee's antennae touch the same spot. This initial brushing may last for more than one minute for a single bee. Then the bee launches off the substrate, hovering, while transferring the substances accumulated on the tarsal brushes to the "basitarsal" comb of the midleg, and then into the slit opening into each of the two hind tibial leg organs. While hovering, a male orchid bee occasionally wipes its mouthparts with the front leg tarsal brushes, perhaps transferring secretions from its labial glands (rather large organs in the bee's head where large amounts of many kinds of lipid substances are synthesized and stored) to the brushes in the process. Lynn Kimsey, in a recent paper appearing in the *Journal of Zoology*, describes in some detail the "grooming" behavior of euglossine bees.

Our findings, and those of other researchers, suggest that the male orchid bee is a virtuoso chemical factory, integrating the lipid secretions from the labial glands in an adaptive fashion with a range of highly fragrant substances obtained from nature, especially from certain flowers and fungus-infected aromatic wood. Lipids from the male bee's body are used as a nonvolatile, nonpolar solvent to enhance the efficiency of fragrance collection in nature, dissolving and retaining these biologically important molecules. Because these highly volatile fragrance substances may otherwise evaporate during the leg action that shunts them into the hind tibial organs, these lipids undoubtedly help to preserve the harvested fragrances in the crucial process of this transfer. (Consider the rapid movements of the bee's wings as it hovers, and the rapid action of its legs, both creating a mini-wind that would easily enhance the evaporation of the collected fragrances, were it not for the presence of these oily carrier molecules.) It is likely that the fragrances are drawn into the hind tibial organs by capillary action, a process that could also be facilitated by the action of the lipid carriers.

Thus we believe that male orchid bees discovered millions of years before humankind the enfleurage technique of gathering up highly evaporative perfumes. Natural fragrances have been collected in the perfume industry by placing large quantities of flowers on sheets of glass coated with grease ("lipids"). The fragrant substances emitted from the flowers dissolve into the greasy film, and the grease is then removed from the glass sheets and extracted to yield the desired floral essence (oil). Our work suggests that male euglossine bees use lipids in a similar manner to collect and retain the fragrant substances they require for their own survival and reproduction. The orchid bees discovered the alluring qualities of perfume scents long before humans, but in this case it is the male bee that exudes the aphrodisiac bouquet to court the female, not the other way around!

When I now see male *Eulaema meriana* displaying its impressively colored body in a rain forest light gap, I am more acutely aware of what this creature may represent in the intertwined cycles of life that comprise the rain forest. In the bee I see the chemistry of life: among the insects and many other creatures dwelling here, the solutions to survival and reproduction are expressed through nature's chemistry, a marvelous font of knowledge operating long before humankind and the inventions of industrial chemistry. Can it be that the chemical bouquet of one male *E. meriana*, *E. cingulata*, or other male orchid bee speaks to the evolutionary fitness of that single bee, compared to other individuals of its own species? Is the bouquet that the bee emits into the rain forest clearing a reflection of its particular genetic heritage, sending a clear message to a female bee of the same species as to its suitability as the father of its offspring?

Such research also suggests that the euglossines, in some ways, may be more ecological generalists than previously perceived by tropical biologists and students of ecological chemistry. If the tropical rain forest is viewed as a large, unexplored, and largely not understood pharmacology laboratory where myriads of species spin off novel combinations of aromatic substances, either as integral facets of their own metabolism or as decay products, male orchid bees can perhaps be viewed as grazers of such biological chemicals from whatever sources are available. This is not to say, however, that from a euglossine-pollinated orchid's point of view the relationship of the male bee with the flower is unspecialized or generalized. The synthesis of a specific set of fragrance compounds in the orchid's body must surely be a specialized genetic commitment, fine-tuned by natural selection over time, to attract a certain kind of pollinating agent, or closely related agents such as several species of orchid bees. But from the bee's point of view, orchid fragrances might just be one of many alternate sources of the fragrant substances they need to reap from the environment in order to make their own chemical sexual attractant signals.

At La Lola I have been impressed by the numbers of several species of euglossine bees found in this largely agricultural habitat. I think the reason for this healthy occurrence of euglossines is the presence of sizable strips of abandoned cacao and patches of older secondary rain forest. Even in the maintained cacao groves, there are still a few giant primary rain forest trees, richly trussed in myriads of dangling lianas and epiphytes. These fragments of natural habitat, together with old, abandoned cacao being invaded by rain forest plants and animals, especially along the borders of La Lola, have kept this place ecologically alive to some extent for euglossine bees. Yet there are no morphoes here, and I hasten to add that what little semblance of nature there is here may be disappearing too.

Mr. Barker's *cacao abandonado* is being changed. In March of 1989, a wide logging trail was pushed through the exact spot where I had watched *Exaeretes* many times—a place too where dozens of species of little skipper butterflies dwelled in the sun-drenched lushness of the glade. The logging trail, put in to allow ready access to *Cordia* (*laurel*) trees that are being sold as timber for interested buyers to build homes, has virtually obliterated the little glade that cut through this old cacao; I do not see *Exaeretes* and the other insects here any more. Now some of the giant trees where I had seen *Eulaema meriana* displaying are fully exposed to the sun, rather than sun-flecked in spots where the bees perched. I am certain too that many of the skipper food plants thrived in the little glade, and not in the heavily shaded cacao. Ironically, the little glade was originally created many years ago as a small logging trail, big enough to allow passage for a team of oxen to haul out the logs. But now, the bigger disturbance is destroying this wedge of life in the abandoned cacao. In the fifteen years since the original logging trail had been put in, there was sufficient time for plants, insects, and other life to colonize the trail once it had been abandoned. Life in nature here lives under a perpetual threat of unpredictability wielded by humans. Perhaps one day soon the logging here will cease and the trail will be closed over with vegetation as it had been for many years before. Then perhaps the insects will return. It remains to be seen whether or not any of the several species of orchid bees found here now, a small slice, I am sure, of the bee fauna that once thrived here when this floodplain was covered with rain forest, can survive the new wave of habitat change along the borders of La Lola.

Volatile substances in plants and animals, toxic substances in plants and insects, and the great diversity of chemistry they emboss upon the interactions among species, reflect nature's unparalleled ingenuity in the broadest sense. Species exhibit a composite of many different

adaptations all aimed at a common goal—to extract limited amounts
of energy from the environment to grow, survive, and reproduce.
What I can see today in Sarapiquí's rain forest, the splendor of the
morphoes weaving along a sun-swept path along the edge of the rain
forest, the succession of cicada species calling from the tops of trees
at different times of the year, the piercing, abrupt buzz of a fat
Eulaema bee scraping mud from a trail in the rain forest, these and
much more are the product of the rain forest's past—of many uninter-
rupted generations of breeding and evolutionary adaptation, all blue-
printed in the genes of these creatures I see today. This is a marvelous
legacy of nature's inherent urge to continue, of its continuity.

Consider the rain forest a stormy, shifting sea, with the tops of
the waves symbolizing the best possible way for a certain species
to survive and reproduce, and the troughs intolerable ecological situations that are nonadaptive for the species. Because the environment
is always changing, the peaks and valleys move around, compelling
every species to continually readapt itself to these new conditions.
Reaching a peak of successful adaptation in the rain forest is largely
a matter of interacting effectively with many other species. In the
tropical rain forest, resources present themselves in disjunct patterns.
For the orchid bees to adapt to the rain forest, each species exploits
a set of plant species and other resources to obtain fragrance chemicals
and nourishment. Different bee species attain different mixes of such
resources in their climb toward a particular adaptive peak on this
rolling biological landscape. How each bee species responds to the
environment is a product of its genetic history as the blueprint for
shaping its morphological, physiological, behavioral, and ecological
traits. How a certain species of orchid bee lives is most likely a mixture of some very generalized traits and some specialized ones as well.
Thus every species of orchid bee may be able to exploit a broad range
of floral types in the rain forest, but each species may exploit some
unique resources. Ecological success in the tropical rain forest for
any species is likely to be a mixed strategy of generalized and rather
specialized traits. This is a reasonable way to survive on the rolling

sea of shifting evolutionary opportunities that rise and fall as the tropical rain forest changes through time and space. Nothing is fixed or static in tropical nature, and the euglossine bees, pharmacological butterflies, and myriads of other insects in the rain forest give insights into the highly textured modes of associations these creatures have with plants, interactions that account for the largest share of biological diversity inherent in the tropical forests of Central America and South America.

Without journeying to this ridge behind the La Tigra cacao, at the edges of the rain forest, I could not have come to appreciate the natural history of butterflies, orchid bees, and much more. It has taken me years to appreciate this and to have the information, just bits and pieces mind you, to share. The tropical rain forest, its ceilings, floorings, and walls, its biological diversity, is something that requires a lot of time and patience to understand. In this place, reverence is expressed by observing and studying the living bricks and mortar, the living fibers and fabric of its statuesque trees, vines, and the immense array of life they support. Life here is camouflaged and secretive, at other times vivacious, bold, and demonstrative. This hidden message is reaffirmed when I catch, in the corner of my eye, the distant flash of red from a butterfly or the instantaneous glimmer of metallic sheen from an orchid bee streaking through the air. There is so much here I will never see. I have no idea how close I have come to stepping on a pit viper, its earthtones concealing it from my gaze. I know how frequently I have flushed feeding butterflies, their conspicuous wing colors concealed as they perched in the recesses of the rain forest. I know that much of what I have found here has come from the unexpected rather than the planned rationale of study.

It has been against Sarapiquí's rolling landscape, bathed for eons in the nurturing tonic of warm tropical rain and sunshine, that I have become enlightened about the sense of discovery. There is a light in the darkness of these ashen afternoon skies, when the rain clouds blow across these foothills with their ancient promise of new life yet to be. To share glimmers of insect life at the edge of the rain forest, to relate one's firsthand experience with tropical nature and its people, is a testament to this light. Let us all therefore strive to be cognizant of the tools of our discoveries, observation, perseverance, and the drive to learn, to feed our natural curiosities about the existence of all species.

EPILOGUE

Here in Sarapiquí I have been very fortunate for many
years. In this valley I began a special journey many years
ago, one that is yet to end. And when it does, I hope
the journey ends right here, where streamers of golden sunlight still
ripple through the lush green canopy of the La Tigra rain forest and
sear through the morning mists clogging the steep ravine at Cuesta
Angel, near the birthplace of the Río Sarapiquí. My journey in
Sarapiquí has allowed me to explore and discover natural history,
and to recognize the specialness of humanity too. Here I have become
more sensitized to the continuum that is life on Earth, to the mysteries
of nature little understood, to the challenge to understand while there
is still time to do so, and to kind, gentle people who live within
the rich, changing fabric of Sarapiquí's patchwork of rain forests,
pastures, and agriculture.

While Sarapiquí today is a land of change, it is still a place where
many memories remain intact. Sarapiquí is stopping at Vara Blanca
for *gallo pinto con huevos* or *tortillas con queso blanco frito* when dawn's
chill is still blanketing the Continental Divide, as I head northeast
toward Cariblanco, La Virgen, and Finca La Tirimbina, my destination. It is the basic constancy of this overland journey that I find
so soothing, something I look forward to every time I come back

to Costa Rica. There is a delightful balance I enjoy between liking Costa Rica for its nature and for its people—it is difficult to separate the two. My fondness for both helped me over and over during my field days, weeks, and months in Sarapiquí.

This caring spirit of Sarapiquí is Challa González, after so many years of greeting one another as effervescent as ever still today when I pull up to his home along the ridge near Cariblanco. Sarapiquí has been for me Dagoberto Alfaro, grinning as he sees me walk into his *almacén-pulpería-cantina* complex in La Virgen, still, after so many years, trying out on me his seldom-practiced English. Sarapiquí is Moncho Morales walking along the dirt road at Finca El Uno at dusk, with an old guitar slung over his shoulder, ready to welcome the end of a long day in the cacao. He and "Don Allen," as he calls me, go back many years. Sarapiquí too is woodsman Jorge Mejías, who enlightened my life on many forays into corners of La Tirimbina's rain forest I would not have found or ventured into, had it not been for Jorge and his willingness to take time and share with me this land of his birth.

Sarapiquí is many other people too, like the strangers who stop and help me fix my jeep, or volunteer to help push it out of the mud. Sarapiquí is the veil of mist that settles every day across the ridges near Vara Blanca, down to the road where the red-haired girl used to peek out from the little red and blue *pulpería*, bundled in sweaters to keep out the chill of the clouds hugging this enchanting place. The Sarapiquí I remember is the bumpy dirt and gravel main road that used to be, but which is now very comfortable asphalt. The bumps in the old road are still engrained in my psyche, and knowing that such discomfort over many years could not deter my interest to return every year to study the *bichos*.

Much of who I am today has been shaped in the mountains and floodplains of the Sarapiquí District. Because of Sarapiquí, I appreciate more at this time my memories of growing up with nature as a child in New York. Forty years ago, bottling live caterpillars of monarch butterflies or black swallowtail butterflies to study their metamorphosis helped to educate me about the interdependence between insects and plants. In Sarapiquí I realized that these childhood moments with nature were still with me. What I began to see and study firsthand in Sarapiquí helped me appreciate the interconnections among species that shape a habitable world for all creatures. The magnificence of the tropical rain forest lives in each of us, for all of the creatures in the rain forest are intertwined with our own existence as a species.

All of nature is a continuum. It is up to us to discover these worlds within worlds, to take the time, to develop the skills and background, to unravel the secrets of life within these interconnected spheres of nature's being, without unraveling nature itself. Even now, more than a century after Thomas Belt's explorations in Nicaragua, there is an urgent call to study the natural history of organisms in tropical forests, where much of life has yet to be discovered, studied, and named. The tropical rain forests are going very fast. Nature's own evolution-molded cycle of life and death in species has its own beauty, a part of which is replacement with other living forms when some go extinct. But the mass extinction of species by humankind is a totally different matter—ugly death, without replacement, not a beautiful death tied to the cycle of life in natural habitats. Human beings abuse nature, taking too much from it, and wanting too much to control and suppress it. These are drives uncharacteristic of the rest of nature. Let the rain forests of Sarapiquí, therefore, teach us all something about the interconnections among species.

It is well past time for us to feel honored to stand on a spot where a *Morpho* soars by on a sunny morning as the cicada sings. I remember well one morning when Sarapiquí gave me an irreplaceable gift. I had arrived at the little footpath leading from the La Tigra cacao near Don Sisto's old house into the rain forest about eleven o'clock in the morning. As I stood in the bright sunshine, I felt almost drugged by the heat. A coating of sweat closed over my face, my blue work shirt plastered to my chest. The light danced strangely on the great many intertangling vines that formed a partially closed canopy over the section of trail in front of me. The portal of dense

Towering rain forest trees, some, like this one, with massive, clinging vines and latticeworks of epiphytes, are today's sentinels of what Sarapiquí's rain forests were once like.

vegetation that pushed up to both sides of the little trail consisted of small trees and the vines. This entrance into the rain forest seemed to have been left untouched by the *finca* workers for several months, giving it an aura of wild abandonment. This little *rinconcito* (little corner) was now a widening band of luxuriant wildness, embossing the zone between the cacao and rain forest with a dense maze of vines and other brush making a tunnel of the trail.

Standing beneath this lush perforated roof, I could make out the shapes and hues of at least eight different species of plants packed into this small area. Flies, bees, and butterflies, of several kinds each, darted and maneuvered through this living maze. Suddenly I spotted a species of *Anaea* butterfly unknown to me, bearing brownish tattered wings with a blue streak down each. The butterfly flitted through the many intermingled leaves above my head, alighting or touching a few but avoiding most. A *Piper* plant—curious to me because as I traced back its leaves to stems and the trunk, I discovered it to be vinelike above and treelike nearer to the ground—seemed to captivate the meandering, searching butterfly. This *Anaea* was certainly a female, her movements and behavior giving her away as a creature in search of places to put her eggs. This odd *Piper*, a species I have not noticed before, seemed a strong candidate, for the probing butterfly alighted the longest here—on the underside of the plant's youngest, most tender leaves, those near the very top of this tangle of foliage. I had to stretch and twist around to catch glimpses of the creature as it continued along to another leaf. She was spending a lot of time here. As I watched her from below, the butterfly appeared and disappeared—first it is there, then it is a shadow, hidden from me. This hide-and-seek went on for many minutes.

Then suddenly a magnificent female *Morpho peleides* appeared— the huge freshly hatched creature just floating over my left shoulder from behind and drifting through the maze of vines and tangled tree branches in front of me. I had seen many morphoes before, but there was something unforgettable about this moment. The big gracious butterfly, its iridescent wings sporting a crisp row of large white dots in the back margins, slowly weaved its way through the vegetation, with little effort, occasionally tapping a leaf here and there, no doubt looking for places to put her eggs. The butterfly left the corridor and swung through the vegetation, coming around again for a second promenade through the gateway into the rain forest. At this very moment, as the *Morpho* flitted under the leafy boughs of the arched canopy just above my head, the sun's brilliance fused with the foliage forming this roof, creating a dazzling, seemingly molten latticework that almost blinded me. I truly felt, at the very moment when the electrifying blue butterfly appeared, that I was gazing into the soul of nature. As I stood here, I felt as if I too became fused into the ethereal magnificence, as if reaffirming, in some small way, humanity's continuity with all of nature.

In the few seconds that the butterfly was there, I felt in this beautiful scene of tropical lushness, diversity of leaf shapes and colors illuminated in the sunlight, cicada calls, the drifting dragonflies, and finally, the stunning blue *Morpho*, the embodiment of what I had enjoyed so much about being here. I had experienced firsthand a complex but elegant beauty much too richly textured to be captured successfully by a photograph or an artist's paintbrush. I had gazed into the fused essence of tropical nature, frozen there before me, just for a few moments, before changing, losing its almost indescribable beauty as the big butterfly flew through the corridor a second time and did not reappear again. Then I felt the drenching sweat again, but this time it felt almost chilly as I walked on, very slowly, into the shady depths of the little swatch of the rain forest I had gotten to know over many years.

I also sense the composite picture of tropical nature in its water, the mighty rivers working over this land windward of the great *cordillera*. In Sarapiquí, great cascades of muddy waters breathe a replenished life into the land. Sometimes I have a vision of tropical soil being a fountain of life. It is the place where microorganisms massage the inorganic and organic breakdown products of the soil, rendering it suitable for nurturing life. In Sarapiquí, claylike, largely inert soils are inoculated, through the cycles of nature, with a plethora of nutrients and microorganisms, which in turn endow this thin skin of the Earth with the ability to support other forms of life such as trees, vines, and animals. In my many days of walking through the rain-soaked forests of Sarapiquí, I have witnessed firsthand this lesson of nature. Rotting leaves, branches, flowers, seeds, and fruits become the nutrients feeding the cycles of life in the rain forest. There it is, as I trek through the forests, beneath my feet a richly textured blanket of brown, orange, and red, the layer of nature's garbage being recycled to enhance the growth of life yet to be. Nurtured by the warmth and rains of Sarapiquí, now and as it has been for thousands of years, the building blocks of life are recycled, decaying leaves becoming millipedes, butterflies, snakes, and toucans. It really doesn't matter, I think to myself. Around me, in these forests of Cariblanco and La Tirimbina, my senses are saturated with the sight and sounds of life. Nowhere else on Earth, I know, than in the American tropics can we come to appreciate and understand the continuity of nature, rudimentary molecules, the breakdown products of decay, becoming new life, crisp and fresh, vibrant and alive.

But whether I look down to the soggy ground or to the rain forest's canopy above, I can see glints of how *Morpho* is intimately connected to the rest of this nature. Take the forest floor, for example. I cannot see it happening or feel its presence, but the forest floor really is alive with debris begetting debris, molded by the action of tiny creatures and macroscopic arthropods sandwiched between pasty layers of mulch. Peeling back the upper strata of mulch I see a fine webwork of hyphae from fungi—nature is at work, feeding the forest giants and all the thousands of other creatures that depend upon them. This fragile webwork, quick to shrivel in the sunlight and die, is what gives the foliage high above our heads life to support even more life. The canopy foliage of each species of giant tree is physically and chemically alien from the others, each one a unique ecological testing ground for herbivorous and other animal species. Then too, there are the overlays of lianas and epiphytes, each one too a microcosm of the evolutionary theatrics that weave through the whole rain forest.

Thus the hidden layers of rain forest below my feet, under the squishy sogginess of the mulch, feed the life of the forest in the canopy. They seem two worlds far apart, yet they are really not separated much at all. I know that a faithful canopy butterfly like the magnificent *Morpho cypris* depends upon the whole rain forest working as an integrated unit. The energy integrity of its caterpillar food plants, legume canopy trees and vines, is linked metabolically to the life-giving respiration of the soil fungi and bacteria, far below the sun-drenched canopy, in a place of darkness where the lofty *cypris* only occasionally touches down. If the soil microflora were to vanish, so too would these giant trees, snuffed out, after all of these centuries, by a missing link in the food chains of their survival. So too would vanish the morphoes and most everything else I see and appreciate. No species lives without the other, especially here.

In recent months I have been living in the Hunters' *cabina* that sits in a little clearing in the rain forest near a bend in the Quebrada La Tirimbina. This is a treat for me. In the room I use in the cabin, I sense the closeness of nature by the loud humming of wasps, their paper nest buried in one of the walls. I feel very much at home here. While I have visited with the Hunters in this cabin for many years, this is the first time I have lived in it, and I especially like seeing

A three-toed sloth ambles across the road between La Tirimbina and Magsaysay. The presence of this canopy-dwelling creature on the road's rain-slicked red earth, juxtaposed with the deep tracks of a log-hauling tractor, is a poignant reminder of Sarapiquí's diminishing rain forests.

Near the Quebrada San Ramón, a large praying
mantis, its cuticle a cloak of forest green, strikes
a conspicuous pose on a fencepost. The
fifteen-centimeter-long creature, like many others,
depends upon the rain forest for its survival.

the walls of the kitchen area covered with the musty, faded covers
of many old *New Yorker* magazines. One of the nicest features of
this cabin is that the front of the living room, which faces out toward
the creek about forty feet away, is a floor-to-ceiling screen wall. I
enjoy sitting in one of the cloth-back rocking chairs and looking
out at the rain forest. We share the cabin with the usual "guests,"

including giant roaches, tarantulas, and a very occasional *ratoncito* whose biggest fault is taking a few nibbles of my bread as its midnight snack. Several species of wasps build their almost innocuous paper comb nests on the outside of the building, usually just under the wooden support eaves of the galvanized metal roofing. The crawl space between the roof and the press paperboard ceiling panels is undoubtedly home for many *bichos*, but this is of little consequence to me. Outside the cabin hummingbirds crisscross the patio, visiting the reddish orange blooms of a potted plant that has since spread itself into the edge of the rain forest.

At night, as I sit in the cabin's living room area, I hear sounds from the rain forest very different from those of serenading animals. These sounds are not unique to the night, but I seem to be more aware of them as I sit quietly and listen, peering out into the inky darknesss. Giant seed pods from a woody legume liana crash into the creek, making loud splashing noises as they hit the water. Large branches, laden heavily with the waterlogged weight of epiphytes, tear away and plummet to the forest floor, making sharp, eerie cries in the night. But the animals keep right on singing without interruption, for these falls of branches and seed pods are a natural part of the rain forest—unlike the wheezing bulldozer sputtering its way through the mud or the screams of the chainsaw. For when the technology-generated instruments of forest death plunder across the land, the melodic sounds of life die too. In the rainy season, when *temporales* hit the Sarapiquí Valley between bouts of dry weather, this forest seems especially alive with branches toppling, even giant trees thundering down. The rain forest swallows up this debris of natural injury and death, claiming its own for its own sustained vitality that will become new life.

Sometimes in the morning, if I am still at the cabin at 8:15, I stand outside in the open, grassy area and listen for the morning LACSA flight heading out of the Meseta Central for Miami, Florida. The jetliner passes exactly overhead on most days. Sometimes, when the cloud cover is broken, I can even spot the plane, a speck of silver climbing northeasterly after passing over Volcán Poás. Here below, I am immersed in an especially rich land, that of the *tierra caliente* where ancient nature is close at hand—a whole different world from the technology symbolized in the sleek jetliner now fading from my view and auditory range. I do not know exactly why, but I enjoy standing here and listening for that morning flight, and sometimes being here again at 2:30 in the afternoon to hear the returning plane descending into the Meseta Central. I believe that it has something to do with the separateness I feel from the rest of the world when I am here at La Tirimbina, and especially now, in the soothing peacefulness of the cabin by the rain-forested creek. The ascending or descending jetliner symbolizes the closeness of the other world, where I spend much of my time, so I am grateful for the time I have here in Sarapiquí. Because of this, I cannot help feeling that my staying at La Tirimbina and in the cabin is a logical complement to that dream that prompted me to write this book. As in that dream, the natural beauty of Sarapiquí and the kindness of people once again come together. The human kindness has been that of Bob and Nancy Hunter and the other people at La Tirimbina. The house in the dream is my home in the *campo* in Sarapiquí, as the Hunters' cabin has now become for me. Like Challa, the Hunters have welcomed me into their home in Sarapiquí. Jorge Campabadal is continuity from the past to the present, a friend who, along with several others, has shared information, insights, and warm feelings about the *tierra caliente*. My dream has been a reality for me—people and nature in Sarapiquí.

At night, in the flickering glow of candlelight in the screened-in living room of the cabin, I see silhouettes of rain forest life on the screens—a giant-sized katydid or cerambycid beetle, even a wasp drawn down from its nest by the light. In the candle's diffuse flame, I feel fused into this ethereal ambience, no longer just an observer or listener. For there is a treasurable oneness occurring here now— you have to grasp it, be ready for it, to know its presence. It is the unity of all living things, of the individual creatures and of their combined total effect, the fabric of nature. The candle's inviting warmth on this cool tropical evening speaks of molten sounds whose sources are heightened by the flickering light on the table. This is a fusion of katydids, crickets, and frogs with the soft glow of *carbunclos*, dances of life and courtship filling the rain forest in front of the cabin tonight. This ambience seems to be too special, too alluring, to last, but it tempts you to believe that this masterpiece of nature will never end! Can it not give us, the custodians of nature, a refreshed wisdom about nature's deepest essence? If only everyone could respect nature, seek to protect the symphony and light show now in full swing outside the cabin.

On cloudless nights the heavens bathe this clearing along the Tirimbina creek in a special hue, the giant *Philodendron* nearby now a silvery, ghostlike creature, as is much of everything else on special nights like this. And when the clouds shut the stars and moon from my sight, the air becomes still and heavy with the promise of rain coming in from the Caribbean Sea not far from here. Then I hear a rushing noise different from that of the gurgling stream near the cabin, then the breezes, then the growing roar of the rain, finally the staccato of rain hitting the metal roof as it sweeps over this spot.

Visiting or living in the cabin helps me to understand the compositeness of the Sarapiquí experience. In the daytime, on sunny mornings, males of *Parides childrenae* do their aerial skirmishes in the patch of secondary-growth vegetation outside my bedroom. High above, I am sure, orchid bees streak through the canopy of the rain forest. The forested sides of the little creek beyond the clearing of the cabin vibrate with the songs of cicadas. I can pluck Ranghpur limes from a tree outside the door and look for midges on the flowers of two cacao trees planted along one edge of the little clearing. Much of what has been my life in Sarapiquí, its elements of natural history, greet me every day right here at the cabin. Bob Hunter no longer lives here as frequently as he used to, for he has moved to Madison, Wisconsin, where he is an honorary fellow in the herbarium at the University of Wisconsin. Bob's stamp is on this place, though, the La Tirimbina farm, now managed by one of his sons, Charlie. Char-

Dr. J. Robert (Bob) Hunter, to the left, and the author at Finca La Tirimbina in the dry season of 1988. Photo with help from Jorge Mejías.

lie is building upon Bob's dream, making the *finca* his own dream, in his own way. This too is part of life's continuities.

In the brightness of La Tirimbina's sunny mornings I can sit out on the patio with a tin cup filled with hot tea and wait for the morphoes to come by, as these creatures follow the little creek's course along the edge of rain forest on the side opposite the cabin, what Bob, Nancy, and I call "Morpho Alley." When the sun suddenly appears, breaking through the clouds in the morning, this stretch of creek springs alive with their aerial dances. Imagine sitting, sipping hot tea, while streamers of brilliant light filter down through a wall of green, the rain forest, rising up, as a living backdrop, from a crystalline stream. Splotches of this sunlight reflect back up toward the sky from the tumbling waters, making smooth rocks protruding just slightly above the water line resemble little luminescent domes. These domes seem like mysterious landmarks for tropical nature's winged creatures, particularly those that haunt this creek rushing across the hills of Sarapiquí. Off to one side of this enticing vista, to the left of our deck, a huge bean pod, about a full meter in length, gently swings back and forth through the air, four or five meters above the stream. This solitary cradle of seeds of future rain forest vines to be belongs to a huge, ropelike liana bridled to the branches of an old *gavilán* tree whose gnarled and twisted trunk juts out over the water. Near this spot Bob Hunter once encountered a large *terciopelo* swimming across the creek. As he tells it, at first he just saw the snake's mammoth, wedge-shaped head arched above the water line, wobbling back and forth as the rest of the reptile's two-meter-long body, hidden beneath the rippling waters, undulated in an opposite rhythm.

But on this splendid morning, like a sampling of many others when Sarapiquí's rain forests are fleetingly drenched in sun, we are not concerned with the close proximity of pit vipers. This is to be a moment of astounding beauty, a moment of the tropics frozen in my mind, an instinctive recording of the human spirit's fusion with the natural world. I wait with baited breath for the first butterfly to appear. Suddenly it is here, a splendid, almost blinding flash of incandescent blue. It is a huge *Morpho amathonte* bobbing up and down in wide arcs above the creek. A few moments later another one appears, headed in the same direction, and later a third. Nancy and I often place friendly bets on how many morphoes will come by their cabin on such a sunny morning. I even encouraged her, on more than one occasion, to keep a running tally.

What a breath-taking scene it is—giant electric-blue butterflies dodging and weaving through the dabble of sun flecks and shade created by tree branches overhanging the creek, a special span of minutes and hours that I wish could be frozen forever. Against the backdrop of the dark green rain forest and silvery-sheened rocks in the creek, a ringed kingfisher came gliding low and silently over the water. First came one bird, then another, perhaps two or three in all, slipping up and down the stream, disappearing into its darkened recesses where the rain forest closes over it, then suddenly reappearing. They are streaks of blurred blueness racing above the water. These kingfishers are there, even when it's overcast or sprinkling a fine mist of rain. The rain forest is filled with the choruses of arrow poison frogs, tiny red and blue creatures hidden in the damp leaf litter and fallen debris beneath the trees. I wonder if the kingfishers could hear these rapid-pulsed alarm-clock-winding chants and the canopy-high shrill of the "rainy day croaker" and other cicadas? I am the audience peeking in on tropical nature. And the unannounced appearance of the morphoes, as if following some unknown cue, with their shimmering beauty, completes this magnificent vignette of rain forest life.

On many evenings at the little cabin, when the sun falls away sharply, heralded by the screeching dusk call of the "sundown cicada" in the rain forest nearby, the daytime vignette of "Morpho Alley" gives way to that tranquil aura of nighttime nature. I feel a part of an exclusive world at such moments. Sometimes Bob Hunter is here with me and we engage in provocative debate, good cheer, and friendship. At other times, when the rain forest at night is filled with the sounds of the world's greatest symphony, that of life itself, and when Bob is not here, I still feel his presence, the presence of a friend who shared his special place with me. Each of us is like a moth being drawn toward the candle's late-night flame on the wooden table in the living room. Like the candle's glow, flickering in one direction and then in another, rocking gently as mounting breezes rushing through the cabin spell out the impending rains, Sarapiquí has helped me to better understand the magnificence of nature. Like a candle's warmth, a composite of many things, so too has been the Sarapiquí experience, instilling in me a diffuse awareness, a raised consciousness of the Earth's greatest story, that of life as seen and illuminated by the interactions and associations between plants and insects in the tropical rain forest, butterflies, cicadas, and other creatures I have encountered in my years of field work in Sarapiquí, and I see the people who have been a part of this tapestry. All of this is very much a part of me, even after the candle's flame has cooled and the soothing night rains have again descended upon Sarapiquí, sweeping in, the way they do, off the Caribbean Sea.

INDEX